James C. Moffat

The Church in Scotland

James C. Moffat

The Church in Scotland

ISBN/EAN: 9783337327637

Printed in Europe, USA, Canada, Australia, Japan

Cover: Foto ©Lupo / pixelio.de

More available books at **www.hansebooks.com**

THE
CHURCH IN SCOTLAND

A HISTORY OF

ITS ANTECEDENTS, ITS CONFLICTS
AND ITS ADVOCATES

FROM THE EARLIEST RECORDED TIMES TO THE
FIRST ASSEMBLY OF THE REFORMED CHURCH

BY THE
REV. JAMES C. MOFFAT, D.D.
PROFESSOR OF CHURCH HISTORY, PRINCETON THEOLOGICAL SEMINARY

PHILADELPHIA
PRESBYTERIAN BOARD OF PUBLICATION
1334 CHESTNUT STREET

PREFACE.

History of the early Irish and Scottish churches lay, until recently, in a state of chaos. A primitive period of intelligent simplicity had left a few honest records of itself. But a long succeeding time of greater pretension had covered those records up with more showy fable. Romish writers of the twelfth and thirteenth centuries, conceiving of no ecclesiastical system but their own, in recounting events of a preceding and different state of things misrepresented them, perhaps unintentionally. Blunders of ignorance mingled with the bias of prejudice to pervert truth, and truthful statements of fact were thrust into the background by the more exciting wonders of legendary lore. In many cases the original narratives, after serving as the basis of some fabulous life of a saint, were suffered to perish. Those that survived were subsequently perverted in the application made of them to suit a fictitious system of history, constructed by John of Fordun in the fourteenth century, further developed by

Hector Boece in the fifteenth, and adhered to by subsequent historians until very recent years.

The period over which this obscurity lies deepest is from the first planting of Christianity in the British Isles to the eleventh century; the churches upon which it rests are the old British, the Irish and the Scottish churches, and deepest of all upon the last.

Recent historical research and criticism have been hardly less wonderfully successful in this field than in that of Oriental archæology. Although Thomas Jones made a beginning in it more than one hundred and fifty years ago, and was followed by Lord Hailes and others at long intervals, the really effective work belongs to men of the present generation. It began in a careful comparison and discriminative treatment of all the ancient books on the subject, resulting in critical editions of the more important under the light of that comparison. In both lines, the prior credit is due to certain scholars of the Irish Archæological and Celtic Society, among whom conspicuously appear John O'Donovan, LL.D., James Kenthorne Todd, D. D., and William Reeves, D. D. Contemporaneously, in Scotland, Dr. Forbes, bishop of Brechin, Joseph Robertson and William F. Skene and others entered the same field.

Mr. Skene's early works were of the utmost

value to the whole enterprise in his editions of the four ancient *Books of Wales*, of the *Chronicles of the Picts and Scots* and other early memorials of Scottish history, and of Fordun's chronicle of the Scottish nation. Such works were accompanied or followed by carefully-written monographs on certain epochs, legal questions and great historical personages, in the list of which Todd's *Saint Patrick* and Reeves's edition of Adamnan's *Life of Columba* stand eminent as masterpieces of historical criticism.

A fourth effort was to combine all the discoveries of research in a consecutive narrative, with every statement supported by critically-defined evidences. So should the whole history be lifted beyond question out of the region of legend. With this view, Dr. Thomas M'Lauchlan in 1865 published his *Early Scottish Church*. He was perhaps too early, for the progress of research went on. John Hill Burton, in the first volume of his general history of Scotland, issued in 1867, found important alterations necessary for his second edition of 1872. And now William F. Skene, in his last work, which he calls *Celtic Scotland, a History of Ancient Alban*, covers the whole of that bewildering period of North British existence with a thoroughly searching narrative, which if not satisfactory on all points certainly distances all competition yet in the field.

The last volume of his three octavos appeared at the close of 1880.

It is presumed that many people would gladly become acquainted with the facts thus elicited who have not leisure to follow the careful and often-retracing footsteps of criticism. To that class of readers is the present volume addressed, in the hope that it may contribute to a popular understanding of the real character of an interesting but hitherto greatly misunderstood portion of the Christian Church.

CONTENTS.

BOOK FIRST.
ANCIENT PERIOD.

CHAPTER I.
PAGE
THE RELIGION OF HEATHEN SCOTLAND 17

CHAPTER II.
INTRODUCTION OF THE GOSPEL 23

CHAPTER III.
CHRISTIANITY ESTABLISHED 33

CHAPTER IV.
NINIAN 39

CHAPTER V.
PALLADIUS 42

CHAPTER VI.
PATRICIUS 47

CHAPTER VII.
PATRICK'S TEACHING 54

CHAPTER VIII.
CHURCH OF STRATHCLYDE 69

CHAPTER IX.
COLUMBA 74

CHAPTER X.
Lindisfarne 88

CHAPTER XI.
Decline of Iona 96

CHAPTER XII.
Constructing the Kingdom of Scotland 108

CHAPTER XIII.
Macbeth 119

CHAPTER XIV.
Malcolm Canmore 124

BOOK SECOND.
PERIOD OF PAPAL RULE.

CHAPTER I.
St. Margaret the Queen 137

CHAPTER II.
The Sons of St. Margaret 144

CHAPTER III.
Introduction of the Romish Church Government . . . 150

CHAPTER IV.
Introduction of Romish Monasticism 160

CHAPTER V.
Papal Scotland.—National Consolidation 174

CHAPTER VI.
Scotland submits to be a Romish Province 184

CHAPTER VII.
Extinction of the Scoto-Saxon Dynasty 193

CHAPTER VIII.
Scotland's Relations to the Papacy during the War . . 206

CHAPTER IX.
Papal Relations of Scotland under Restored Independence. 225

CHAPTER X.
Progress of Education.—Rise of the Scottish Universities. 237

CHAPTER XI.
Closing Summary 253

BOOK THIRD.
CAUSES WHICH LED TO THE REFORMATION.

CHAPTER I.
Decline of Clerical Piety 263

CHAPTER II.
Clerical Morality 272

CHAPTER III.
Truth and Error 287

CHAPTER IV.
John Major 296

CHAPTER V.
Patrick Hamilton 303

CHAPTER VI.
Cardinal Beaton 312

BOOK FOURTH.

THE REFORMATION CONFLICT.

CHAPTER I.
GEORGE WISHART AND CARDINAL BEATON 341

CHAPTER II.
ALLIANCE WITH FRANCE 367

CHAPTER III.
THE LORDS OF THE CONGREGATION 383

CHAPTER IV.
MARY OF LORRAINE AND THE PEOPLE 400

CHAPTER V.
JOHN KNOX 420

CHAPTER VI.
THE FRENCH INVASION 429

CHAPTER VII.
THE VICTORY 439

MAPS.

	PAGE
BRITAIN UNDER THE ROMANS	*Facing Title.*
NORTH BRITAIN IN THE TIME OF COLUMBA	*Facing* 75
NORTH BRITAIN IN THE TENTH CENTURY	" 119
ROMISH BISHOPRICS	" 155

A LIST OF THE KINGS OF SCOTLAND, WITH THE CONTEMPORANEOUS KINGS OF ENGLAND AND POPES, FROM THE NORMAN CONQUEST TO THE CLOSE OF THE FIFTEENTH CENTURY.

Scotland.	England.	Popes.
A.D.	A.D.	A.D.
1057. Malcolm III. (Canmore).	1066. William I. (the Conqueror).	1061. Alexander II.
	1087. William II.	1073. Gregory VII.
		1086. Victor III.
		1088. Urban II.
1093. Donald Bane.		1099. Pascal II.
1094. Duncan.		
1095. Donald Bane (restored).		
1098. Edgar.		
1107. Alexander I.	1100. Henry I.	1118. Gelasius II.
		1119. Calixtus II.
1124. David I.		1124. Honorius II.
	1135. Stephen.	1130. Innocent II.
		1143. Celestine II.
		1144. Lucius II.
1153. Malcolm IV.	1154. Henry II.	1145. Eugenius III.
		1153. Anastasius IV.
		1154. Adrian IV.
1165. William.		1159. Alexander III.
		1181. Lucius III.
		1185. Urban III.
		1187. Gregory VIII.
	1189. Richard I.	1188. Clement III.

LIST OF KINGS AND POPES.

1190. John.	1191. Celestine III.	
	1198. Innocent III.	
1214. Alexander II.		
1216. Henry III.	1216. Honorius III.	
	1227. Gregory IX.	
	1241. Celestine IV.	
	1243. Innocent IV.	
1249. Alexander III.	1254. Alexander IV.	
	1261. Urban IV.	
	1265. Clement IV.	
	1271. Gregory X.	
1272. Edward I.		A.D.
	1276. Innocent V.	1276. Adrian V., John XXI.
	1277. Nicolas III.	
	1281. Martin IV.	
	1285. Honorius IV.	
1286. Margaret.	1287. Nicolas IV.	
1292. John Baliol.	1294. Celestine V.	
	1294. Boniface VIII.	
1296. English Usurpation.	1303. Benedict XI.	
		1305. *Papal court removed to Avignon.*
		1305. Clement V.
1306. Robert I. (the Bruce).	1307. Edward II.	
		1316. John XXII.
	1327. Edward III.	
1329. David II.		1334. Benedict XII.
		1342. Clement VI.
		1352. Innocent VI.
		1362. Urban V.
		1370. Gregory XI.
1371. Robert II.		
	1377. Richard II.	

A LIST OF KINGS, POPES, ETC. (Continued.)

Scotland.	England.	Popes.		
		Rome.		*Avignon.*
		A.D. *Return to Rome, and the Papal Schism.*		A.D.
		1378. Urban VI.		1378. Clement VII.
A.D.		1389. Boniface IX.		
1390. Robert III.	A.D.			1394. Benedict XIII.
	1399. Henry IV.	1404. Innocent VII.		
1406. James I.		1406. Gregory XII.		
			Popes of Bologna.	
			A.D.	
			1409. Alexander V.	
			1410. John XXIII.	
	1413. Henry V.		1414.⎱ Council of Con-	
			1418.⎰ stance.	
	1422. Henry VI.	1417. Martin V.		
		1431. Eugenius IV.		1424. Clement VIII.
1437. James II.		1447. Nicolas V.		
		1455. Calixtus III.		
1460. James III.	1461. Edward IV.	1458. Pius II.		
		1464. Paul II.		
	1470. Henry VI. (restored).			
	1471. Edward IV. (restored).	1471. Sixtus IV.		
	1483. Edward V.			
	1483. Richard III.			
	1485. Henry VII.	1484. Innocent VIII.		
1488. James IV.		1492. Alexander VI.		

BOOK FIRST.

ANCIENT PERIOD.

THE CHURCH IN SCOTLAND.

CHAPTER I.

THE RELIGION OF HEATHEN SCOTLAND.

NORTH BRITAIN, in her most ancient recorded times, was a forest, and her religion a religion of the woods. Her people, like those of South Britain and the neighboring isles, were of Celtic stock, and, although called by Roman writers Caledonians, were comprehended under the common classification of Britons. Like the primitive Hebrews, Hindoos, Greeks, and perhaps all nations of earth's early history, they worshiped in the open air, the temple being only a space designated by some religious ceremony. Among the Britons it was a dark grove, and never reached a more formal structure than that of a grove enclosing a circle of stones surrounding the sacred area, sometimes with an avenue of approach bounded in like manner, and within the circle a broad flat stone, called the "cromlech," supported, like a table, by three or more stones set on edge. In some parts of Scotland these structures have been removed to make way for the plough. Still, especially in the Central Highlands, a great number of them have been allowed to remain.[1]

Their priests, called Druids, probably from two Celtic words signifying "spokesmen for God," observed a Nature-worship, after the style of the Vedic in India and pre-Homeric in Greece, but which also had some features peculiar to itself. They rejected the worship of images, and taught the doctrine of one supreme God, but not to the exclusion of other divine beings regarded with an inferior degree of veneration. They believed in man's responsibility to God, in the immortality of his soul, in his liability to sin, and in rewards and punishments ever changing in future states of transmigration. Of God the chief emblem was the Sun, the giver of light and warmth and the supporter of life. To him, and to fire as a secondary sign, were the most solemn ceremonies of worship paid. Annual festivals were observed in his honor. The Beltane, meaning perhaps "the fire of Bel," was lighted upon high places on the first day of May and on Midsummer Eve, accompanied by sacrifice.[2] A similar solemnity was observed on the last of October or first of November.

A mark of Oriental origin was also retained

---

[1] *Gazetteer of Scotland*, Introd., p. 52.
[2] *Statistical Account of Scotland*, iii. 105, v. 84, and xi. 620.

in the religious feeling with which the serpent was regarded. The Druids are said to have attached great religious virtue to the serpent's egg. Veneration was also paid to certain trees, especially the oak—to mountains, springs and rivers. Spiritual beings were conceived of as animating matter and as disembodied in the air. To certain plants a mystic and sacred character was ascribed, as to the mistletoe when found growing upon the oak, which was believed to be an antidote for poisons and a cure for all diseases. It was cut with ceremonies of mysterious solemnity. "A Druid clothed in white mounted the tree, and with a knife of gold cut the mistletoe, which was received by another standing on the ground in his white robe." In their worship, as in most other ancient religions, the principal elements were sacrifice and prayer. But sacrifice, as practiced by Druids, must have been appalling. Their favorite victims were human beings. Criminals, after imprisonment for years, were offered as sacrifices by being impaled and burned in great fires. They also "immolated prisoners taken in war." On certain great occasions, making a gigantic image of wickerwork, they would fill it with men and animals, and burn it with all its contents in one terrible holocaust. Sometimes, inflicting the fatal wounds in such a manner as not to produce instant death, the priests deliberately took their auguries from the contortions of the dying agony of the victim.

Druidical discipline was severe, and was maintained by punishments of various degrees. One of the most remarkable was what may be called excommunication from their sacrificial observances, implying also prohibition from all civil rights and privileges—equal, in short, to expulsion from the nation.

Druids were also the learned class of the people, and used an alphabetical system of writing consisting of seventeen letters—most likely the primitive Greek alphabet derived from Phœnicia. Their legal and religious instructions and liturgies, however, were not read, but recited, and were in verse. Only in common business was writing employed; their sacred literature was to be treasured in the human mind, not written. Such was the amount of it that a novitiate of twenty years was ordinarily spent in getting full command of it by memory. For, besides religion, it treated of law, of medicine and of astronomy, or rather, perhaps, of astrology.

Superstitious in their religion and cruel in some of its observances, the Druids were yet careful practical correctors of morals and gave much attention to moral and natural philosophy. Within their own order they were of three classes, as bards or poets, prophets and common Druids. Diodorus makes only two classes by including the prophets under the head of bards. A president of the whole was elected by suffrage of the rest, and invested with supreme authority.

Druid women also were of three classes, some being married and living with their families; others married, but devoting themselves to long periods of religious seclusion; and a third class being under vows of perpetual celibacy.

Cæsar, about the middle of the first century before Christ, described this sacerdotal order of the forest as being then held in profound reverence among the Celtic people of Britain and of Central Gaul, and stated that the Druids of Britain excelled in the learning upon which their power reposed. Welsh tradition affirms that they brought it from the far East, whence they had come with the Kumri (or Cymri), that branch of the Celtic race to which the Welsh belong. Their religion was not accepted by all the nations of Gaul, only by those of the centre and west, who received their instruction from Britain. In the British Isles the most authoritative of their seats of learning was Anglesey, on the coast of Wales. From that island they were extirpated by Suetonius Paulinus in the sixty-first year of the Christian era. Those who escaped the slaughter fled, it is thought, to the Isle of Man, and thence, following the fortunes of the independent Celts, found refuge among the adherents of their faith in Ireland and Scotland.

The progress of Roman arms and imperial edicts continued to diminish the territory of Druidical rule, and Christianity, following after, impaired its moral power. In the next three hundred years it declined even under its own laws and among its own free tribes, until it became little more than a public superstition. Its later feebleness prepared the way for the accession of Christianity. Many Druidical practices and beliefs, however, continued long afterward to retain their hold upon the Celtic people. Some were converted into the number of Christian observances, with a real or fancied Christian meaning. From neither Irish nor Scottish Celtic populations are they entirely eradicated to this day.

Cæsar, *Bel. Gall.*, vi. 13-18; Pliny, *Nat. Hist.*, xvi. 95; xxiv. 62; xxx. 4; *Gazetteer of Scotland*, Introd., 52; *Pictorial History of England*, b. i. chap. ii.; G. Higgins, *Celtic Druids*.

CHAPTER II.

INTRODUCTION OF THE GOSPEL.

THERE is no record of the means whereby Christianity was planted in Britain, for the traditions and disguised guesses recounted by early annalists cannot command belief. Bede[1] mentions briefly a story about a British king named Lucius applying to Pope Eleutherus to be made a Christian, and that he obtained his pious request. Nennius[2] and the *Anglo-Saxon Chronicle*[3] mention it still more briefly, each in one short sentence. Geoffrey of Monmouth,[4] after his own fashion, spins a pretty little romance out of it. Gildas,[5] who is older than the oldest of them, makes no allusion to the story, and, from the way in which he speaks of Christianity as slowly dawning upon Britain, most likely had never heard of it, notwithstanding Geoffrey's complimentary reference to his treatment of the subject. The story of Donald, king of the Scots, making a similar application to Pope Victor I. is a baseless fiction.[6]

[1] *Hist. Ecc.*, b. i. ch. 4.　　[2] *Hist.*, ch. 22.　　[3] Under A. D. 167.
[4] *British Hist.*, b. iv. chs. 19, 20; v. i.　　[5] *Hist.*, chs. 8, 9.
[6] Innes, *Civil and Eccles. History of Scotland*, p. 14.

The earliest reliable mention of the gospel in Britain belongs to the beginning of the third century, and is by Tertullian. The reference, however, is merely incidental, giving no definite information as to dates or agencies, and is contained within a somewhat boastful statement of the extent to which Christianity had been accepted. Yet it testifies, beyond all doubt, to the fact that the gospel had gained some foothold in the island before the date at which it was written. The passage occurs in Tertullian's answer to the Jews, where he zealously defends the position that Christ has come, and is as follows: "As, for instance, by this time the various races of the Gætulians, and manifold confines of the Moors, all the limits of the Spains, and the diverse nations of the Gauls, and the haunts of the Britons, inaccessible to the Romans, but subjugated to Christ, and of the Sarmatians, and Dacians, and Germans, and Scythians, and of many remote nations, and of provinces and islands, many to us unknown, and which we can scarce enumerate. In all which places the name of Christ who is already come reigns, as of Him before whom the gates of all cities have been opened."[1] In the next sentence it is added: "In all these places dwell the 'people' of the name of Christ." A few sentences farther on he writes: "Christ's name

---

[1] *Answer to the Jews*, ch. vii.

is extended everywhere, believed everywhere, worshiped by all the above-enumerated nations."

A similarly incidental remark of Origen,[1] written in or soon after the year 246, implies the same. "When did Britain, previous to the coming of Christ, agree to worship the one God? When the Moors? When the whole world? Now, however, through the Church, all men call upon the God of Israel."

By both writers it is presumed to be an undisputed fact that people in Britain had at least as early as the beginning of the third century adopted the religion of Christ. Both wrote of what existed in their own time. Communication between Rome and the provinces was then free and frequent. Over excellent Roman roads and upon abundant Roman shipping military forces and supplies were passing continually and news was transmitted without impediment.

No distinction existed then between England and Scotland, the whole island being called by the common name Britain. The people lived in separate tribes and governments, and were known by different local names; but Roman dominion had created a division of the whole into two great sections which has existed ever since, though not always in the same propor-

---
[1] *On Ezekiel*, Homily iv., xiv. 59.

tions any more than for the same causes. In the latter years of the first century the boundary-line had been drawn between the Clyde and Forth. All north of that line remained independent and British. South of it were conquered provinces. Some of these were precariously held, but after the victories of Agricola it could not be said that any British nation south of the Clyde and Forth had been unvisited by the Romans. The remark of Tertullian, therefore, asserts that Christianity had, in his time, been carried north of that line. Tertullian is prone to color highly, but there is no ground for charging him with falsehood; and when he says that there were, when he wrote, parts of Britain subdued to Christ which were not subject to Roman arms, we cannot take him to mean less than that Christians were to be found among the independent Britons north of the Roman line.

By what means Christianity had been carried into Britain is nowhere directly stated by any reliable authority; but certain probabilities are obvious. More than a hundred and fifty years before these words of Tertullian were written Roman armies had been maintained in the land. Dispersed over it in camps, many of which have left their names to the towns that grew up around them and under their protection, many of the men necessarily came into acquaintance with the natives. In the second century earnest Christians were soldiers in the Roman legions. Britons were also enlisted in the army, and marched to other provinces or to the capital. Whilst some of those who returned doubtless brought evil with them, others may have learned Christ and brought back with them the message of the gospel. From the nature of the Christian impulse we may safely infer that those who had learned of Christ did not remain silent amidst a heathen people visibly suffering the penalties of a cruel religion. Much may have been done by humble pious soldiers, whose names were never known to history, because they labored not by public efforts, but quietly, each in conversation with his own little circle of acquaintances. Nor is it likely that, among the Christian men who in various departments of business must have visited and resided for years in Britain, not one devoted himself of more set purpose to the work of the missionary. It was a period of great activity in missionary enterprise, when speaking for Christ was not confined to the clergy. The British churches in after years bore marks in doctrine and worship, as well as in the ministry, of having been planted in an age not far from that of the apostles.

It was the part of Scotland lying south of the Clyde and the Forth which participated in that benefit, though not to the exclusion of some conversions farther north on the eastern coast. Agricola achieved his victories in that part of the island between the years 81 and 85 A. D. He also constructed a line of defences between the Forth and the Clyde.[1] In 121 the emperor Hadrian visited Britain, and built another wall farther south, across the island from Carlisle to Tynemouth. By order of Antoninus, in 138 the fortified line of Agricola was strengthened with a connecting wall; and in the beginning of the third century Septimius Severus enlarged and strengthened that of Hadrian. His successor, Caracalla, in the year 211 surrendered all the territory north of that rampart. During the one hundred and twenty-seven years from Agricola to Caracalla the south of Scotland between the two walls was subject to Roman rule.

After that act of Caracalla we hear nothing more of Britain until the appearance of Carausius in the reign of Diocletian. But that successful naval leader, whom the senior emperors—the *Augusti* in the Diocletian system—thought best to recognize as an associate in government,[2] is himself the only theme of the history which touches the country in his days. In 293, Carausius was murdered by Alectus, and Alectus, at the end of three years,

---

[1] Tacitus, *Life of Agricola*, ch. 23.
[2] Gibbon, i. 320-322, Paris ed.

was defeated by Constantius Chlorus, to whom the administration in Britain had been transferred by the same imperial authority. Constantius died at York in 306, and the Roman army of Britain elected his son Constantine to the honors of Augustus.

The persecution which began in the latter part of the reign of Diocletian, and continued long in the East, extended also to the Western provinces, but for a briefer time.[1] A few British names are recorded in the list of victims. The martyrdom of St. Alban is referred to the year 305. But the story of it is entirely traditional, not appearing until a hundred years after the date when the event is said to have occurred. It is placed in the reign of the mild and Christian-loving Constantius, and so burdened with miracles that a nimbus of doubt surrounds it.

The interval from Caracalla to Carausius, about seventy years, seems to have been entirely free from northern invasion, and that part of Scotland once subject to Rome remained in peace. The planting of Christianity there within the preceding one hundred and twenty-seven years would best account for this long uninterrupted tranquillity.

Meanwhile, the Scots, a people from Ireland, were securing settlement, by war or treaty, among the southern Hebrides and on the ad-

---

[1] Bede, *Ecc. Hist.*, i. 7, 8; Geoffrey of Monmouth, v. 5.

joining mainland. The first clear historical mention of them is made by Ammianus Marcellinus as pertaining to the year 360. But that author gives his reader to understand that it was not the first time they had joined the Picts in ravaging the province.

No history records the origin of the Scots, and only probabilities testify to their ethnic relationship. Their long residence in the north and east of Ireland would account for their use of the Erse language without implying Celtic descent. In some respects their character was strikingly different from the Celtic. Not an impulsive people, they were cautious, patient, ready to seize an advantage when it occurred, and far-seeing to provide for such occurrences. In being brave in defending what they had acquired they were only like their neighbors. From their subsequent relations to the Picts, it is probable that they came into the Hebrides as allies of that people, or, with the same motive, made invasions upon the Romanized Britons. Some of them were perhaps Christian, but in mass they were heathen.

The name "Pict," as applied to the Caledonians, appears first in the address of Eumenius to the emperor Constantius Chlorus upon his victory over Alectus, A. D. 296. Eumenius distinctly applies it to the inhabitants of North Britain before the time of Julius Cæsar.

Under Roman rule in its best days Britain consisted of three sections: First, the completely Romanized provinces to the south of the wall of Hadrian, divided into four provinces; second, the midland or debatable territory between the wall of Hadrian and that of Agricola; and third, all that lay north of the wall of Agricola, which was held by the independent Caledonians, with some of the allied Scots. The people of the midland were reduced to subjection, but the northern Caledonians, though worsted in battle often, never submitted, and frequently retaliated invasion upon the Romans; and the midland was the principal seat of war between them.

In the time of Tertullian the part of Britain not subjugated by the Romans was that of the Caledonians. And if there were Christians among them when he wrote his treatise against the Jews, their conversion could not have been later than the end of the second century, perhaps earlier. The style of Christian teaching which reached them in the days of Polycarp, of Justin Martyr or of Irenæus may have been very little altered from that of the apostles.

While the people of the provinces were affected by religious changes in the capital, Christians among the Caledonians were cut off from such influences by the constant attitude of hostility in which their nation stood to the Romans, and by the broad belt of debatable land between them. Whatever may have been the extent to which the gospel was accepted among the people between the two walls—and it does not seem to have been universal, certainly, beyond their northern bounds—it was only the dissent of a few from the established heathenism.

Beyond any reasonable doubt, Christianity came first into the south of Scotland, as in England, through Roman occupation of the country, in the ordinary intercourse of business, by the capture of prisoners in war and otherwise. Nor can we exclude the probability of conversions through positive missionary efforts.

CHAPTER III.

CHRISTIANITY ESTABLISHED.

THE army which carried Constantine in victory to Rome, and first elevated the military banner of the cross, began its march from Britain. How much of a British element it contained we cannot say. But it indicates the convictions prevailing in the province that Constantius, who treated Christians with favor, was greatly beloved by the people. If Constantine was not then himself a believer in Christ, he evinced his belief that the Christians were the stronger party by attaching himself to their side; and the army under his command consisted, beyond all doubt, largely of Christian men. Eight years later, at the Council of Arles, there were three bishops from the British provinces south of the Tyne—that is, south of the wall of Hadrian—but none from the north. As long as connection with Rome existed its ecclesiastical progress was communicated to the provinces. But Christians of the farther north, cut off as foreign by the receding of Roman dominion and by frequently recurring wars, had few opportunities of obtaining relays of religious instruction from the imperial city, and had to remain fixed in what was originally taught them. Whatever new practices grew up among them were not dictated from that quarter.

Another hundred years of imperial rule was that of emperors professing and protecting Christianity. Roman Britain was now fully recognized as a Christian country.[1] But it was obscure. The great interests of the Empire had been attracted to the East by the planting of the new capital on the Bosphorus, and ecclesiastical discussions centred there or in the schools of Antioch and Alexandria. The Western churches were less conspicuous in the controversies of the fourth century, and the British Isles were the farthest extremity of the West. Moreover, the people, like the subject races in Gaul and Spain, were poor, exhausted by the drain of supporting foreign rulers and armies which annually carried their exactions out of the country.

Little is known of the British churches for the hundred years after the reign of Constantine. Indirectly, it appears that through the Arian controversy they remained orthodox. "In 363, Athanasius could reckon the Britons among those who were loyal to the catholic

[1] Bright, *Early English Ch. Hist.*, p. 10.

faith," although three of their bishops took part in the Council of Ariminum, and accepted the half-Arian formulary there propounded. In that they did not truly represent their Church at home, and "appear to have returned to the Nicene position." Jerome subsequently declared: "Britain worships the same Christ, observes the same rule of truth, with other Christian countries."

These remarks touch only the Roman provinces in Britain. And they, from the time of Constantine, were governed by the constitution which he impressed upon the whole empire. They belonged to the jurisdiction of the prefect of Gaul. "And his deputy, who bore the title of vicar of Britain, resided at York. Under him were presidents of each of the four great divisions" or provinces "of the island."

From the accession of Constantine, in 306, for half a century, the internal tranquillity of the island was little disturbed, except occasionally by the exactions of an unprincipled imperial officer. But in the year 360 Picts united with the Scots—who now, for the first time,[1] appear on the records of Britain—broke over the wall of Severus, and, continuing their ravages for the next seven years, ultimately reached the extreme south and threatened the city of London. By order of the emperor Valentinian

[1] Skene, i. 97, 137.

I., the great general Theodosius transported an army from the Continent, with which he defeated the invaders, and drove them back over the wall of Severus and farther north, until he had re-established the rampart of Agricola. By the year 370 the country between the two walls was once more a Roman province, now called Valentia or Valentiniana, in compliment to the emperor. But that was of brief duration.

After the imperial forces were withdrawn their persistent enemies from the north again recovered possession of the debatable land. When the Roman army returned the invaders were driven back. But the wall of Severus was subsequently the northern boundary of the imperial dominion. And as soon as the Roman army was out of the way, even that was crossed and invasion repeated to the south. But as Rome became involved in serious conflicts near her own gates the protection of her distant territories had to be surrendered. Early in the fifth century her rulers in Britain collected all their treasures—"some they hid in the earth," "and some they carried with them into Gaul"—and in 418 abandoned Britain for ever.

From the time of Agricola they had ruled in the island three hundred and thirty-five years, but their residence was south of the rampart of Severus. The province north of that was never a safe possession. And yet it was sufficiently subjected, and for a long enough time, to receive substantial elements of civilization, and certainly to some extent the gospel.

By the imperial constitution of Constantine the Christian Church was woven into the web of general government as the state religion. In its own sphere, like the civil and military departments in theirs, it extended over the whole field of Roman dominion. Corresponding to the civil prefects, the great bishops of the capital cities —Rome, Constantinople, Antioch and Alexandria, with Jerusalem—were elevated to the highest ecclesiastical authority next to the emperor. But by that constitution they could have no power over Christians beyond the bounds of the Empire. In the general Council at Constantinople in 381 that fact was recognized, and action taken accordingly, in a canon ordering that churches planted among barbarians should continue the practice they had been taught by their founders—that is, the missionaries under whom they were converted. That was the position of the British Christians north of the Tyne and Solway during the greater part of the Roman dominion in the island. And as Roman power waned in the south, so were they the more frequently subjected to new incursions of Scots from Ireland, who formed settlements on the west and joined the Picts in raids upon the Roman provinces. Strength was thereby added to the heathen element, while the Christian was diminished and depressed. On the eastern side of the island the invasions of Saxons had already begun.

CHAPTER IV.

NINIAN.

THE first positive facts of Scottish church history now emerge into light.

On the extreme south of Galloway, which looks over the Irish Sea, the coast of Scotland is divided into three capes by the bays of Luce and of Wigton, with the Solway firth. The middle cape terminates at Barrow Head in an embankment of sea-worn rocks about two hundred feet high. North-east and north-west from that point the rugged barrier girds the coast for thirty miles. The general level of the country lies at a corresponding elevation above the sea, and, without possessing mountains, rises irregularly into a multitude of isolated hills. Up the eastern side, about three miles from the blunted apex of the cape, there is a break and depression in the rocky wall, forming a natural harbor of small extent, made safe by a little island lying nearly across its entrance. On that point of land, and by that little harbor of Whithorn, in or about the year 390, landed Ninian, the first Christian missionary to Scotland known by name.

And yet Ninian did not come to an entirely heathen country. More than a hundred years before, Christians had been settled in that province. But lack of religious instruction and the devastations of heathen invaders had no doubt deranged their order, whatever it was, and greatly diminished their number. Ninian was a native of Christian Britain, probably of North Wales, where the churches were in a flourishing condition, according to the venerated practices established by their founders. At Rome he had sought a more complete education than his own country could afford. His residence in that city must have been in the pontificate of Damasus I. or of Syricius, or in part of both. The constitution of Constantine was then in full force, and the hierarchical system in union with the State, although still new, had already shaped itself into the likeness of the civil government. On his return through France, Ninian visited Martin, bishop of Tours, from whom he could not fail to hear more and other lessons on the merits of sacerdotal and monastic orders. He arrived at Whithorn, there can be little doubt, with ideas of Christianity formed, to some degree, upon what was to be found in Rome under Syricius. But nothing is credibly recorded of him at variance with the simple practice of earlier Christians. He built a house for residence and worship and for the education of youth, and preached the gospel there, as well as elsewhere in the country of the southern Picts.[1] Many of that people had heard the message of grace before, but ere Ninian's work closed all of those living to the south of the mountains of Dumbartonshire, and perhaps farther north on the eastward, had, in the language of Bede, "forsaken the errors of idolatry and embraced the truth."[2]

The death of Ninian is assigned to the year 432. His successors and the results of his labors are lost to the eye of history for many generations. His mission-station subsequently came into possession of the Saxons, and, like Lindisfarne, was reconstructed after the Romish model. Bede mentions it again at the end of his history, and says that it had then, in 731, been lately constituted an episcopal see, and had Pecthelm for its first bishop.[3]

[1] Skene, ii. 419.   [2] *Historia Ecclesiastica*, b. iii. 3.   [3] Ibid., b. v. 23.

CHAPTER V.

PALLADIUS.

SHORTLY before the date assigned to Ninian's death Palladius arrived as an emissary of Rome—sent not to convert heathen, but to conform existing churches to the Romish model. John of Fordun writes: "The Scots in Scotland had long before been believers in Christ, but had as teachers of the faith and administrators of the sacraments only presbyters and monks, following the rite of the primitive Church."[1] But in the middle of the fifth century the residence of the Scots was in Ireland. And by Irish accounts Palladius was sent by Pope Celestine to collect and organize into church order the few scattered Christians among them.

In 429 the Pelagian heresy was taking effect upon some of the clergy in South Britain. At the instance of Palladius, who was then a deacon, the pope sent Germanus, bishop of Auxerre, to bring them back to the Catholic faith. His attention being thus turned to that quarter of the world, in the second year afterward he

[1] Todd's *St. Patrick*, p. 282.

ordained Palladius a bishop and sent him to the Scots.

Prosper of Aquitaine, a contemporaneous writer, by whom these facts are stated, records in his chronicle, under the consulship of Bassus and Antiochus (A. D. 431), that Palladius was ordained by Pope Celestine, and sent to the Scots believing in Christ to be their first bishop. In another work, referring to these two missions of Celestine, he adds that the pope in ordaining a bishop for the Scots, while endeavoring to retain the Roman island Catholic, also made a barbarous one Christian. By the "barbarous" island the writer cannot, in that connection, mean any other than Ireland; the Latin word *barbarus* designated it as never having been reduced to Roman government. The Scots of Ireland were still heathen. All the pretended evidence to the contrary has disappeared before the light of sober criticism. There is no testimony to indicate more than a probability that a few believers may have been found amid the mass of a heathen public. To unite these into a Church was the mission of Palladius. He was not sent to convert heathen, but as a bishop to Christians. It proved, however, upon his arrival in Ireland, that Christians were not numerous enough in the country to make his enterprise practicable. Encountering much hardship, he became disheartened, and leaving Ireland crossed over to Britain. By a storm at sea, or, quite as likely, by intelligent choice, he was directed to the eastern coast north of the wall of Antonine, where there was a Christian community still without a bishop. Fordun in Kincardineshire became the centre of his operations. There he remained, according to the common account, only a short time, but all the rest of his life, for he there died, as the ancient *Book of Armagh* says, in the territory of the Britons,[1] 432.

The missionary enterprise of Ninian began when Roman arms were finally withdrawn from the debatable province between the walls, but not from the country south of it. The success of his long and popular ministry was probably due in part to his being himself a Briton, in sympathy with the national feelings of the people and their earlier religious instruction, where they had received any, earlier than that communicated by himself. Palladius came after the Romans had entirely withdrawn from the whole island. His failure to enforce the Romish ecclesiastical rule as it then stood may have owed something to the fact that he was a foreigner. Romans never were favorites on the north side of Antonine's wall. The people may have been apprehensive that in complying

---

[1] A later writer for "Britons" puts "Picts," Todd, 288.

with the wishes of the emissary from Rome they might be submitting to the Roman empire, and thereby yield to an artifice the independence they had so bravely defended with arms. A persistent enemy no longer able to use force might be suspected of craft.

The efforts of Palladius were addressed to the clergy, whom he sought to instruct in "the Christian law." But there is no account of any conversion to the law, except that of Servanus (St. Serf), who must have been already a Christian. He is said to have accepted consecration as a bishop at the hands of Palladius.[1] He also baptized and instructed Ternan, a youth of noble birth, who afterward became a presbyter, and later a bishop. But the story of Ternan is entangled in impossible anachronisms. Both Servanus and Ternan were reputed miracle-workers, and most of what passes for biography of them consists of silly and incredible fables. In short, the undertaking of Palladius seems to have been a failure which later Romish writers attempted to disguise.

Moreover, in the *Book of Armagh* an ancient annotator on the life of St. Patrick states that Palladius was also called Patricius, and distinguishes between them as the first and the second Patrick. Many contradictions found in the biographies of the apostle of Ireland have

[1] Todd, *St. Patrick*, p. 302, Note 1.

been thereby reasonably accounted for, as due to importations from the life of Palladius.[1]

After the final withdrawal of the Romans, barbarian invasions deranging all the countries between Britain and Italy, pirates infesting the seas and plundering the coasts, the British churches were completely severed from that of Rome—a separation which in North Britain lasted over two hundred years. During all that time the churches in that quarter, conducting their inner affairs in their own way, and allowing great freedom in mission enterprise, contracted customs and established an ecclesiastical system of their own. Meanwhile, those upon the Continent were still more active in building up a structure of a different style—in some things better, in some worse, but in all more powerful. When they next met the difference between them was found to be irreconcilable.

[1] Todd, 289; also, 305-345.

CHAPTER VI.

PATRICIUS.

WHILE the missionary work of Ninian was going on in Galloway and among the southern Picts, incursions of heathen Picts into the province continued, and heathen Scots from Ireland still harried the western coast. The Scots at that date seem to have been in quest not so much of territory as of plunder and slaves. In one of their raids a youth of sixteen years of age, named Succat and also Patricius, was carried off to Ireland, and sold or assigned to an under-chieftain of the O'Neil, in the county Antrim, who put him to the task of tending cattle.

By his own account, Patrick was a native of Britain. And that he meant the island of Britain, and not Brittany, admits of no doubt. He does not say in what town or other locality he was born, but the country of which he was a native he names, and also the place where he was taken captive by Irish pirates. The latter was a village called Bonavem Taberniæ, near which his father had a little farm.[1] Bonavem

[1] *Confession*, c. i.

Taberniæ has not been successfully identified with any recent name. An ancient Irish hymn, attributed to Fiacc, a younger contemporary of his, states that "Patrick was born at Nemthur;" and the scholiast upon the hymn explains Nemthur as a "city in North Britain, namely Alcluada," now Dumbarton, on the firth of Clyde.[1] The country of his nativity Patrick mentions incidentally, but plainly. He calls it *Britanniæ*, using the plural, as the Romans did in reference to the provinces into which they had divided Britain. Thus, having recounted his escape from captivity in Ireland, he says that he was again *in Britanniis* with his parents, who received him as a son, and besought him never again to leave them.[2] In another place, writing of his wish to go from Ireland to Britain, he again uses the name in the plural, *in Britannias*, and calls that country his *patria*—that is, his native land—where he would meet with his parents (or relatives); and adds that he would be glad to go even as far as to the Gallias—that is, to Gaul, also designated in the plural—where he could visit brethren and see the face of the saints of the Lord—that is, Christian brethren.[3] But Armorica, or Brittany, was a part of Gaul. And Gaul was at some

[1] Todd's *St. Patrick*, 355.
[2] *Confession*, Migne, x.; *Patrol.*, vol. 53.   [3] Ibid., xix.

distance farther away from Ireland than Patrick's native land.

It is a tradition consistently retained in Scotland that the place of Patrick's birth was on the Clyde, a few miles above Dumbarton, on the north-western frontier of the Roman province of Valentia, and within what afterward became the native kingdom of Strathclyde.[1] He was the son of a Christian family in a Christian community, who must have derived their Christian instruction from a date earlier than Ninian. His father was a deacon, by name Calpurnius, who had also held the civil office of decurio,[2] and his grandfather, Potitus, had been a presbyter. Their names, as well as that of Patricius himself, being Latin, seem to imply (not certainly that they were of Roman birth, but) that their connection had been with the Roman occupants of their neighborhood, and that their Christianity must have reached them through the same channel.

Patrick writes of himself and his young companions as not faithful to the religious education they had enjoyed.

The hardships of bondage revived and intensified his early religious impressions. After six years he escaped, and carried with

---
[1] Todd, 353-358. See argument for Patrick's Gallic birth in Lannigan's *Eccles. Hist. of Ireland*, i. 103, etc.
[2] *Epistle against Coroticus.*

him the purpose to prepare himself for returning and preaching the gospel to the barbarous people of Ireland. His process of preparation is not very clearly recounted, but it seems to have occupied a number of years; after which, in compliance with repeated admonitions of the Lord, he entered upon the execution of his design—at what date is not closely ascertainable. That commonly given is 432, but some authors argue for an earlier[1] and some for a later year—not plausibly later than 442.[2]

With a few assistants Patrick landed at the south-west extremity of Lough Strangford, in the county Down. By divine blessing upon the energy and prudence with which he prosecuted his mission the gospel was soon carried over that and the adjoining counties. In his ministry of thirty (some say forty or more) years there were few places in Ireland where it had not been preached and churches organized. Heathenism was not eradicated, but Christianity was planted in every tribe.[3]

Christianity, as preached by Patrick, observed the simple rites once common to all the churches, Roman as well as the rest, but longest retained in the old, out-of-the-way British churches with-

---

[1] Killen quotes the "Old Catholic Church" for the date 405: *Eccles. Hist. of Ireland*, i. 13, Note 4.

[2] Todd's *St. Patrick*, 391 and fol.   [3] Ibid., 499.

in which Patrick had received his education. He went to Ireland, not to propagate a sacerdotal system, but from love to Christ and to the souls of men. Of a commission from Rome or from any human authority he makes no mention, but says that it was Christ the Lord who, in a vision, commanded him to go, and the admonition of the Holy Spirit which retained him in the work when once begun. He entered upon his work as a presbyter. Concerning his episcopal rank, where and by whom it was conferred, he does not say. And the pretension that he set up a primacy in Armagh has been shown to be unfounded.[1] Those whom he ordained to the ministry he calls clerics, without saying of what rank. Writers of succeeding times classified them according to their own ideas, making five thousand of them presbyters and three hundred and fifty bishops. Of course, in so small a country as Ireland, and at that time so thinly populated, their number declares what kind of bishops they were not. Under the late Established Church thirty-four dioceses of moderate size included the whole island. The present Catholic distribution covers it with twenty-nine. And yet, in a sense not intended by prelatic writers, Patrick's clerics were no doubt many of them bishops; that is, among other ministerial duties they discharged those of the pastor-

[1] Todd, Introd.; also 475.

ate and general oversight in the tribe to which their fraternity belonged.

On the shores of Lough Strangford rise certain low grassy hills called "downs." On one of these, at a later time, was erected the stately cathedral consecrated to the name of Patrick. About two miles from that stood his first preaching-place, given by Dichu, his first convert. It was an old barn constrained to accommodate worshipers, but soon replaced by a more ecclesiastical structure, though it still bears the name Sabhal, shortened to Saul, meaning in the Celtic tongue barn or granary.[1]

At Armagh, upon the "hill of willows," and on ground given by Daire, chief of that district, he erected the edifice in which he most frequently ministered.[2] And, after all his manifold labors for Ireland through her length and breadth, upon those two points where they began were their latest efforts expended. He died at Saul, and was buried at Downpatrick, as is generally believed, near the spot where now stands the cathedral of Down; in what year is not certain. The event has been put at various dates from 455 to 495. Many arguments are urged in favor of 465, March 17.[3]

Such a man was of course, in the records of the Middle Ages, credited with prophetic and

[1] Todd, 407, 409. [2] Ibid., 472 and fol.
[3] Lannigan, i. 355–363; Killen, i. 13.

miracle-working powers. Everything done by him is done in some preternatural way; and such a mist of absurd fiction is thrown around him that his very existence has been called in question. Careful criticism has winnowed out some grains of truth, but in the mass his mediæval biographies cannot be accepted as history.

Fortunately, Patrick in his old age felt constrained to defend himself "from the charge of presumption in having undertaken such a work as the conversion of the Irish, rude and unlearned as he was." In that *Confession*, as it is called, the motives which actuated him to his missionary enterprise, and some points of his life concerned with it, are recounted in a plain, modest and indubitable way. An open letter also written by him in reference to the barbarous conduct of Coroticus, a Welsh chieftain, contains a few more statements which may be safely trusted. His honors of saintship were conferred at a long subsequent time, when papalism, in effort for universal dominion, deemed it expedient to adopt and claim credit for all earlier Christian achievements, disguising them with its own colors and decorations.

CHAPTER VII.

PATRICK'S TEACHING.

THE external form of Christianity, as carried by Patrick to Ireland, differed from that which prevailed on the Continent at the same date. Confusion was subsequently introduced into the history by attempts of later Romish writers to cover up that difference, or make it appear as little as possible. Because if Western Christianity came from Rome, as they all believed it did, they thought there could be no difference. Patrick was not a heretic nor a schismatic. And yet from his own writings, as well as from some events in the state of the later Scottish Church, which the chroniclers could not omit, it is plain that there were differences. That fact, however, did not amount to the argument which they apprehended against the Roman origin of the British churches. For the Christianity of Rome in the fifth century differed on several points from itself in the second. That the practices in the Church of Strathclyde were not, in the sixth century, the same in all respects as those of Rome, nor of the national churches elsewhere on the Continent, is not now denied; nor that the churches in Ireland within the same period agreed with that of Strathclyde on points whereon they differed from others.

Why did they so agree together, and so differ from Rome?

The answer is, That elsewhere there had been progress in definition and statement of doctrine, in construction of formal orthodoxy, in definition of heresies, in multiplication of rites in worship and sacramental ceremonies, in clerical practices, in distinctions of clerical ranks, and in the development of a great sacerdotal system in union with the Roman imperial government. In Britain the country lying between the walls had never been Romanized, as were the provinces to the south of it. Its communication with the Christian Continent never was as free. A great part of the time, and repeatedly, it was the battle-ground between Romanized and independent Britons. It was cut off from such intercourse the more completely as the Roman force declined, for so the more daring was the heathen force which overran it. According to the best that historical criticism can ascertain, Patrick was a native of the extreme north-western frontier of that debatable land. It was therefore to be expected that the Irish and Strathclyde churches should agree with each other, as well as that they should differ, in some respects, from those on the Continent.

In the interval of time between the second Christian century and the fifth changes had taken place in the great Church of the Roman empire. Heresies had arisen, new terms had been adopted in statement of the common faith, and controversy had given to certain phrases a conventional meaning which they had not before. But there is no evidence that the Easter controversy, the rebaptism controversy, the Arian or Semi-Arian or Apollinarian controversy, had ever reached the secluded community in which Patrick learned Christ.

To such a degree was Patrick's work disconnected from the ecclesiastical system of the Continent that his very name seems to have been unknown there. For several generations after his death scarcely an allusion is made to him by men of the Roman Church. "Not a single writer prior to the eighth century mentions it."[1] But for his undoubtedly genuine autobiography, the reality of his life might have been totally lost in the depths of mythical cloud with which mediæval writers have actually obscured it. To the same document also are we indebted for any positive information about the type of doctrine he taught.

[1] Skene, ii. 16.

At the beginning of his narrative the aged missionary gives a brief statement of his theology, upon which he says that he cannot be silent:

"For after we have been corrected and brought to know God, we should exalt and confess his wonderful works before every nation which is under the whole heaven—that there is no other God, nor ever was, nor shall hereafter be, beside God the Father, unbegotten, without beginning, from whom is all beginning, upholding all things, as we have said; and his Son Jesus Christ, whom we acknowledge to have been always with the Father, in an ineffable manner begotten before all beginning; and by him were made things visible and invisible; and being made man, and having overcome death, he was received into heaven with the Father. And he (the Father) hath given unto him all power, above every name, of things in heaven and things in earth, and things under the earth, that every tongue should confess that Jesus Christ is Lord and God, whom we believe, and look for his coming, who is soon to be the Judge of the living and the dead, who will render unto every man according to his works; and has shed in us abundantly the gift of the Holy Spirit and the pledge of immortality; who makes the believing and obedient to become the sons of God the Father and joint heirs with Christ, whom we confess and adore, one God in Trinity of the holy name. For he himself has said, by the prophet, 'Call upon me in the day of thy tribulation, and I will deliver thee, and thou shalt magnify me.' And again he says, 'It is honorable to reveal and to confess the works of God.'"[1]

This seems to be an original confession of faith. Except in containing the same fundamental doctrines of God and Christ, it bears no marks of relation to the Nicene or Constantinopolitan Creeds drawn up by the doctors of the Empire, nor to the so-called Apostles' Creed. It differs from them in laying stress on the "ineffably begotten before all beginning," but none on the begotten of the Virgin Mary, not even mentioning the virgin mother, while all the three Catholic creeds press the latter into conspicuous place. It also differs from the Nicene and Constantinopolitan Creeds in saying nothing about Christ being of the same substance or of similar substance with the Father, and lays no emphasis on the distinction between begotten and made. In short, it evinces no knowledge of either Arian or Semi-Arian controversy. Nor is there anything in it which implies acquaintance with the Pelagian belief. It has more resemblance to the summaries of doctrine to be found in the early Fathers, especially to that of Irenæus; and yet it is not a

[1] *Confess.*, c. 2.

copy of any of them. This is remarkable for such a production in the latter half of the fifth century, and could not have occurred had its author been educated in France or Italy, where among ecclesiastics those controversies had long enlisted the fiercest partisan zeal and determined certain forms of expression on both sides, heretical and orthodox.

Of the imperial system of church government sanctioned under Constantine, with its authoritatively graduated ranks of clergy, Patrick and his helpers seem to have had little knowledge. In his statement his helpers were all clerics, without any distinction of rank. He is himself, in his old age, a bishop—how constituted or by whom he does not say, but believes that he had received from God what he was.

Bishop is a word which has belonged to Christian history from the days of the apostles. Nor can there be any completely organized Church without a bishop. The word is a scriptural word, but it has gone through a variety of meanings in the progress of church history.

1. In the first instance, when an apostle constituted a church in any city he ordained presbyters in it, and immediately it was competent to manage its own affairs, because the presbyters, in their pastoral duties, were the bishops of that church, and were sometimes so called.[1]

---
[1] Acts xx. 17-18; Philip. ii. 1; 1 Tim. iii. 1; Tit. i. 7.

2. It became necessary in the meetings of those presbyter-bishops that some one should preside. They might have taken that service turn about in routine, but it was quite as natural for them to elect one of their number as permanent president. And that method was soon adopted in all the churches. Pastoral supervision came thereby more immediately into his hands, and of the two titles the one significant of pastoral duty as overseer was naturally appropriated to him, while his colleagues retained the title presbyter.[1]

3. Further on, the presiding brother among the presbyters of a congregation came to be recognized as occupying a higher rank than the rest. And thus the principle was established of having only one bishop in one church.

4. In a large city, when the church increased to such numbers that they could not all meet in any one of the houses at their disposal, separate congregations were set off, and a presbyter appointed to minister in each. But from the beginning it was a principle of Christian brotherhood that all the Christians in one city should constitute but one church. Accordingly, all the congregations in one city, though worshiping separately, were only branches of one church, and one bishop presided over them all. Thus two principles were firmly established—namely,

[1] Jerome, *Ep.*, 82 : *Com. on Titus*, 1, 7.

one bishop in one church, and one church in one city. From these seeds the growth of prelacy was inevitable.

5. A fifth degree was occasioned by the mission churches planted outside of the cities. In any one of those the missionary sent out to minister in it, when constituted permanent, became its bishop, being pastor in the church of a separate town or village. At the same time he was held to be subordinate to the bishop of the church from which his mission proceeded. And in the neighborhood of some great cities such mission churches were many. The bishop of the great city became thereby a bishop over bishops—a metropolitan. Other country churches, for the most part, in the course of time fell in with the method prevailing at the great centres of population.

6. Thus, before the time of Constantine the Church had grown into a structure of government whereby she easily conformed to his great system for the civil power, and readily furnished a still higher rank of bishops to preside each over the ecclesiastical affairs of an imperial exarchate, thereby providing a double rank of archbishops presiding respectively over dioceses and subordinate provinces of the Empire.

7. The four greatest divisions of the Roman dominion, called prefectures, gave greater dignity to the bishops of the capital cities—Rome,

Constantinople, Antioch, and, as there was no capital for the most western prefecture, Alexandria took her place among the high ranks of the Church. Accordingly, the bishops of those capital cities, with the title patriarch, stood at the head of ecclesiastics. In course of time Jerusalem was revived and added to the patriarchates.

8. Meanwhile, a higher honor among the patriarchs was conceded to Rome and Constantinople—a metropolitan patriarchate.

From that summit of ecclesiastical authority the ramifications of clerical office adapted themselves to all the territorial divisions and subdivisions of the Roman dominion, down to the smallest parochia (parish); and the power of the trunk permeated the branches to their farthest extremities.

So far had the hierarchical development proceeded on the Continent when the work of Patrick in Ireland began. It was a development ruled in its outgoing by the territorial distribution of the Empire. But the Empire had never extended to Ireland or to Britain north of the wall of Antonine. An entirely different structure of government was needed for the missions of Patrick, as being addressed to a different state of social and civil order.

The population of Ireland consisted of an aggregate of great families, each family, in all its branches, recognizing the relationship as a bond of organic union. All the rights of the father in the family were held to be inherited by his heir as head of the clan. His authority was absolute. Clansmen had only to depend and to obey. There were rules to be observed, but constitutional privileges of the governed there were none. The tribes possessed lands, but the tribal, and not the territorial, distribution was the basis of their organization. "Clanship," says Dr. Todd,[1] "is the key to Irish history."

Patrick proceeded with prudence and adapted his church to the constitution of society. He always addressed himself first to the chieftain. To have attempted the conversion of the clansmen without consent of their prince would have been to excite rebellion not likely to succeed. But when the chief accepted baptism, the example went far with his dependants. Patrick framed the structure of his churches to correspond with that of the clans. His clerics he associated in groups, each group for a clan, the members of it living together in common —a little Christian tribe within the tribe, setting an example of Christian society, and distributing among themselves the religious duties for the tribe, usually by the order and under protection of the chief.[2]

[1] *St. Patrick*, 226, 227.   [2] Ibid., 503.

The imperial style of prelacy was perfectly in accord with the style of society and government under the Roman empire; and its growth was natural from a few determining principles. But from the structure of society in Ireland it was utterly alien. There, every clan was in itself a separate power. No plan of union comprehended them all. Each clan was liable to be at war with some of its neighbors. Headship of all was to be brought about, if ever, by force of arms. Internally, each clan respected only the authority of its chief. How, in that condition of affairs, was the island to be parceled out territorially on one common principle into peaceful dioceses and parishes? The churches had to be distributed after the fashion of the tribes. A group of bishops with their respective churches in one neighborhood was quite as accordant with the monastic residence of the clergy as under the Empire the rule of one church in one city and one bishop in one church.

When, long afterward (five or six hundred years), Ireland came under papal rule, writers whose ideas had been formed upon the papal system thought that in Irish church history they must find all the prelatic ranks from the beginning, and, not finding them, called what they did find by their names. So, Ireland is forthwith supplied with diocesans and a subordinate parochial priesthood, and Patrick himself is constituted a great metropolitan, and Armagh the seat of a primacy over all.

Neither was there in the minds of those writers any conception of ecclesiastical growth. Everything must be from the first all that they knew it to be in their own time. Patrick, they say, ordained three hundred and fifty bishops or more, five thousand presbyters, and constituted seven hundred churches. That may be true or not. He says nothing of the kind. It was not true as they meant it, measuring out, according to their own notions, the proportion of bishops and presbyters for seven hundred separate churches.[1]

Out of Patrick's missionary stations, partaking of the monastic character, grew up, after his death, a system of monasteries connected with the tribes and modified by an influence proceeding from Wales. Founded by some person of eminent piety, and endowed by him or by some Christian family, each monastery fitted itself to the regulations of the tribe to which it belonged. Its abbot[2] was not elected by its members, but followed his predecessors in right of the family of the founder. If that failed to furnish a suitable person, the succession passed over to the family which had furnished the endowment. If the family of the founder was also that of the donor, the in-

[1] Todd, 28. [2] From the Semitic *abba, abbas*, father.

heritance of election remained with its members, who were under obligation to provide a person duly qualified for the duties. The abbot might be either a clergyman or a layman, but in either case he was the highest governmental authority in the church of his tribe. The episcopate was merely a rank among the collegiate brethren, and not only void of jurisdiction, but necessarily subject to the abbacy in as far as respected the collegiate rules. A bishop's duties of confirmation, administration of the Eucharist with rites of the greatest pomp, and ordination to clerical office, the abbot did not usurp, but he held the discharge of them under his direction.[1]

This was equally true of the rule of an abbess over her nunnery. Brigid of Kildare employed a bishop, whom she held as subject to her laws, in his place, as were her nuns in theirs.

The members of the association were called brethren, and the number under one abbot (father), generally amounting to one hundred and fifty or more, were the family. They constituted a regular Christian community in each tribe, to which the members of the tribe were drawn by the attractions of kindred and greater security.

No one of these fraternities ruled over the rest. They stood to one another in the relation of a federal union, and no central head was

[1] Todd's *St. Patrick*, 5, etc.

acknowledged save Christ. The monastery had certain claims upon its tribes for support, while the tribe had claims upon it for clerical duties and for instruction by recital of the word of God to all who would listen to it.

Every such clerical fraternity was also a seminary of learning, and besides its family maintained a body of youth in the course of instruction. It was still a missionary system, designed to set an example of Christian life in a state of self-denial and the practice of Christian virtues and affections, and to furnish protection for persecuted converts. Its accommodations were humble, consisting mostly of huts made of wattles and earth or boards; but it was "defended by a wall of veneration, and belief prevailed that the peace of the religious society could not be violated with impunity."

Care of scriptural instruction was an inheritance from early Christian times faithfully retained by the great missionary to Ireland, and by the clergy who succeeded him. As stated by Columbanus, a monk of the second period, their Church insisted upon knowledge of the Scriptures, and accepted as a standard of doctrine nothing beyond the teaching of the evangelists and apostles. Concerning a daring controversy of his time, he said that, "excepting those statements which either the law or the prophets or the Gospels or the apostles have made known to us, solemn silence ought to be observed with respect to the Trinity. For it is God's testimony alone that is to be credited concerning God—that is, concerning himself."

CHAPTER VIII.

CHURCH OF STRATHCLYDE.

WHILE Patrick was pursuing his mission in Ireland new settlements of heathen were forming in South Britain. Saxons already had their colonies planted along the whole eastern coast from Kent to Northumberland, extending successively to the districts on the Tweed and Forth, while Norsemen had begun their invasions on the farther north-east. What is now Scotland was greatly distracted by invasion. Scots from Ireland on the west, and Saxons on the east, expelled or subjugated the earlier inhabitants. The Romanized and Christian Britons of the south-eastern coast were driven to the central mountains and their congregations broken up. The people north of the great firths were still chiefly heathen. Galloway, embracing what is now Kirkcudbrightshire, Wigtonshire and the southern part of Ayrshire, was inhabited by an ancient British race, Christian perhaps to some extent in Roman times, together with a recent Pictish immigration, converted under the preaching of Ninian. A large colony of Scots from

Ireland had settled in the West Highlands and made themselves masters of what is now Argyllshire.

Thus, by the middle of the sixth century North Britain was divided among six or seven different groups of population—heathen Norsemen on the north-east; heathen Saxons on the south-east; Picts, partly Christian, on the intermediate east coast; Britons, partly Christian and partly heathen, in the south centre; Christian Britons and Picts in Galloway; Picts with Scots, partly Christian, in the south-west Highlands and Hebrides; and Picts, purely heathen, in the Highlands of the north-west and north centre.

The history of Scotland as a nation had not yet begun. It was to take shape and consistency from the slow process of unions, subjugations, annexations and amalgamations of different races, and their conversion to Christianity. At that date the principal seat of Christian profession was the south centre, from the firth of Clyde to the Solway, and Galloway. Of the former the inhabitants were chiefly of Kymric descent, and recognized their religious as well as ethnic relations with the people of North-west England and of Wales. But they were weakened by division under several petty kings, and the Church within their bounds suffered greatly from neglect and long-continued warfare with the heathen on both north and east, while their clergy were disorganized. It was the period of intensest conflict between Britons and Saxons—the time of King Arthur's legendary wars, described by Geoffrey of Monmouth as the most successful resistance ever made by Christian Britons to the aggressions of their heathen foes.[1] Arthur's twelve great successful battles seem to have been real, and fought in defence of the Kymric south of Scotland against Picts on the north and Saxons on the east.[2] These contests gave to the hills and valleys of the Clyde and Tweed—countries subsequently fertile in themes of romantic fiction and poetry—a foundation for heroic history. The death of Arthur is referred to A. D. 537, soon after which period a revival of Christianity began among the people whom he had defended.[3]

The birth of Kentigern, an event no less deeply covered with the mirage of mediæval fable,[4] must be referred to the same period. Kentigern, also called Mungo (the Beloved), received his education in connection with that ancient Church north of the Tay once visited by Palladius, although his ordination by Ser-

---

[1] Geoffrey's *British Hist.*, b. ix., x.
[2] Veitch, *History and Poetry of the Scottish Border*, chap. ii.
[3] Ibid., p. 68.   [4] M'Lauchlan, 107-115.

vanus, who had been ordained by Palladius, involves an interval of time which is incredible. Called by the king and clergy of Lanark, with the Christian people, then reduced to a small number, he consented to be their bishop. A bishop was invited from Ireland to ordain him.[1] Thus he entered upon his pastorate five or six years after the death of King Arthur. With long-sustained zeal he carried forward the revival of Christianity within the little kingdom, in opposition to encroaching idolatry. A number of youths, accepting their education from Kentigern, followed his example and aided in the execution of his plans. They did not escape persecution from enemies at home. A strong party in favor of the old Druidical worship divided the nation,[2] and during the rule of a king of their persuasion, Kentigern had to take refuge in Wales. There he remained similarly employed until after the accession of a Christian king in Lanark, Rhyderch Hael, and Rhyderch's victory over the princes, leaders of the heathen party, in the battle of Ardderyd in the year 573. By that victory the Kymric tribes[3] from the firth of Clyde to Derwentwater were united in one kingdom under the name of Strathclyde, with

[1] Skene, ii. 184.
[2] Veitch, 101 ; Todd's *St. Patrick*, 33, etc.; M'Lauchlan, 115-118.
[3] Veitch, 101 ; M'Lauchlan, 123-125.

its fortress-capital Dumbriton, now Dumbarton, in the religious interest of Christianity.

Kentigern was welcomed back to his former charge. At first he took up his residence at Hoddam, in Dumfriesshire, no doubt to encounter approaching heathenism on that frontier of Saxon occupancy. From thence he went into Galloway, and, as Jocelin says, cleansed from the foulness of idolatry and contagion of heresy that home of the Picts. Afterward returning to Glasgow, he continued to pursue his evangelical enterprise without interruption until his death. The principal dates in his life—his birth in 518, his ordination in 543 and his death in 603—are only approximate.[1] His extant biographies—the fragment and the life by Jocelin—were not written until the twelfth century, more than five hundred years after his time, and are full of absurd miracles in the conventional mediæval style. But, setting these aside, there is no good reason to doubt that Mungo was the main support of the Christian cause in the south of Scotland at a time when it was declining there under the fierce assaults of heathen enemies. His long-sustained reputation for knowledge and piety procured him influence in missionary excursions beyond the bounds of Strathclyde.

[1] Skene, ii. 198.

CHAPTER IX.

COLUMBA.

WHILE heathenism in North Britain was still resisting the work of Kentigern, the princes of Ireland were defenders of the Christian faith, and some of them its ministers. It was one of the latter who proved the messenger of an effectual gospel to the unconverted Picts, whom no missionary's voice had yet addressed.

Columba, of royal descent in the family of O'Niel, was born in December, 521, at Gartan, in the county of Donegal.[1] "As he grew up he exhibited various qualities, as well of body as of mind, fitted to excite the admiration of his countrymen. He was of lofty stature; he had a clear and commanding voice and a noble bearing. He could express himself with ease and gracefulness; he had a quick perception and a sound judgment. He was an ardent student, and had great powers of application. His temper was hot, and he sometimes gave way to gusts of passion; but with all he was just and generous, and his indignation was

[1] Reeves's *Adamnan.*

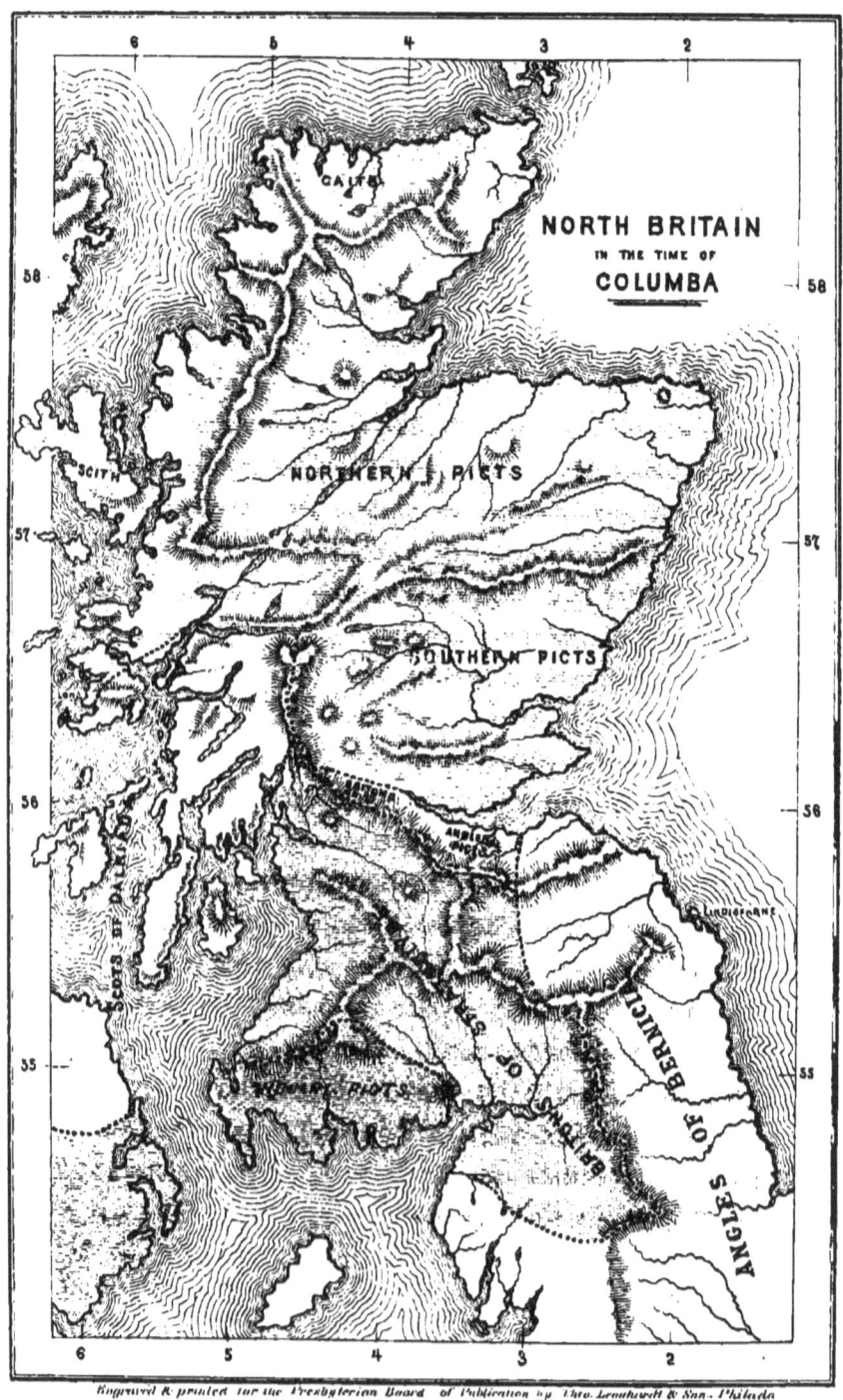

never so much excited as by the perversity of the wicked." His honorable birth and "personal endowments soon placed him in the position of a leader, and more than once he was able to control the political movements of the Irish princes."[1] Though he early resolved to attach himself to the service of the Church, his youth was greatly divided between it and the political and military conflicts of parties.

As Columba approached middle age he broke away from all secular interests to devote himself solely to the work of the gospel.[2] From the lofty headlands of his native county, far over the intervening ocean, could be seen the grayish-blue mountains of the southern Hebrides—Islay, Jura, Colonsay and others. On some of those Columba knew that there were colonists from Ireland, converted before leaving home, but now without religious instructors. Others were descended from people who had left Ireland before Christianity reached it. And far out of sight beyond, under the cold dark blue sky of the north, on islands and mainland, lay tribe after tribe of Picts in a state of utter heathenism. Columba resolved to set apart the remainder of his days to preaching the gospel in those spiritually destitute regions. At the age of forty-two he found himself in condition to carry his design into effect. As a pres-

[1] Killen, *Eccles Hist. of Ireland*, i. 30, 31.   [2] M'Lauchlan, 150-151.

byter of the Irish Church (a higher clerical rank he never bore), and accompanied by twelve assistants, in the year 563 he set sail in his *currach*, and after landing at several intermediate points fixed his residence upon Iona.

That little island, about three miles and a half in length and one and a half in width,[1] lying off the south-western extremity of Mull, from which it is separated by a sound one mile and a half wide, and on every other side lashed by the free sweep of the Atlantic Ocean, was for Columba conveniently situated within the territories acquired by his countrymen, where they already had a church, and yet not far from the borders of the Picts, whose conversion he had in view.[2] At that point also he was protected by the chief of a Scottish colony, who gave him the island and was prepared to welcome his Christian instructions. There, he and his assistants erecting for themselves such houses as they needed of the humble materials of wattles and earth, Columba set up one of those missionary schools which formed a feature of the old Irish and Scottish churches. Monastic institutions they were in a certain sense—namely, in that their inmates lived together in common, with a degree of ascetic self-denial and in obedience to their own superior; but not monastic in the sense in which that term is most likely to

[1] Skene, ii. 89. [2] Ibid., ii. 34. 86-88.

be taken at the present day, inasmuch as they were under neither episcopal nor papal authority, and acknowledged no human superior outside of their own body, and in that the constituent members of their fraternity were clergymen, having a view to missionary and pastoral work. Their separation of themselves from the world was not to secure merely their own salvation and power with God, but to present before the heathen an example of Christian life as pure as possible, separate from the ways of sinful men, and to prepare missionaries and pastors, provide a central home for them, and oversee them and the affairs of the churches which they planted.

It would misrepresent their character to call them monasteries without discrimination. Their monks were in reality all the clergy their Church had. Vows of obedience were exacted, but only to the president of their own college. Under his direction they were held, the lay members to their work for the community, and the clerical in readiness for missionary or pastoral duty as he and the fraternity saw fit; or as students they pursued the course of preparation for the ministry. They always made the monastic college their home. The plan, in short, was that of a well-regulated missionary station, and church extension consisted in multiplying such missionary stations.

As they were planted among a people living in clans, they addressed themselves to the clan system. Instead of dividing the country into sections for distribution of Christian work, the missionaries accepted the natural grouping of the people. The clan was one great family, including its branch families, and for the most part inhabiting adjoining districts. The missionary college was a little family of clergymen with their students adapting itself to the clan organization to carry religious instruction through all its ramifications. Accordingly, there was no call for a territorial distribution of parishes and dioceses or presbyteries. The missionaries used the order they found. And even when carried beyond the clans their method still had regard to the people rather than to the divisions of the land.

Roman monasticism, with which that of Ireland and that of Iona are liable to be confounded, had only begun its career under the hand of Benedict. But even the older style of monastery had always been subject to the bishop of the diocese in which it was situated, or to the council, or to the bishop of Rome. Without the approval of one or the other it had no right to exist. Latterly, all that control fell into the hands of the pope.[1] In the Scottish Church there were no territorial bishops, no provincial, diocesan or general councils, and the pope was

[1] Gieseler, i. 510.

nothing more than a venerated name. The clerical fraternities were themselves the heads of ecclesiastical authority.

Such an institution was now set up in Iona, from which to direct the operations of missionary enterprise, and in which to prepare men to be pastors for the future congregations. It was after the example of the Irish, but differed from them in that it was not planted for the benefit of a kindred tribe, and in that it was supported by the industry of its own members. It had no place for a territorial episcopacy or a presbyterian republic. It was itself the Church. Its brethren were the clergy, associated with a presbyter as their principal. In another aspect it was a missionary station cultivated into a theological college, on a manual-labor plan. Columba was not sent by the Church of Ireland, though he, and Iona after him, always cherished filial relations to it. For the mission upon which he entered he had accepted his orders from the Lord, whose gospel he preached. And he acknowledged no standard of doctrine save that of the evangelists and apostles. The foundation of his instructions and of his preaching, his great instrument in the conversion of the heathen, was the word of God. He and his assistants did their Lord's work under their own responsibility, as they understood their Lord's commission.

In his house on Iona, Columba ruled and instructed his clergy and assigned them to their places of duty—with authority, but not without consultation. As he was not a bishop, but a presbyter, so all succeeding Scottish abbots of Iona were presbyters, and yet in the government of the Church took precedence of bishops. Bishops, in that connection, were recognized as of a superior rank in the ministry, but assigned to an insignificant position in the work of the Church. One of them could ordain a bishop or administer the Eucharist without an assistant, and his superior rank was held in honor. But presbyters could ordain presbyters, and a presbyter could also administer the Eucharist without an assistant if he chose.[1] The bishops were under the monastic rule, and as such were, in respect of jurisdiction, subject to the presbyter-abbot as the head of the monastery.[2] In short, bishops were only occasional visitors in Iona; the system was one which had no place for them, and, although admitting their rank, never knew properly what to do with them.[1] As little had it any place for a church session, a presbytery or a synodal government. Its ruling power was the missionary college.

The government of the early Scottish and Pictish churches was neither papal, episcopal nor presbyterian, as those systems now stand,

---

[1] Skene, ii. 94.   [2] M'Lauchlan, 169, 170.

but monastic, or rather collegiate, in which theological schools were the rulers. They educated the clergy, assigned them to their missionary or pastoral places, and were the authorities consulted when difficulties arose. In their college the clergy had their home, their place for study and their books. Out from it they went in their respective directions with instruction and pastoral service for the clan in which they ministered, and thither they returned for rest and further preparation. All the religious houses of the Scottish Church were constituted after the example of Iona, to which they all voluntarily conceded a primacy of honor.

Ascetics were to be found, who withdrew to desert places, lonely islets in the ocean, and lived in utter solitude; but in so doing they were outside of the church system, and not to be counted as belonging to a monastic order. They were mere voluntary anchorets.[1]

Columba began his evangelical work with preaching to the men of his near neighborhood, and for a revival of religion among the long-destitute Christians of the Scottish colony— long destitute of the means of grace.

At the end of about two years from his leaving Ireland, and when his college, upon which all his other plans depended, had been put in working condition, the zealous missionary found

[1] M'Lauchlan, 176-180.

the way prepared for his enterprise of addressing the gospel to the northern Picts. His first step was to visit the court of their king to obtain his consent. The journey was long, for King Brude was then residing in the neighborhood of Inverness, one hundred and fifty miles away, and much of that distance had to be traversed on foot.[1] At first, the king was not disposed to listen to his application, and forbade him admission. The miracles whereby Columba overcame that opposition are the conspicuous events in Adamnan's narrative.[2] They seem to have been uncalled for; the royal resistance was neither cruel nor obstinate, and the Pictish people were, for the most part, ready to give a hearing to the gospel.[3]

The Pictish king Brude, when converted, became zealous in the cause, and gave its missionary his hearty support. Columba had already the friendship of the Scottish colony in his neighborhood, and used his influence to secure them in possession of their territories, and obtain for them recognition of their independence from the head-king of Ireland. With these advantages he extended the operations of his Church as far as those friendly princes ruled, by planting new religious houses in both kingdoms of Scots and

[1] M'Lauchlan, 155, 156.
[2] Adamnan's *Life of St. Columba*, Reeves's ed., lib. ii., c. 35, 36.
[3] M'Lauchlan, 157-159.

Picts, in the islands as well as on the mainland, and in Ireland. By the end of twelve years his enterprise was almost complete, as far as profession was concerned. The western and central Highlands were brought under Christian instruction, and the whole nation of the Picts was formally added to the Church.[1]

Subsequently, evangelical work was carried more in detail through the heart of the mainland to the east, and relations were established with Kentigern and the Church of Strathclyde. When prosecuting his work in that direction down the river Tay, perhaps in the year 584, Columba took occasion to visit Kentigern in his residence at Glasgow. He was received with warm affection. The two devoted Christian workers spent several days together, "conversing on the things of God and what concerned the salvation of souls."[2]

The area covered by the missions of Columba and his companions, added to that of Strathclyde and Galloway, where the inheritance of the older British churches had just been revived, constituted all that is now Scotland, except the Saxon and Scandinavian settlements on the eastern coast.

Columba died on Iona in 597.[3] His burial-place continued long afterward to be the most

---

[1] Skene, ii. 127.   [2] Ibid., ii. 194-196.
[3] Reeves's *Adamnan*, lib. iii., c. 23.

venerated cemetery in Scotland, the chosen resting-place of chiefs and kings. His little isle became an illustrious seat of Christian learning, from which went out ministers of the gospel, with evangelical and educating influences, over all Scotland, island and mainland, and far beyond its bounds.

Columba was a man of superior education among the men of his time in his own country, and the Irish Scots were then the lights of civilization for the British Isles. He wrote both verse and prose in Latin and in Irish, and his Latin style was marked by accuracy and ease. His ecclesiastical system was also educational. After the example of the Irish monasteries, his mission-stations, planted at many different places for convenience of Christian work, were also colleges for the education of youth and the culture of religious literature.[1] The work of the school consisted in the study of the Latin language, of religious Latin literature, and especially of the Latin Bible, with the doctrines of revelation as then classified and defined, the practice of religious duties, observances of devotion, and the training necessary to the proper exercise of ministerial functions. The standard of doctrine was the Bible. Much time was devoted to copying it or portions of it, and in the study of it help was ob-

[1] Skene, ii. 75, 127, etc.

tained from such commentaries and summaries of its contents as their learned men had prepared. Some of the brethren gave part of their time to original composition and to keeping a record of passing events. But the great theme of their studies at home and their preaching among the people was the gospel of salvation.

Of the parts of their public worship, and what order they observed in it, little can be ascertained. Among the books mentioned as studied in Iona there is no word of a missal. Perhaps their missionaries demanded a freedom in adapting means to unforeseen circumstances more than would be compatible with a prescribed formulary.[1] But doubtless there was an established order for all ordinary occasions. The elements of which the daily service consisted were recitation of psalms, and sometimes perhaps passages of other Scripture; and prayer, of such frequent occurrence with them on other occasions, could not be absent from their social worship. On the Lord's Day the principal part of the service was the Eucharist. When several presbyters were present, one was selected to officiate, who might invite a brother-presbyter to break bread with him. If a bishop ministered, "he broke the bread alone."[2] But that was in the social service of the fraternity. Before the people to

[1] M'Lauchlan, 188.   [2] Skene, ii. 102.

whom their mission was addressed, beyond all doubt the chief part of worship was preaching the gospel. They made no use of pictures or images as helps in devotion; they did not appeal to the intercession of saints nor adore the Virgin Mary.

Yet it would be a mistake to conceive of those brethren of Iona as entirely free from the superstitious notions accumulating in their time. Celibacy they might have defended as a state more expedient for them in the enterprise they had undertaken, but they certainly deemed it holier than that of God's own institution. Their tonsure, or peculiar cut of the hair, shaven close over the fore part of the head, had nothing but superstition to recommend it. Their use of the cross as a holy sign amounted to an incantation. Living in colleges or monastic cells they looked upon as especially favorable to devotion and service acceptable to God. Some of their practices were peculiar to themselves and the Irish Church to which they belonged, such as their monastic tonsure, and their observance of Easter after the example, as they understood it, of the apostle John. But the greatest errors of the Catholic Church, so fast accumulating in the sixth century, had not yet corrupted their faith.

After the conversion of the northern Picts, and the revival of Christianity among the

Scottish colonists from Ireland, the Columbite missionaries followed the course marked out by their founder, and extended their enterprise to the interior of the mainland south, until their religious influence united with that of Strathclyde and touched the borders of the Teutonic settlers on the eastern coast, who were still heathen.

CHAPTER X.

LINDISFARNE.

IN the year 635, Oswald, heir of the Saxon kingdom of Northumbria, having been converted to Christianity during a residence of several years among the Scots, succeeded to the throne of his fathers. Earnestly desiring to have his subjects instructed in the gospel, he applied to the Scottish Church for a missionary. One of the brethren from Iona was sent to him, but proved to be of temper too severe, and, meeting with no success, returned in discouragement. His place was better filled by Aidan, another priest from the same school, and a man of singular meekness, piety and moderation, who was received with high respect by both king and people. His progress was rapid and of sound effect. Oswald gave him a residence not unlike that which he had left in the Highlands.

Eight miles south of Berwick, at the foot of the seaward hills of Northumberland, and separated from them by a belt of water about two miles broad, but at one place almost entirely withdrawn at low tide, lies the island of Lindisfarne. It is only seven miles in circumference, and contains a smaller proportion of arable land than Iona. One-third of it, to the north, is only a group of sandbanks. On the south-east a lofty rock rises precipitously from the plain, crowned with a castle looking southward, while on the south-west a high rocky embankment runs east and west close to the water's edge. Between these two elevations lies a convenient little harbor for small craft. From the rocky embankment extends a stretch of rising ground along the western side of the island until it joins the sandhills of the northern extremity. On that rising ground did Aidan build his modest home, close under the shelter of the embankment. The finer structures that followed took their places successively farther to the north, and there now moulder their ruins, save those of Aidan's house, which, afterward rebuilt by Finan of wood and thatched with reeds, is entirely gone. On that same rising ground, a short distance from the ruins to the north, stands the village of the present day. There other Scottish clergy came to the assistance of Aidan, and younger men were educated for the ministry. Lindisfarne became another seat of Christian learning, an Iona for Northumbria, and out from it proceeded missionaries who traveled in all directions through the provinces over which Oswald ruled, preaching the gospel. But those provinces of Northumbria then extended along the eastern border of the Strathclyde kingdom as far to the northward as the firth of Forth.

Aidan, founder of the mission college on Lindisfarne, died in 651, after having planted and conducted the affairs of the Church in Northumbria for sixteen years. Finan, another monk from Iona, took his place and proved a worthy successor.

South of Northumbria lay another Teutonic kingdom—that of Mercia, sometimes called of the Middle Angles, and east of Mercia that of the East Angles, corresponding nearly to the present Norfolk and Suffolk, and farther south that of the East Saxons. To all these the same Christian enterprise extended.

In 653, Peada, heir to the crown of Mercia, was united by marriage with the royal family of Northumbria, and upon hearing the gospel preached declared himself a believer in it. Missionaries, at his request, were sent from Lindisfarne to instruct his people; and so readily was their doctrine received that before the year elapsed Finan could afford to withdraw one of their number for the purpose of sending him among the East Angles. Finan himself went to preach among the same people, and baptized their king, Sigibert, together with his immediate followers. And the planting of Christian congregations went on, going southward into the land of the East Saxons.

Iona was now at the height of her influence. Christian zeal had carried the gospel over Scotland to the conversion of its heathen and the revival of religion among nominal Christians, and into the Teutonic settlements of England from the Forth to the Thames. Care had also been taken to set up or to continue colleges for ministerial education. To those at Whithorn,[1] Culross and Abernethy, that of Kentigern at Glasgow and of Ternan at Aberdeen, and many of less dintinction elsewhere, were now added Coldingham and Melrose among the Saxons on the Tweed, and for the farther south the greater institution on Lindisfarne.

But another missionary enterprise was at the same time advancing from the south. In the year when Columba died (597) a party of Benedictine monks, with Augustin and Lawrence at their head, landed on the coast of Kent. They came directly from Rome, sent by Pope Gregory I. Ethelbert, king of Kent, influenced, it is said, by his queen, a Christian princess of the royal house of the Franks, received them favorably, and after a short interval professed his belief in their creed. His example was followed by his people, ten thousand of whom were bap-

---
[1] Bede, v. 23.

tized on the following Christmas. Canterbury was constituted an archbishopric, and Augustin its first incumbent.

The plans of the Romish monks wrought prosperously. Proceeding northward, it was not long until they encountered the missionaries of Lindisfarne. On several points their teaching and observances were found to differ. In the controversy which arose, Lindisfarne, sustained from Iona, was ill matched with Canterbury, backed by all the weight of Rome. The Romish monks, proceeding northward and by way of the centre of England, and among the Christian Britons of the west, strove as much to bring the British churches into conformity with their own practice as to convert the heathen. On the eastern side of the country, while Aidan was in the midst of his work in Northumbria, they had succeeded in planting a missionary as far north as York; but so little was he encouraged by success that he soon withdrew, and the ground was forthwith occupied by men from Lindisfarne. Reinforcements were sent out from Canterbury, by whom the Scottish missionaries were charged with error on the subject of their tonsure and in their way of observing the Easter festival.

During the administration of Coleman as principal of Lindisfarne, King Oswy of Northumbria called a conference of clergy, constituted of representatives from both sides, to settle the dispute. It took place in 664, in a convent near Whitby, and was attended by King Oswy and his son Alfrid, the former favoring the Scottish and the latter the Romish side. The chief speakers were Wilfrid, a Saxon priest, and Coleman. For the Scottish practice Coleman pled the example of Columba and his predecessors, traced back to the apostle John. Wilfrid endeavored to show that the Scottish way of observing Easter did not entirely coincide with that of John, belittled the name of Columba, and urged for the authority of the pope that he was the successor of the apostle Peter, to whom Christ had said, " Thou art Peter, and upon this rock I will build my Church, and the gates of hell shall not prevail against it; and to thee will I give the keys of the kingdom of heaven."

At that point King Oswy turned earnestly to Coleman with the question, "Is it true that these words were spoken to Peter by our Lord?" "It is true, O king," Coleman replied. "Can you show any such power given to Columba?" asked the king. Coleman answered, "None." Then, addressing both the debaters, the king inquired, "Do you both agree that these words were principally directed to Peter, and that the keys of heaven were given to him by our Lord?" They both answered, "We do."

Without waiting for any further explanation or discussion, he forthwith gave his judgment: "I also say unto you that he is the doorkeeper, whom I will not contradict, but will, as far as I know and am able, in all things obey his decrees, lest when I come to the gates of the kingdom of heaven there should be none to open them, he being my adversary who is proved to have the keys."

In that decision most of those present coincided. Only the keeping of Easter and the tonsure were discussed on that occasion. But the Scottish Church differed from the Romish on more vital points than these, as appeared in a broader conflict at a later time.

Coleman, defeated but not convinced, retired from Northumbria, and spent the rest of his days among his own people. Tuda, another Scottish priest, more compliant with the southern discipline, succeeded him in office for a brief term, but died of the pestilence in the same year.

The conformity of those who came after Tuda proved to be all that Canterbury could desire. The island school of Northumbria, with its missions, passed entirely out of the Scottish Church and took its place as a Romish monastery.[1] The most effective agent in bringing about that change, and in persuading the brethren to become Romish monks, was Cuthbert, who received his reward in the most miraculous honors of sainthood.

[1] Bede, *H. E.*, iii. 25, 26.

CHAPTER XI.

DECLINE OF IONA.

AFTER the conference at Whitby calamities fell fast upon Iona. First came the loss of her missions in England, with their principal college on Lindisfarne, which within the next ten years were all gathered into the net of the Roman fisherman. The Scottish ministers, who could not submit to that transfer, withdrew into their own country. The Saxons of Northumbria extended their rule into Galloway, where early in the next century they created a bishopric with its seat at Whithorn, and subjected it to the metropolitan of York.[1] The ambition of their king, Egfrid, prompted him to push their fortune in war along the northeastern coast. In 685 he invaded the territory of the Picts beyond the Tay, but encountered a ruinous defeat, which compelled the withdrawal of his boundary to the south of the Tweed.

That great gain to the Picts decided the weight of political power in their favor over both Scots and Britons. Their victorious king, Nectan, assumed his position accordingly. Observing

[1] Bede, *H. E.*, b. v. 23.

that the Saxon churches had all separated from Iona, he entered into particular inquiries on the subject, and in 710 sent into Northumbria, to Ceolfrid, abbot of Jarrow, desiring instructions touching the proper tonsure for the clergy and the proper observance of Easter, and asking for architects to build a church in his kingdom after the Roman manner, which he would dedicate to St. Peter. He also promised that he and his people would follow the custom of the Roman Church as far as they could obtain knowledge of it in their remote quarter of the world and imperfect acquaintance with the Roman language. Ceolfrid complied with the request, and sent full instructions on the points of inquiry by the hands of the architects who were to build the church. The king accepted them, and forthwith decreed the Roman observance of Easter and the tonsure called that of St. Peter for the clergy.[1] A few years later (718) the Columbans, who refused to submit, were banished, and their institutions thrown open to Saxon monks, or others who felt free to conform to the new law.

Repeated attacks were made upon Iona herself from the same quarter. Adamnan, one of her own fraternity, and abbot from 679 to 704, having traveled in England and visited the same Ceolfrid of Jarrow, was by him persuaded to ac-

[1] Bede, *H. E.*, b. v., c. 21.

cept the Romish ways. Upon his return he tried to introduce them at home, but succeeded in only creating a schism, which ended in the victory of the Scottish party. Twelve years after Adamnan's death, Egbert, a Saxon priest, went to Iona and resided among the brethren thirteen years—long enough to convert them, as far as the proper time for Easter and the place and shape of the tonsure were concerned, and having done so died in peace.[1]

Controversies about a monkish way of shaving a part of the head and the precise day of observing Easter may be considered of importance by some persons, by others of none; but in this case they demonstrate one thing worth notice—namely, that the Scottish Church of those days, with Iona at her head, held no relations to Rome and recognized no binding force in the pope's authority; and when some of her people conformed to Romish practices, it was through persuasion of their Saxon neighbors or obedience to an arbitrary king, and not because their Church acknowledged a papal right to their allegiance.

The Picts could not, as a whole, have been satisfied with the violent measures of Nectan. Their Church fell into disorder. It was left almost destitute of a ministry. To supply it with Saxons was impracticable. Whatever the

[1] Bede, *H. E.*, b. v., c. 22.

king's charity might be, it was not reasonable to expect that his people should willingly accept their religious counsels and consolations from the ranks of their bitterest hereditary enemies. Some of the vacated or partly vacated Columban houses were seized by laymen, and under the pretence of providing a ministry turned to the account of their own temporal interests. Nectan withdrew from the strife of business to spend his last days in exercises of religion.

In that embarrassed condition of the Pictish Church a new class of clergy made their appearance, with an organization similar to that of the Columban, and filling their place in conducting the more spiritual parts of worship.

From the time of the immediate successors of St. Patrick the practice of solitary asceticism prevailing on the Continent extended also to Ireland. Men of earnest but gloomy piety sought lonely places in some wilderness or far-off islet in the ocean, where in solitude they devoted their days to religious exercises and meditation. Not belonging to any monastic order nor bound by obligatory rule, they lived each according to his own plan. On the Continent such independent ascetics were in great numbers scattered about in desert places, but some also in the neighborhood of cities. Most of them, no doubt, earnest, godly devotees, they all enjoyed the reputation of extraordinary piety, and were often, as a class, termed *Deicolæ*, that is, God-worshipers, meaning that they were men who minded no other business than the worship of God. To the Irish recluses the same name was applied, but in the reverse order of its component parts—*Ceilede*, servants of God.

The vast increase of such solitaries, and their irrresponsible character, created anxiety in the Catholic Church, and several councils in the seventh century took action with a view to bring them under some common restraint and to diminish their numbers. Among those of Irish and Scottish connection—for there were many such belonging to the Columban Church—a similar feeling began to actuate some of themselves. They had come to the belief that it would be profitable for two or three of them to occupy cells in each other's neighborhood. Accordingly, numbers of such little neighborhoods of hermits grew up in Ireland. Without surrendering their solitary habits and freedom, their vicinity to one another must have exerted over them an influence of regulation, and principles of community came to be agreed upon.

It was an association of this kind which appeared in the land of the Picts soon after the expulsion of the Columban ministry, and soberly taking their place, which they continued to fill acceptably, and with high reputation for some of the best features of a pastoral ministry. Among the Picts they were called *Keledei*, which in course of time changed to Culdee, of the same meaning with the Irish and continental terms.

Like the Scottish brethren, they were cœnobites, but not regular monks. They were secular clergy, and their institutions were colleges, not monasteries—more like cloisters of secular canons in the Catholic Church. Yet their freedom was greater than that of secular canons. They were under no vow of celibacy, and some of them were married. So nearly did their fraternities resemble those of the Columban type that, although not quite the same, it is not surprising that the two should have been identified by writers both mediæval and recent, Roman Catholic and Protestant. Having their origin also in the same Irish Church, the Columbans and Culdees held to the same theological doctrines.[1] In their way of living they were "accustomed to fastings and sacred vigils at certain seasons, intent on psalms and prayers and meditation on the divine word, and content with sparing diet and dress," they suffered no time of the day to pass without its proper employment.

[1] Skene, ii. ch. vi.; M'Lauchlan, ch. xix.

Although by the victories of Nectan, and afterward of Angus, who succeeded to the Pictish throne in 731, the superiority in force of the Picts over both Scots and Britons was proved, and Saxon dominion was pushed back to the south of the Tweed, the Saxon people were not driven out, nor did Saxon invasion cease. The country between the Forth and Tweed continued to be the seat of war. Tradition narrates that in a campaign within those bounds King Angus had a vision of St. Andrew or heard his voice in the air, promising him victory "if he will dedicate the tenth of his possessions to God and St. Andrew." Putting faith in the saint, he proved victorious. On his way home he was "met by Regulus, a monk from Constantinople, with relics of St. Andrew."[1] And the king, thus providentially constrained, recognized his obligations, and founded a new religious house at Mucross in Fifeshire, which he dedicated to St. Andrew as the patron saint of his kingdom.[2]

Early in the ninth century the people of North Britain first beheld the swift-sailing ships of the Vikings. In their long wars with Charlemagne the northern Germans had been compelled to settle on the lands assigned them or to retreat beyond the reach of the emperor's conquests. Those who chose the latter found themselves

---

[1] Skene, i. 296, 297.   [2] Ibid , ii. 272.

confined to wildernesses, mountains and marshes, where a brief summer and a scanty and unkindly soil left little to be hoped from culture. Daring enterprise looked out upon the sea. The land could supply them with timber, iron and pitch and the safe refuge of harbors. For everything else they trusted to the sea. Fish were to be gathered from its waters, an inexhaustible supply, and its surface could carry them to partake in the harvests and collected products of lands more highly favored. They had been driven by violence from their own possessions; might they not indemnify themselves from the surplus of others? Sweeping over the ocean from the fiords of Norway, their ships flitted along the coasts of Scotland and England and swarmed among the islands and the sea-lochs of the western Highlands. Pushing into some inviting scene on land, their warriors would leap ashore, rush upon whatever they found available for plunder, hurry it on board, and disappear as swiftly as they came. Churches and other religious houses, usually containing wealthy deposits, the gifts of grateful piety, were a favorite quarry for those hunters of the sea.

Iona had become a much-frequented shrine of pilgrimage, enriched by donations, favored by kings—some of whom were proud to enroll themselves among the brethren—and sought as the place of sepulture for those whom their friends or the Scottish nation desired to honor. The little isle had ceased to enjoy the safety of poverty and insignificance. It was the most conspicuous mark for piracy. As early as 802 its religious houses were visited by the sea-kings, plundered and burned. Four years later the invasion was renewed, the island ravaged and many of the brethren slain. The richness of the booty attracted other adventurers of the same class, and the repeatedly repaired buildings were subjected to repeated desolation.

In 814 a new Columbite church was completed at Kells,[1] in the county of Meath in Ireland, which became a refuge for residents of Iona when harassed in their own exposed situation. In Scotland also, for greater security, as well as for other reasons, much of the weight of Columbite churchism was about the same time transferred by Constantine, king of the Picts, to Dunkeld,[1] although even that inland town was not entirely safe from piratical ravages. The island sanctuary was subsequently revived, and continued long to be a highly venerated seat of Christian learning, but its primacy came to an end, divided between Ireland and the Scottish mainland.

In the early part of the ninth century the

[1] Skene, i. 305.

Pictish kings had put their people at the head of the nations in Scotland. But a great calamity followed soon after. Disastrously defeated, in 839, by a piratical invasion of the Danes, they were unable to sustain themselves in war with their Scottish neighbors. Upon the death of the last heir of their dynasty, in 844, Kenneth, king of the Scots, succeeded to the Pictish throne.[1] The Scottish seat of destiny was removed from the palace of Dunstaffnage to the Pictish capital at Scone, and the two crowns were permanently united.[2] At first the new kingdom was that of the Picts and Scots, but in course of time the name "Pict" fell out of use, and that of "Scot" covered the whole; and that very naturally in days when the king was the chief bond of nationality. The united kingdom received the name Alban or Scotia.

Meanwhile, the old British kingdom of Strathclyde, with its head of authority at Glasgow, still retained its separate independence, although, together with Galloway, greatly weakened by incursions from their northern neighbors and from the Saxons of Northumbria. Between the Forth and Tweed, the eastern part of the country, called Saxonia, was still a debatable land, and those who contended for it on both sides were equally harassed by Northmen from the sea.

[1] Skene, i. 308-310.   [2] Buchanan, lib. vi. LXIX. Rex, near the end.

It was in the reign of the Pictish king Constantine, who died in 820,[1] that the new college at Dunkeld was founded,[1] being the third among that people, Abernethy being the first and St. Andrews the second. Afterward, when Scone became the capital of the united kingdom, and Dunstaffnage was deserted, Iona was left at a distance from all protection. As a place of royal sepulture it also became inconvenient. Lying, as it did, in the way of the Vikings as they swept through the Western Isles to the coasts of Ireland, nothing but poverty could save the lives of its inhabitants. In consequence of the union of the Scots with the Picts the connections between the royal families of the Scots and those of Ireland became relaxed. From neither side could Iona be maintained in its former rank.

The Scottish king Kenneth, on coming to the throne of the Picts, resolved to restore the Columban Church to its power among that people, from whom it had been expelled in the foregoing century. To that end he selected Dunkeld, perhaps as the most central seat for ecclesiastical supremacy over the Columbans in his dominions, and, there erecting a new church building, or perhaps renewing that of Constantine, removed to it a part of the relics of Columba.[2]

[1] Skene, i. 305.   [2] Ibid., ii. 307.

At first the Scandinavian invaders were heathen, but as time went on intercourse with the Christians among whom they lived brought about the conversion of their settlers, who became Christian according to the instructions proceeding from Iona. Later immigrations from Norway brought Christians after the type of Romanism planted in their native land by the successors of Anschar.[1] But that in the Hebrides was a small element of population, and created no discord in the religion of the country. They now ceased to be plundering Vikings. Shetland and the Orkneys were completely under Norwegian rule, and continued so to be until the fifteenth century.[2]

Scottish clergy of the Columbite school had carried the gospel to those northern islands, but, exposed to the full storm of Norwegian warfare, they seem to have been early exterminated. Tales are told also of their missions to the Faroe Islands, to Iceland and to Greenland, and even of their enterprise, or desperate flight from persecution, beyond the ocean to the coast of North America.[3] Such traditions bear testimony at least to a prevailing belief in the greatness of their missionary courage and devotion.

[1] Maclear, *The Northmen*. [2] Ibid.; Skene, i. 375-379.
[3] *Brit. and For. Evangel. Rev.* for July, 1881, iii.

CHAPTER XII.

CONSTRUCTING THE KINGDOM OF SCOTLAND.

OVER Europe in general the tenth century was a period of great depression. Ignorance prevailed. There was no popular education. Even among families of wealth and high rank only the members designed for the priesthood were instructed in letters. For the rest it was deemed enough to learn how to manage a horse and wield their weapons. Ecclesiastics, content with their superiority of intelligence and the submission of the multitude, indulged their indolence. Spiritual enterprise lay torpid. The energies of the great Catholic Church were expended chiefly upon the enlargement of her endowments and increase of her subjects and power. The proper work of the gospel languished, and ecclesiasticism became secular. The Scottish severed from the Catholic Church, and thereby saved from partaking in her evils, suffered from other evils native to itself.

Among the many peoples who divided the territory of North Britain, the Picts had hitherto been strongest. By the arrival of the Northmen their superiority was divided with a dangerous competitor. The friendly colony of Dalriad Scots had grown into a kingdom. Although a warlike people, their progress had not been alarming to their neighbors, but rather connected with the diffusion of Christianity. Iona was within their bounds, and their seat of royalty was not far off at Dunstaffnage in Lorn. In respect to religion the Scots had long submitted to a grievance from their Pictish neighbors, whom their missionaries had converted. Kings of the Picts, becoming acquainted with Romish practices from Saxon monks, had imposed them on the Scottish Church in their dominions, driving the Scottish clergy into banishment and alienating the institutions they had founded.

Union of the two nations in one kingdom under a Scottish dynasty formed a new power which might hope to resist the Northmen. But it needed compacting by a sense of satisfaction on both sides. Among the measures necessary to that end, agreement on the subject of religion was most of all necessary. Of that the early kings of the united kingdom seem to have been well aware. By Kenneth, the first of that line, freedom was at once secured for the Scottish clergy in his Pictish provinces, and, as far as practicable, restoration of the religious houses from which they had been expelled. And on the other side, the place of Iona as a religious centre was given to Dunkeld in the land of the Picts, and where already stood a Pictish church.

As another element of compromise, the abbot of Dunkeld was made also bishop over the territories of the Picts which had come under Kenneth's rule. Thus the same person, "as abbot of Dunkeld, occupied toward the Columban monasteries in Scotland the same position as had belonged to Iona," while as bishop "he was the recognized head of the Pictish Church."[1] In the next reign these offices were separated, the episcopal office being transferred to Abernethy, but still in the land of the Picts, and only one bishop for the whole kingdom.[1]

Girig, the fifth king in that list, although apparently of foreign birth, is honored on the ancient record of the Picts and Scots as he who first gave freedom to the Scottish Church, which until that time had been in bondage under the law and usage of the Picts.[2] Perhaps he added to what Kenneth had done the relief of church property from the bondage of secular exactions which it had suffered under Pictish rule.[3]

Seven Scottish kings reigned within the tenth century over the united kingdom, now called Alban. Of these the first and most eminent

[1] Skene, ii. 308.   [2] Ibid., i. 333.   [3] Ibid., 320–323.

was Constantine, second of that name in the Scottish line. In the beginning of his reign Norwegian invasion upon the centre of his kingdom was finally repelled, and Danish pirates in East Lothian were constrained to retire farther south from the territory over which he ruled. In both of those hard conflicts the standard was the pastoral staff of Columba.[1]

Constantine was less successful in his wars with the kingdom of Wessex. On that side he had to contend against the illustrious Saxon monarch Athelstan, who met his movements southward by a retaliating raid upon the heart of his dominions, and finally, in 937, terminated his campaigns by the disastrous battle of Brunanburh.

After his early success in war with the Norwegians and Danes, Constantine gave much care and labor to the consolidation of his kingdom and to the obliterating of national distinctions among his subjects, endeavoring to put all upon a fair legal and religious equality. In the sixth year of his reign he convoked a great assembly on the Moothill, near the "royal city of Scone," in which he and Kellach, a bishop, assumed a solemn obligation to observe the laws and discipline of the faith and the rights of the churches and of the gospel, and that they should be maintained on a footing of

[1] Skene, i. 347, 348.

equality with the Scots.[1] By this declaration the Pictish and Scottish churches were to be united, and one bishop set over them, whose residence was to be in St. Andrews. Kellach was himself the first of that line of bishops. His jurisdiction was the whole united kingdom of the Scots and Picts, then called Alban, afterward Scotia. That kingdom, under Constantine, included all the mainland from Loch Broom and Dornoch Firth on the north to the Forth and Clyde and the extremity of Kintyre on the south. Caithness and Sutherland, with all the island groups—Orkney, Shetland and Hebrides—were in possession of the Norwegians. South of the Clyde and Forth, the east was occupied by Saxons, the extreme south-west by Celts of Galloway, and the centre, from the firth of Clyde and the Atlantic Ocean to the Solway, constituted the kingdom of Strathclyde, otherwise called that of the North Cumbrian Britons. The Isle of Man was held by the Danes, who had also possessions in Ireland. After a busy and agitated reign Constantine II. withdrew from the cares of state, and spent the last nine years of his life in the duties of religion among the clerical fraternity of St. Andrews.

Malcolm I., the successor of Constantine, attempted to extend the borders of his kingdom

[1] Skene, i. 340; ii. 323, 324; M'Lauchlan, 308, 309.

on the north, to include all the mainland in that direction. But he failed to carry them north of Moray, nor even in that province was his rule firmly established. Meanwhile, further additions were made on the south. The Danish kings of Ireland were making effort to annex Northumbria to their conquests. Landing on the coast of Cumbria (the present Cumberland and Westmoreland), they overran it and made it their path to a greater object of their ambition. For the Northumbrians had chosen "Olaf of Ireland for their king." But Edmund, brother of Athelstan, and his successor on the English throne, defeated their plans, and in 944 removed all resistance to himself from Northumberland. The next year, to break off its communications with Ireland, he reduced Cumberland, and gave it to Malcolm, king of the Scots, on condition of co-operating with him both by land and sea.[1] Upon Edmund's death, Edred Atheling brought all Northumberland under English rule (954). And thus the border of England was carried to the Tweed, while the dominions of the Scottish king extended on the south into Cumberland and Westmoreland.

The same year Malcolm lost his life in a further attempt on Moray. In the succeeding reign of Indulph (954–962) the Scots obtained possession of Edinburgh,[2] a strong base for

[1] Skene, i. 361–363.   [2] Ibid., i. 365.

movement upon the Saxon settlements to the south-east. And after the less important reigns of Duff and Cuilean, the next king, Kenneth II., actually turned his enterprise in that direction. His ambition was to reduce the intervening territory and annex Northumberland to Scotland, while the English king insisted upon his claim to the eastern coast as far as the Forth. Battles were fought, but the permanent change on either side was small. On the north, Norwegian dominion had returned to the southern borders of Moray, under the valorous leadership of Sigurd the Stout, who held his hereditary earldom of Caithness in spite of all the force of the Scots, and annually made his expedition to the Hebrides and to Ireland, and added to the territory of his fathers the provinces of Moray and Ross, with a large extent of country down the western coast into Argyll.

Kenneth, thus limited by strong enemies on both north and south, was constrained to confine the efforts of his long reign to the consolidation of the internal power of what he already possessed. His successor, Constantine IV.,[1] was slain in a battle with an opposing party of his own subjects before the end of his second year. Kenneth III. met the same fate after a reign of six years, but meanwhile had maintained the

[1] Sk ne, 374-380.

boundaries of his kingdom as it came into his hands, and transmitted it unimpaired to his successor, Malcolm II. And Malcolm, by his great victory of Carham over the Northumbrians in 1018, carried the boundaries of his kingdom from the Forth to the Tweed; and, with the previous extension of Cumbria southward, his grandson Duncan, king of Cumbria, from the same date reigned on the west as far south as the Derwent and over more than half of Westmoreland.[1]

The royal line of Strathclyde—which must now be called Cumbria—had hitherto proceeded from an ancient family claiming Roman descent. In 908 that dynasty came to an end, and Donald, brother of Constantine II. of Alban, was elected king.[2] In the third generation a grandson of the Scottish king succeeded as heir to the same throne,[3] and on the death of his grandfather inherited that of the Scots. Thus in 1034 the kingdoms were united under the Scottish dynasty.

In those days of spiritual inactivity the political and social standing of the Scottish Church was high. Churchmen were on an equality with the noblest of the land. An abbot of Dunkeld marries the daughter of a king, and their son takes his place in the royal succession; and the abbacy of a Columbite monastery, or even a

[1] Skene, i. 394, 398, 399. [2] Ibid., 346. [3] Ibid., 392.

place among the brotherhood, is held to be not unworthy the dignity of a retired monarch.

Iona continued her ecclesiastical existence—still the link between the Irish and the Scottish Church—but under deep depression, and only as aided by other institutions of the connection. Sometimes an Irish abbot, as of Raphoe or of Armagh, would be constituted also abbot of Iona as chief of the Columbite fraternity. But for a long time it is doubtful whether any of them made his abode on the island.[1] Later in the century it appears that there was a resident abbot at the same time with the chief in Ireland. In 986 the Danes put to death the successor of Columba at Dublin, and in an expedition to the Hebrides slew the abbot of Iona with fifteen of his clergy.[2] Norwegians and Danes had now obtained complete command of the sea between Ireland and North Britain, and the formerly intimate relations between the churches of the two countries ceased. With the rise of Dunkeld and Abernethy and St. Andrews on one side, and the obstruction of communication with Ireland on the other, Iona was shorn of her power, but even under the heaviest adversity had not ceased to be the most venerated shrine in the land of the Scots.

There was now a Scotland, comprehending the greater part of North Britain. It had

[1] M'Lauchlan, 310-312. [2] Skene, ii. 333.

grown from the little Scottish kingdom of Argyll, by union with the best of Pictland, then by victory securing the land of the Saxons on the lower Tweed, and by dynastic relationship annexing the whole of Cumbria. Still, much was lacking of completeness. Galloway stood out as a separate state, and Caithness and Sutherland and a large tract of the western coast and all the islands were in the hands of the Northmen.

The northern invaders were still for the most part heathen, but in the land from which they came the work of the Gallic missionary Anschar was making progress—greater than it had made during his lifetime—although slow in reaching Norway; and those who had secured settlements on the islands and coasts of Scotland were gradually brought into conformity with the Christianity prevailing around them. In course of time a change took place whereby the Northmen settled in the islands began to claim an interest in the ecclesiastical institutions which their forefathers had plundered. This took place chiefly in the Shetland and Orkney islands after the eleventh century; but already, in the tenth, one of the Danish kings of Dublin went on a pilgrimage to Iona, where he died "after penance and a good life."[1]

Later immigration from Scandinavia came

[1] Skene, ii. 333.

with profession of Christianity after the style carried there by Romish priests; and while Malcolm II. was still upon the Scottish throne Canute, a Christian Dane, was reigning in England.

As respects religion, the component parts of the new kingdom of Scotland were, in the main, of one mind. Christian doctrine, as believed by the Scots, had been accepted by the Picts, and coincided with that of the Cumbrian Britons. Some practices and elements of government had been copied from England by Pictish kings and enforced upon their clergy. But the early princes of the united kingdom sought to restore agreement. In the reign of Constantine II. the Church of the Picts was united on an equal footing with that of the Scots, only one new element being added— namely, that of a bishop over the whole. That bishop seems to have represented not an ecclesiastical demand, but a royal idea. It was the monarchical principle appended to the Church rather than filling any place created by its wants. For the monastic system of the Scottish Church continued to be the system of the united Church. The bishop's place could therefore be only a higher honor than any other clergyman in the kingdom had a legal right to claim.

CHAPTER XIII.

MACBETH.

THE long-protracted warfare of Scots and Saxons for sole dominion between the Forth and Tweed was decided by the campaign of Malcolm II. and the battle of Carham in favor of the Scots. Cumbria, dynastically connected with Scotland, was already a sub-kingdom of that growing power. Her king, a kinsman of Malcolm, was with him in the battle, and was there slain or died soon after. His successor, Duncan, grandson of Malcolm, sixteen years later (1034) inherited also the crown of Scotland.

In this newly-constituted union of kingdoms Cumbria, though oldest in profession of Christianity, and when the rest were heathen distinguished among Christians for simplicity of ordinances and government, had fallen under great depression. Diminished in strength by the removal of multitudes of her people into Wales, she tacitly submitted to a dominion which was creeping step by step over all.

Duncan's right to the throne of Scotland was through his mother, a daughter of Malcolm II., for that king had no male heirs; but Malcolm had secured it for himself by the issue of war, in which he had defeated and slain his predecessor, Kenneth IV.; and now there was still a claimant from that side, who stood as nearly related to Kenneth as Duncan stood to Malcolm. The son of Kenneth was dead, but a daughter of that son was living, who had been married to the mormaer of Moray, and after his death carried her claims, with the guardianship of her son, to her second husband, Macbeth, son of a former mormaer of Moray. If Duncan was the son of a daughter of the late king, Gruach, wife of Macbeth, was the daughter of a son of the preceding king. As respects nearness of relationship they were on precisely the same footing. And if a woman might not in those days wear the crown herself, she might presume to transmit the right to her husband as truly as to her son. Such most probably was Gruach's view of the case. Nor could she fail to regard Malcolm II. as an usurper, and the occasion at least of her grandfather's death. He certainly had grasped for himself all the profit to be secured from it. Lady Macbeth, as Shakespeare calls her, viewed herself as the heir of a royal inheritance of which her family had been unjustly and by violence deprived. Her descent, moreover, was from the older branch of the royal family of Alpin. But Duncan's father, Crinan, abbot of Dunkeld, also represented the mormaership in the ancient house of Athole, whose weight proved the greater in a threefold rivalry. For, to complete the story, another piece of genealogy is needed: Finlay, the father of Macbeth, had been, some thirty years before, mormaer of Moray. He was defeated in battle by Sigurd, the Norwegian jarl of Caithness and Sutherland. King Malcolm II. was pleased with the event, and gave one of his daughters to Sigurd in marriage. After Sigurd's death his son Thorfinn was confirmed by Malcolm in possession of the two northern counties. Thorfinn, when his cousin Duncan came to the throne, did not feel disposed to submit his independent territory as a province of the Scottish kingdom, and no doubt thought that as a grandson of the late king and the son of a distinguished soldier he had as good a right to the sovereignty as the son of the abbot. For one cause or the other, or both, he refused the submission or tribute which his cousin demanded. Duncan assumed to depose him, and appointed Moddan in his place, sending an army to enforce the substitution. The army was worsted, and Moddan betook himself to Duncan. A new expedition was organized, which issued in disaster and the death of Moddan.

In these circumstances Thorfinn moved a

force across the boundary of his own domains. Duncan hastened in person to encounter the insurrection. But again his forces were defeated, and the rival kinsman pressed on his victorious march to the south.

At this juncture Macbeth, who was probably commander of the royal army then, conceived the project of securing his own claim. The son of Sigurd was his hereditary enemy, but if the king were out of the way might agree with him in dividing the whole territory of North Britain—Scottish and Scandinavian both —between them. Duncan was murdered somewhere in the neighborhood of Elgin on the 14th of August, 1040. Soon afterward the division of the country took place, the north being assigned to the Norwegian earl, and the centre to the mormaer of Moray with the honors of king of Scotland.

The abbot of Dunkeld did not quietly submit to the fate of his son. Five years later he fell in a battle fought apparently for the restoration of his house.[1]

But the murdered king was destined to transmit the contested inheritance. Duncan had married a sister of Siward, the Danish earl of Northumberland, and with that uncle his family found protection after his death. His children were then young, but at the end

[1] Skene, i. 404, 405, 407.

of fourteen years Malcolm, the oldest, was carried into Scotland by Siward at the head of a great army of Saxons. The issue of war put him on the throne of Cumbria and Lothian. Macbeth retired northward, and sustained himself two years longer, no doubt by aid of Thorfinn. In 1057, Thorfinn died. Malcolm renewed the war with native forces, and pursued Macbeth into the Highlands, where he defeated and slew him on the 15th of August, 1057.

Macbeth reigned seventeen years, and is not, by the old records, charged with injustice in administration of the government. The country is said to have enjoyed prosperity under his rule. To the Church he was eminently liberal, conferring extensive lands upon "the Culdees of Lochleven, from motives of piety and for the benefit of their prayers."[1] He was the first of Scottish monarchs to offer directly his services to the bishop of Rome. There is some reason to believe that both he and Thorfinn visited Rome, and obtained absolution from their sins; and there is no doubt that Macbeth expended money liberally among the Roman poor. Nor are these facts incredible of the murderer of Duncan. In neither earlier nor later times has the Church been ignorant of conscience-money.

[1] Skene, i. 406.

CHAPTER XIV.

MALCOLM CANMORE.

MALCOLM III.—called Canmore, or Great Head—son of the murdered Duncan, succeeded Macbeth as king of Scotland. Early in his reign, which began in 1057, he married the widow of the recently deceased Thorfinn, earl of Sutherland and Caithness. The defeat of Macbeth, and seven months afterward of his stepson Lulach, had reduced the protracted resistance of Moray, and thus the northern part of the mainland was formally connected with the Crown.

Malcolm III. stands in a clearer historical light than any of his predecessors. Changes took place in his time which went to put the kingdom into nearer relations with the general current of European history. The Norman Conquest of England in 1066 was of hardly less importance to the government and people of Scotland than to those of England, and of more importance to the Scottish Church. It imposed the feudal system upon England, and gave occasion to its partial adoption in Scotland, where it afterward divided the kingdom

with the old national patriarchy. A great
change was also made in the material of
population in both countries. A Norman element was added to that of England, and a large
Saxon, and eventually a Norman one also, to
that of the south of Scotland. In the former
country it was an addition of conquerors, who
were constituted the nobility and rulers; in the
latter, an addition of refugees, most of whom
came as commoners and servants.

From the severities inflicted by the Conqueror multitudes of English people, some of high
birth, fled to the northern kingdom. Among
those fugitives came the Saxon heir of England,
Edgar the Ætheling—that is, the crown prince
—with his mother and two sisters. They were
kindly received by King Malcolm, who also
aided Edgar in attempts to retrieve some part
of his fortunes. But a campaign made into
Northumberland, and carried as far as York, resulted in only adding to the number of refugees,
vast multitudes of whom followed the returning
army. They were distributed throughout the
south of Scotland. Rare was the family in
which English slaves were not to be found,
many of them sold by themselves to secure
the means of subsistence.

Malcolm's first wife died young. He subsequently married Margaret, sister of the fugitive
Saxon prince. Her brother he also protected

and provided for bountifully, more so than the weakling deserved. He never succeeded in pushing his raids into England farther than York, nor in lessening the power of the Conqueror, but he limited the northward advance of conquest. The territory embraced by Northumberland, Durham, Cumberland and Westmoreland by his aid successfully resisted the establishment of Norman rule. Malcolm did not secure the annexation of it to his own kingdom, but during the time of William I. he prevented the Normans from adding it to theirs. It was ravaged by invasions from both sides. Provoked by that resistance, William in 1072 broke through the debatable land and brought the Scottish king to terms of peace, and forced him to give his son Duncan a hostage for their observance.[1] Edgar also, at Malcolm's advice, made his peace with William, who entertained him at his court and gave him lands in Normandy.

Thus was the conflict settled for the time. But in 1091, William the Conqueror died, and his successor, William Rufus, expelled Edgar from his estates. The Ætheling had recourse to his royal brother-in-law,[2] who once more led an army into England to assert his cause.

In the course of successive campaigns Malcolm again ravaged Northumberland; William

[1] Skene, i. 424.   [2] Ibid., 428.

seized the lands south of the Solway belonging to the king of Scotland as part of the ancient British kingdom of Strathclyde, and at a conference of the two kings at Gloucester treated the Scottish king with indignity. Resenting the insult, Malcolm withdrew, and brought another army into Northumberland. The campaign ended in his death and that of his son Edward, it is said by the treachery of Morel of Bamborough, who, under pretence of surrender, lured him into his power, Nov. 13, 1093. Queen Margaret died upon receiving the tidings.

The reign of Malcolm Canmore is one of the most important epochs in Scottish history, covering thirty-five years, within which the kingdom was extended from the lower Tweed and the Cheviot mountains and the Solway on the south to Caithness on the north, and over all the Hebrides.[1] And that change in the Church was commenced which eventuated in its displacement before the Romish. In the latter movement the principal actor was Queen Margaret, a woman of high intellectual endowments and earnest piety, with a degree of ecclesiastical learning uncommon among her sex in that day. Her thinking, moulded by the Romish Church, enabled her to defend it before the majority of men who admitted its traditional

[1] Skene, i. 431-433.

interpretation of Scripture. It had been her wish to enter a nunnery and spend her whole life in devotion; and hardly was she persuaded to forego that purpose by the offer of a throne, and, of what must have weighed more in the estimation of such a woman, the love of a brave, true-hearted and generous man. Becoming queen of Scotland, she took under her special care the interests of religion. The Saxon princess, from the nature of her education, could not fail to condemn many things in the Scottish Church, however they might have been estimated on their own merits.

Christianity was still taught in Scotland, north of the Clyde and Forth, by the Church of which Columba had planted the seeds in Iona, for the Culdees in Pictland had substantially maintained the succession. But it had not escaped the hands of the innovator, the ravages of war, nor the effects of natural decay which will befall any Church unquickened by revivals of spirituality. Changes adopted from the Saxons had only marred the development of its native constitution. As far as they pertained to organization, they were incongruous elements in the clan system, embarrassing it without securing any proper province for themselves. Territorial distribution of dioceses and parishes was quite foreign to it. Its priesthood had always been collegiate. Episcopacy had no virtual place in it, and could never be more than functional. In course of time it dwindled into a mere representative bishop for the kingdom, and that, being really unnecessary, was finally abandoned. The bishop of St. Andrews, who died in 1093, was the last of that line. The attempt to engraft Romanism upon the Columban Church had proved an utter failure.

Frequent internal wars and the devastation of a great part of the country by heathen invaders had destroyed many of the properties of the Church and crippled others, breaking down or displacing the clans to which they pertained. In many cases "the lands with the ruined buildings fell into the hands of laymen, and became hereditary in their families, until at last nothing was left but the mere name of abbacy applied to the lands, and of abbot borne by the secular lord for the time."[1]

From such causes the Scottish Church of the eleventh century was greatly reduced in efficiency, and from some parts of the country removed entirely. The Culdees were the clergy, a society of secular priests, who, occupying the churches and their properties not otherwise appropriated, discharged all public religious duties, maintaining divine service and providing spiritual advisers for the people. Dr. Reeves

[1] Skene, ii. 365.

says of the *Kelede* of Armagh that they continued to be the officiating clergy of the churches there, "and by degrees grouped themselves around the great church, where they became the standing ministers of the cathedral. They were presided over by a prior, and numbered about twelve individuals."[1] Of the same nature was their place in the Scottish churches. And well was it with those which enjoyed the ministrations of Culdees. Where the Columban clergy had been expelled in war, and their places usurped by laymen, ministration of the gospel must have ceased.

On some points of doctrine, on the manner of administering the Eucharist and observing the Lenten fast, in the ranks of the ministry on the source of ecclesiastical authority and the monastic orders, the Scottish Church still differed from that of Rome. Scripture was held to be the sole authority in faith; the Catholic claimed an hereditary authority of her own —traditional in a line of apostolic bishops. The time of observing Easter had, from the eighth century, been conformed to the Roman; but the Roman mass had not been introduced, and the Scottish Lent was a continuous fast. In their ministry and their government the churches differed still more widely.

[1] Dr. Reeves *On the Ancient Churches of Armagh*, p. 21; Skene, ii. 359.

The Scottish Church in its constitution stood entirely apart from the State. Its ministers were supported by the free gifts of the worshipers and by their own industry. Nor did they claim to derive their sanction from any earthly sovereign, ecclesiastical or civil. The king might be their friend or protector or benefactor; he was not their head. The bishop of Rome was allowed to be the greatest among bishops, but Scotland was no province of his, and from some of his practices they dissented. The intermeddling of Saxon monks and Pictish kings had produced great confusion, but had not substantially altered the organization. In the eleventh century the Scottish Church still retained its distinctive features as inherited from the missionary society of Iona. The Culdees had taken the place of the Columban clergy, or the Columban clergy had gradually merged into Culdee societies. Their occupations among themselves were still chiefly devotion and study of the Bible and other matters pertaining to ministerial duties, in accordance with which the "practice of clerical worship" seems to have been "deemed their special function."[1] From their common residence they attended to the instruction and other spiritual wants of the community in which they were planted.

[1] Reeves, *Ancient Churches of Armagh*, p. 21.

Their societies were not monastic in any sense accepted as true at that date. The brethren were not bound by vows of celibacy; they might hold property, and their institution had no relation to the papacy by sanction or otherwise. It would better serve the purpose of clearness, and avoid the risk of confounding two classes of things quite different, to call them colleges (*collegia*), for, whatever else they were, ecclesiastical colleges they certainly were, and nothing else were they so much. The Scottish Church was founded upon *instruction*. Theological colleges were its only seats of power. Bishops as well as presbyters were recognized, but presbyters alone were the working clergy. And yet it was not a Presbyterian Church. It had no parochial distribution of clergy and congregations, nor organic classification of them into presbyteries. The clan system, though greatly disorganized, was still the type of government. Not strong at best, as compared with the Catholic, rather like the ganglionic system of nerves in the human frame as distinguished from the spinal, it was ill suited to present an effective resistance to a compacted force like that which was soon to be arrayed against it.

That ancient Church, we must not forget, had come from Ireland, and the Irish Church was the first of a mission from the old British

Church, which at one time extended from the Clyde southward all the way through the Roman provinces, and still in the eleventh century held its ground in Cumbria and down the west of South Britain through Westmoreland, Lancashire, Wales and Cornwall. All these affiliated churches were still free, retaining their earlier doctrines and their ecclesiastical independence. Though not in all respects identical, they were of one common type and entirely harmonious in their relations with each other. The Saxons, who then possessed the east and centre of England, having been converted by missionaries sent from Pope Gregory I., were entirely Roman Catholic, and their religion, together with their settlements, prevailed also in the district immediately to the north of the Tweed.

Such were the ecclesiastical relations of the British Isles when the Celtic king of Scotland married a Saxon princess.

BOOK SECOND.

PERIOD OF PAPAL RULE.

INTRODUCTION OF ROMANISM.

CHAPTER I.
ST. MARGARET THE QUEEN.

THE religious condition of her husband's kingdom became to Queen Margaret a matter of great concern. In her eyes the doctrines taught and the practices observed were heretical. It was her wish to abolish them and in their place to establish those of Rome. The king complied. At her instance councils of the Scottish clergy were called, in one at least of which she appeared in person and maintained her positions in an oral address. "Her biographer tells us that 'at the principal council thus held she, with a few of her own ecclesiastics, contended for three days with the sword of the Spirit, which is the word of God, against the supporters of those strange customs; while her husband, who was equally well acquainted with the Anglic language and with his native Gaelic, acted as interpreter.'"[1]

In the annual commemoration of the Lord's

[1] Skene, ii. 346, from Turgot.

passion the various parts had been gradually shaped in a long course of time. The process of growth was not the same in all churches. Differences existed touching the order of the Easter observances, the date for beginning them and the length of the preceding fast, which varied greatly from time to time, until finally fixed to the sacred number of forty days. During the latter centuries of that prolonged growth and controversy the Scottish Church, cut off from communication with those on the Continent, adhered to the style of observance which prevailed in the British churches before the Romans withdrew. And the British churches then were still marked by features of the third century. Within the long interval until the eleventh century the Roman Church had settled many questions and adopted many practices unknown, or imperfectly known, or disapproved of, by the theologians of the far West. Among other things, the controversy of Easter had been determined by adoption of the Romish rule. And in the main the Scottish Church had conformed, but not perfectly. Now, so long had that rule been observed as to give the general impression among Roman Catholics that it had existed from the beginning. The multitude had lost the memory of controversy on the subject. Fully under that conviction, the pious queen set to work to bring the

Scottish Church into line with the Roman Catholic as a matter indispensable to salvation.

For the fast of precisely forty days she argued Christ's example and the practice of the Catholic Church. The Scottish clergy did not reject either, but said that they complied correctly with Scripture. But the queen found fault that they counted in the Sundays, and the Catholic Church never fasted on Sunday. If the Scots would subtract the six Sundays, as they ought, they would find that the Lenten term did not amount to forty days. So the queen was right by Roman Catholic rule. But if the Lord's forty days' fast were the law, the Scots were right, for his was a continuous fast, without excepting Sabbaths.

Against their refraining from communion upon the specially solemn occasion of Easter Day, lest they should eat and drink judgment to themselves, the queen reasoned scripturally, but assumed also the erroneous ground that the communicant was prepared, having been washed from the stains of his sins by the preceding long fast and its duties.

A third point was the mass, which the Scots were charged with celebrating in a barbarous manner. No description is given of what is thus called "barbarous." But nothing unscriptural is necessarily understood in it. For the same term is applied by Roman Catholics of the present day to the manner of observing the Lord's Supper in all Protestant churches. The Latin word *barbarus* classically signifies only that a thing is neither Greek nor Latin. The sacrament was ordered to be celebrated after the Romish rite, with acceptance of the elements as changed into the real body and blood of the Lord.

It seems to have been customary in the Celtic churches of early times, in Ireland as well as Scotland, to keep Saturday, the Jewish Sabbath, as a day of rest from labor, and Sunday, commemorative of the Lord's resurrection, as one of rejoicing, with exercises of public worship. In that case they obeyed the fourth commandment literally upon the seventh day of the week —the day on which the Lord lay in the grave— and did not understand the precept about resting from labor to apply to the day of rejoicing over his resurrection. On the latter, people did not feel under obligation to refrain from any of their ordinary occupations consistent with their attending upon public worship. The queen insisted upon the single and strict observance of the Lord's Day. People and clergy alike submitted, but without entirely giving up their reverence for Saturday, which subsequently sank into a half-holy day preparatory for Sunday.

A practice which to some extent prevailed without rebuke of the Church, supporting itself upon Hebrew example, whereby it was not unusual for a man to marry a deceased brother's widow or a widowed stepmother, was also, at the instance of the queen, censured and forbidden.

Among the changes introduced by the pious queen, it is remarkable that priestly celibacy was not included, nor the rule of poverty enforced upon the inmates of the Church colleges. That they were not has been conjecturally imputed to the priestly descent of her husband or the ecclesiastical position of her son, still a minor. It may have been so. But from what is told of Margaret's character it is not probable that her censure would have been withheld from the breach of a solemn vow. More likely, she knew that those vows were not concerned in the case, and that the government was not yet prepared for such a revolution as the attempt to institute them would create.

Her husband sustained the queen on those points, and added the weight of his royal sanction to the consent obtained from the councils. How far the acquiescence of the clergy became practical, and how far the changes were accepted into the real faith of the people, we cannot say. But it is worth remarking that the Saxon party of the court was intensely hated by the Celtic population, as appeared immediately upon Malcolm's death in the wars to exclude Margaret's sons from the throne; that the Saxon queen, with all her excellence, was not popular among the Scots; that in the high places of the subsequently-introduced hierarchy Scottish ecclesiastics had little share; and that long afterward, when the Scottish people once more took the regulation of their Church into their own hands, they rejected all the changes made by Margaret and her sons, except those touching marriage and the Lord's Day.

When her proposed reforms were accepted many Scottish institutions experienced great favor at the hands of the queen. Several ecclesiastical buildings, by her influence with the king, were erected or repaired. Iona, after the Hebrides had been restored to Scotland, enjoyed her patronage. Some of the houses, repeatedly subjected to plunder and latterly suffering from neglect, were restored and provided for. The king and queen, and the bishop of St. Andrews in the same spirit, also enlarged the endowments of "the hermit *Keledei* on the island of Lochleven, living there in the school of all virtues devoutly and honorably." Solitary anchorets were objects of her highest veneration. And as they would accept no donation at her hands, she honored them by complying with their religious wishes and admonitions. Crucifixes and other objects used in Romish worship were introduced into the churches by her example, and in some cases, as in those of Dunfermline and St. Andrews, by her donation.[1] Every encouragement was given to the practice of pilgrimage to holy shrines. Houses were erected and servants paid to wait in them for the accommodation of pilgrims to St. Andrews.

Queen Margaret was the first among the sovereigns of Scotland to interfere with spiritual matters in dictating faith and forms of worship. Rome, in whose interest her work was done, recognized the service and rewarded it with the honors of canonization. A learned ecclesiastic of that connection composed a glowing biographical eulogy of the royal saint, in which her good works are made to appear, as Alban Butler says, "more wonderful than her miracles," with which she was also adorned. She died upon receiving the tidings of her husband's death, and was buried at Dunfermline, where the king's body, when brought home, was also laid.

[1] Skene, ii. 345–353.

CHAPTER II.

THE SONS OF ST. MARGARET.

THE long and prosperous reign of Malcolm Canmore closed in gloom. In the same year the Western Isles were again ceded to Norway. The Scots, who had long beheld with jealousy the increasing influence of Saxons at the court of their king, and the enforcing of Saxon opinions upon themselves, with good reason apprehending the risk of losing all authority in their native land, immediately upon the death of Queen Margaret rose in arms to set Donald Bane, the brother of Malcolm, on the throne, as being one of their own race, in opposition to any of the sons of the Saxon queen. The rising was successful. The Saxons were expelled, and Donald Bane set up as king, and with such haste that the deceased queen was carried from Edinburgh Castle to her burial through armed bands by stealth, under cover of early dawn and of a dense morning mist.

Donald reigned six months, when Duncan, the oldest son of Malcolm by his first wife, asserted his claim, which was regarded with more favor by the people of Lothian and Cumbria. Duncan had been a hostage at the English court from his childhood, but now, with permission of King William II., and professing the fealty demanded, he marched to the north at the head of a force collected among Saxons and Normans, dethroned his uncle and took his place.

But English dependency in any degree was revolting to the Scots. At the end of six months their leaders banded together against Duncan and slew him, and again set up his uncle. A compromise was made with a view to unite the two parties, whereby Donald accepted as his colleague Edmund, one of the sons of Queen Margaret, who had taken part in the plot against Duncan. Alban or Scotia—that is, Scotland proper—at that time was the country between the Forth and Spey. Lothian, with its Saxon population, and Cumbria, the old kingdom of Strathclyde, were recently-annexed dependencies. In Lothian the dominion of a son of their much-admired queen was gladly accepted, while Donald was the choice of his Celtic countrymen.

To neither party perhaps was that divided rule entirely satisfactory. After about three years Edgar Ætheling, with an English force, carried his nephew Edgar, another son of Malcolm and Margaret, into Scotland. In a hard-fought battle he defeated Donald, took Edmund prisoner, and, having made Edgar king, returned to England. Edmund was doomed to perpetual imprisonment, and Donald, after two years, falling into Edgar's hands, was blinded and consigned to the same fate.

The kingdom of Malcolm Canmore was again united as to the mainland. Norway held dominion in the isles.

Edgar's reign extended from 1097 to 1107. It was uninterrupted by wars or party broils. When Magnus Barefoot, king of Norway, appeared a second time in the western seas, Edgar renewed to him the cession of the islands which his father had made. In his third year (1100) his sister Matilda was married to Henry I., king of England—an event of more importance to both countries than many expensive and bloody wars. By the Saxon population Matilda was regarded as one of themselves, a daughter of their own royal line. Her education had been almost entirely English. Her marriage went far to reconcile them to their new masters. Once more their race had an interest on the throne; the daughter of their princess Margaret was now queen of·England. The Norman king strengthened his own hand by a step which went to unite the conquered with the conquerors, and to create some check thereby upon his arrogant Norman barons;

and, added to other causes, it contributed, for one generation at least, to more friendly relations with Scotland. Through Matilda, by the marriage of her daughter with Geoffrey of Anjou, the powerful dynasty of the Plantagenets obtained their right to the English crown.

Upon Edgar's death his brother Alexander succeeded him, while David, a younger brother, was constituted, by Edgar's request, ruler of Cumbria, with the title of earl.[1] In the beginning of Alexander's reign another uprising of the Celtic party took place. But their army was pursued into the north, and finally defeated and dispersed beyond the Spey.[2] When Alexander died in 1124, David became king of both the north and south of Scotland, retaining the earldom of Northampton, which he had received with his wife, and other estates in England.[3] Within the period covered by these three reigns, from 1097 to 1153, the religious revolution begun by Queen Margaret was completed, and the kingdom subjected to a feudal government.[4]

David, while a youth, had followed his sister Matilda into England, upon her marriage with King Henry. Her deep religious feeling seems to have had much to do in the formation of his character. During many years' residence at

---

[1] Skene, i. 446.
[2] Ibid., 452.
[3] Ibid., 444-458.
[4] Ibid., 433-457.

the English court he was trained, "with the young Norman barons, in all the feudal usages, so as to become, by education and association with the young English nobility, imbued with feudal ideas and surrounded by Norman influences."

To the Celtic race that was far from agreeable. But another element of population had begun to enter Scotland, which, without the religious devotion of the Saxon, proved of more regulative effect in the government. The Norman friends of his youth were not forgotten by David when he came to power in his native land. Many of them were introduced to places of rank and emolument in his earldom and afterward in his kingdom. By marriage and otherwise he was himself a wealthy English nobleman. Through these means many Norman families were added to the higher ranks in Scotland, bringing with them their ideas of feudal distinctions, rights and privileges. Thus did the Somervilles, Lindsays, Bruces, Comyns, Avenels, Baliols and others receive their earliest settlements in the northern kingdom. It was as friends or guests of the king that they came. In some quarters they were endowed with large estates, as Robert Avenel in Eskdale and Robert Bruce in Annandale, and others elsewhere.

When David had been six years on the

throne an attempt to repel the foreign intrusion was made from the north, headed by Angus, a descendant of Lady Macbeth, as representative of the ancient mormaers of Moray, together with Malcolm, a natural son of the late king Alexander. In the reduction of that rebellion the whole territory of Moray was taken into possession of the king. But the discontent was not allayed, nor did it cease to break forth in successive insurrections for a hundred years.

CHAPTER III.

INTRODUCTION OF THE ROMISH CHURCH GOVERNMENT.

QUEEN MARGARET'S changes in the Scottish Church pertained to doctrine and observances; all the rest of the revolution was the work of her sons, Edgar, Alexander and David.

In the year 1093 the sole bishop of Scotia died. The kingdom was left without a bishop fourteen years, until the death of King Edgar —a defect in the eye of the monarchy, but not intrinsically in the national church system. It was not the intention of the monarchy now to continue that system.

In the Scottish Church all right to demand the attention and compliance of men was, from the first, treasured in the Holy Scriptures, in the duties of making their teaching known to the people, and in keeping their ordinances before the public mind. That Church was now, without discussion and by royal will alone, to be set aside for one which claimed a right to command obedience and belief by virtue of divine authority resident in her priesthood.

Establishment of the Catholic system was commenced by Alexander, and, as far as respects the mainland, carried forward almost to completeness by his brother and successor, David. The method generally pursued was that of reviving old bishoprics, British, Scottish, Pictish, not upon the old clan method, nor upon any compromise with it, nor as having any relation to it, but upon the simple parochial and diocesan plan. All the territory of the kingdom was to be divided into dioceses, and those subdivided into parishes. Each diocese was to have one bishop—no longer a mere functionary, but an actual ruler—and every parish its own priest. The tithes from the parishes were to sustain all.

Various predispositions of the old Church, into the details of which we cannot enter, facilitated these new divisions. Old Scottish abbacies could be changed into bishoprics by substituting a bishop for the abbot. Other members of the fraternity, where willing or desirable, could form the chapter of the diocese, or they could minister in parishes separately, as they had done hitherto collectively, for the clan or for a group of neighboring churches. Where such a transformation was not acceptable the old ministry was entirely superseded.

Consultation with the existing clergy was no part of the plan. No synod was called, although it was an age in which synods were common. The ecclesiastical transfer of a whole nation was not trusted to ecclesiastical authority, but conducted by the civil arm alone.

The three Celtic kingdoms were now united in one, together with a Saxon district. With the last there was no difficulty in the way of Romanism. Of the Celtic kingdoms, one was that of Strathclyde, now called Cumbria; another was that of the Picts; and the third, that of the Scots, latterly the ruling race. Each of these had at some time acknowledged one bishop. But the see of Cumbria at Glasgow and that of Abernethy had long ago been discontinued. The latter, when the Scots became masters in the north, had to part with its honors to Dunkeld, and Dunkeld, in the further progress of the same people, had to yield to St. Andrews. The Scottish bishopric at St. Andrews had been vacant since the death of Malcolm Canmore. At the accession of Edgar there was no bishop in any of those united kingdoms. As that rank of the ministry, though recognized among them, was not necessary to the completeness of their ecclesiastical order, it was easily allowed to fall into disuse when no special effort was put forth to keep it in place. Edgar did not attempt to supply the lack—" did not attempt to introduce a parochial church north of the Forth," but limited his ecclesiastical enterprise to the Saxon dependency between the Forth and Tweed.[1] In that quarter he refounded the monastery of Coldingham and established some churches on the parochial plan. But when his brothers— Alexander as king to the north of the great firths, and David as earl in the south—succeeded him, their mother's policy of assimilating the Church in their native land to that of Rome was at once resumed.

Alexander in the first year of his reign (1107) filled the vacancy in St. Andrews by appointing Turgot, prior of Durham, his mother's confessor and biographer, to the bishopric, and created two new sees, one for Moray and the other for Dunkeld. Moray was an earldom scarcely yet assured to the Scottish crown from its old hostility, continued in the family of Macbeth. The new ecclesiastical establishment, when in time it took effect, went to strengthen the ties of allegiance. Dunkeld was the seat of an old church rebuilt by Kenneth MacAlpine, founder of the Scottish dominion over the Picts. It was a Columbite institution, and for a time the head of Scottish ecclesiasticism in the land of the Picts. With the rise of St. Andrews it lost that place of honor. Still, it occupied a rank of some distinction in having given the reigning dynasty to the kingdom.

[1] Skene, ii. 368.

It was now transformed into a Romish bishopric by substituting a bishop for the Columbite superior. The ample territories still in its possession were such as to endow the new foundation with consistent dignity and completeness.

Upon St. Andrews, however, the higher honor was conferred, and to its bishop were "the fate and fortunes of the Culdee establishments" throughout the kingdom committed.[1] Most clearly, from the beginning of that reign, was it the royal intention to abolish the Scottish Church to make place for the Romish.

Meanwhile, during the whole of Alexander's reign in the north, David was pursuing the same policy in the southern dependencies "over which he ruled as earl." About 1115 he restored the diocese of Glasgow, and directed an inquiry to be made "by the elders and wise men of Cumbria into the lands and churches which formerly belonged to the see." Upon the information thus obtained he reconstructed the bishopric, in 1120 or 1121, to include all the territory of Cumbria then belonging to Scotland and as far as the Tweed. Lothian was chiefly Saxon, both by blood and religion, and was assigned to St. Andrews. Galloway, though belonging to Scotland, was under the ecclesiastical jurisdiction of York.

[1] Skene, ii. 372.

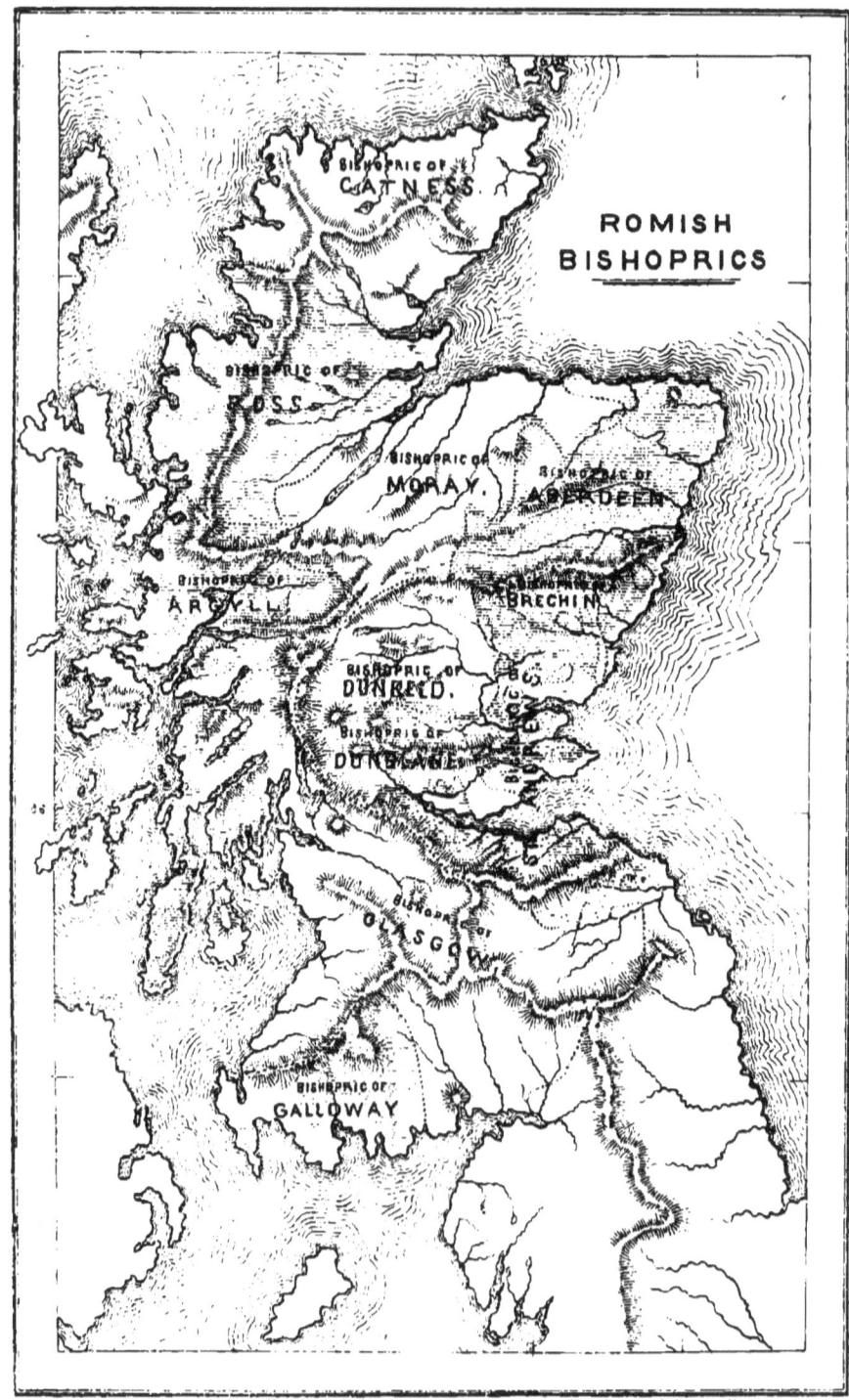

David, after he had become king of the whole country, continued to prosecute his work for the Church with increasing zeal until it amounted to a war of extermination against everything belonging to the native establishment. The disjointed style of government in the Scottish Church, now enfeebled by internal decay, was unable to present an effective resistance to the intrusion of such a compacted ecclesiastical host, marched in upon it with such steady persistence.

In King David's long reign of nearly thirty years the diocesan system was completely established over the whole kingdom, with parish boundaries prescribed for separate presbyters or vicars in their respective cures.

In constructing the dioceses all native institutions were seized and turned to the service of the intruder. Glasgow, St. Andrews, Dunkeld and Moray were already created or reconstructed when David began to reign—all except Moray being the conversion, each one, of the single bishopric of a formerly independent kingdom. In a few years more the rest of the work was done. A bishop of Ross between 1128 and 1130 held jurisdiction over the breadth of the mainland south of Sutherland, sustained by the transfer of an ancient Columban college with its revenues.[1] The diocese of the two north-

[1] Skene, ii. 377, 378.

ern counties, Caithness and Sutherland, was constituted in the early part of the same reign, though perhaps not fully established until the end of it. And by appropriation of several preceding institutions was that of Aberdeen created. Brechin and Dunblane were constructed out of fragments into which the old Pictish bishopric of Abernethy had been broken down.

The example of King David was, in this respect, followed by his powerful but refractory noble, Fergus, lord of Galloway, and his rival, Olaus (Aulay), Norwegian king of the isles. By the former the diocese of Galloway was reconstituted, subject to the archbishop of York; and by the latter, that of the Sudreys (Sodor) and Man about the year 1134. By Sudreys was meant the Hebrides, as lying south from the Orkney and Shetland groups. The Isle of Man was the residence of the Norse king of the isles.

At the death of David, in 1153, the transformation was complete. Nine episcopal sees comprehended the whole territory of the kingdom to be thus disposed of—namely, St. Andrews, Glasgow, Dunkeld, Dunblane, Brechin, Aberdeen, Moray, Ross and Caithness. The Shetland and Orkney isles, being under Norwegian rule, were not brought into the system until the next century, and the diocese of Argyll, or Lismore, was not separated from that of Dunkeld until 1222.[1] Whithorn was still ecclesiastically connected with York. Twelve dioceses covered the utmost extent that Scotland ever reached.

Upon the whole, as many of the Scottish clergy as submitted were assigned to subordinate places, generally perhaps as priests or curates to minister in the parishes. The native monastic system being abolished, the superintendence and working of the new system was put into the hands of aliens. It was doubtless perceived that the foreign Church could be best managed by foreigners, at least until the nation should be reconciled to it.

Of course the service instituted for the dioceses, as well as the cathedral constitution, was foreign. Both were, for the most part, copied from England. "Glasgow and Dunkeld followed the model of Salisbury; Moray, Aberdeen and Caithness that of Lincoln. The Breviary and Missal of Salisbury formed the ritual of all the Scottish dioceses."[2]

In the establishment of prelacy after the English model it followed that the English metropolitans claimed jurisdiction over the bishops in Scotland. But to admit that would have been to surrender the national independence, and on

---
[1] Skene, ii. 396, 397; *St. Giles Lect.*, p. 73.
[2] Joseph Robertson, *Quarterly Rev.*, June, 1840.

the part of the king the control of what he had himself created. One step more must be taken. A Scottish primacy must be constituted. The necessity was early perceived, and action taken in regard to it by Alexander I., who turned the revenues of St. Andrews into an endowment for the new metropolitanate. Turgot, the first incumbent, was a Saxon, who had been a monk and prior of St. Cuthbert's in Durham. He found much difficulty in getting his office into satisfactory relations with the English metropolitans and Romish practices on the one hand, and the royal authority, the priests and practices of the Scottish Church on the other.[1] He was appointed in 1107, when still the only bishop in what was then called Scotia, and was consecrated at York in 1109, with reservation of the rights of both sees. After six years of trouble he went into England for advice, and never came back. The see was again vacant until 1120. His successor, Eadmer, also a Saxon, a monk of Canterbury, found the same difficulties. Some clergy of his native country advised him to comply with the usages of the Scottish Church as far as he could "without dishonoring his character or hazarding his salvation." In their estimate, it seems, the difference between the Scottish Church and the Romish, on some points, was vital. Eadmer preferred to abandon the strife,

[1] Skene, i. 450.

and returned to England. Again the see was left vacant, and after Eadmer's death, in 1124, Alexander again chose a Saxon,[1] but one better acquainted with the country, having been some time prior of the monastery of regular canons at Scone, established by Alexander in the beginning of his reign. The king wanted a Scottish primacy without dependence on England; could he not find a Scotsman able and willing to take that honorable place? It seems not, or that he felt unwilling to trust any of them with so much influence over his plans. Robert the monk had to contend with the same difficulties which discouraged his predecessors, but he weathered through them, and in the fourth year of King David was consecrated by the archbishop of York, "as Turgot had been, reserving the rights of both churches," and held the office until his death, in 1158 or 1159. The bishop of St. Andrews, however, did not reach full recognition of his metropolitan honors until long afterward. The archbishop of York persisted in the claim of superiority over all the bishoprics of the north, nor at first would the pope interfere to restrain his ambition or to enforce compliance.

[1] Burton, i. 423.

CHAPTER IV.

INTRODUCTION OF ROMISH MONASTICISM.

DURING the same reigns another branch of the Romish ecclesiastical empire was planted in Scotland. Monachism is not an integral part of the Roman Catholic Church. It is rather a foreign resident which has obtained naturalization under severe conditions, never entirely removed. And yet in a large part of her history Roman Catholicism has fostered the regular monastic orders as valuable auxiliaries. But the royal sons of St. Margaret thought the Church not complete without the monastery, and set up the two side by side, as if they had been the two halves of a unit.

To neither the diocesan nor the monastic system were the Scottish clergy held to belong. They were set aside to make way for the bishops, and totally ignored when bringing in the orders. If the bishoprics in Scotland were every one constructed on an English model,[1] and an Englishman was appointed to preside over their working, the monasteries were a

[1] Joseph Robertson, in the *Quarterly Rev.*, June, 1849, p. 117.

wholesale importation, entirely of foreign material. Buildings for them were erected after the example of those in England or on the Continent, and the monks and nuns were imported from abroad. The work of their multiplication was carried forward by Kings Edgar, Alexander and David parallel with their reconstruction of the Church, until the land was full of them. Edgar had no sooner secured himself on the throne than he began (1098) by restoring the monastery of Coldingham among his Saxon subjects on the English border, providing it with abundant endowment and supplying it with Benedictine monks from Durham. He also founded a priory at Dunfermline, which was afterward remodeled by King David, who made it an abbey and placed in it Benedictine monks brought from Canterbury.[1] In 1114, Alexander erected an abbey for regular canons of St. Augustine at Scone, and in 1123 another for the same order on Inchcolm, and others elsewhere.

But in abundance of this kind of work David I. distanced all rivalry. In 1128 he established an abbey of Augustinians at Edinburgh, which, being dedicated to the Holy Cross, was called of the Holy Rood. He built at Melrose, upon the ruins of the old Columban institution, an abbey for Cistercian monks brought from

[1] *Gaz. of Scot.*, i. p. 389; Skene, ii. 392.

England; also the abbey of Cambus Kenneth for Augustinian monks from France; also that at Kelso, that at Jedburgh and others, besides priories in various parts of the kingdom. He furnished establishments for Knights Templars and Knights of St. John, whom he was the first to bring into Scotland. He also erected monastic houses for Cistercian nuns at Berwick, Three Fountains, and at Gulane in East Lothian.

Again the example of the monarch was imitated by some of his wealthy nobility. Fergus, lord of Galloway, founded for Premonstratensian monks the abbey of Soulseat near Stranraer, and another at Tungland, and one for Cistercians at Dundrennan. Hugh de Moreville, constable of Scotland, erected the abbey of Dryburgh on the Tweed, and that of Kilwinning in Ayrshire. Cospatrick, earl of March, built a convent for Cistercian nuns at Coldstream, and another at Eccles in Berwickshire.

In brief, when this enterprise of extinguishing the Scottish Church was complete, "not less than one hundred and fifty religious houses of all kinds" were established within the bounds of Scotland, "many of them richly endowed." A large portion of the best soil of the country had been transferred to foreign monks and nuns.[1] That many of the earlier monks were

[1] Dr. Campbell's *St. Giles Lecture.*

skillful farmers and generous landlords was so far good, but the time came when they were neither; and irrespective of that consideration, certainly the conduct of the king was the most extraordinary imposition ever inflicted upon an unsubdued people.

Whether it might not have been better to reconstruct the Scottish Church, and reform what needed reformation in it, would at that date have been unprofitable speculation. Its enemy was on the throne. That the change turned out to be for good in a great crisis of the national history will appear in the subsequent narrative. But, however well intended or however turning out, it looks to us at this distance of time and place as a singularly high-handed course of conduct. No doubt some of its details were as cruel as its general policy was arbitrary. Considering what Scotsmen are in spirit and independence, the serenity with which they, or some of them, write about the innovation is not a little remarkable. The king who seizes their entire Church and all its property, turns out their whole national clergy, and without consulting the religious preferences of the nation intrudes upon it a foreign Church with a great array of expensive foreign dignitaries, on whom he not only confers all that belonged to the national Church, but also lays an enormous burden of taxation upon the country to sustain the rank of the new and expensive class of nobility, is, in the language of some of their writers, "the saintly David." People in the ordinary way of speaking about such a ruler would use less complimentary terms. King James VI. said of David that he was "a sair sanct for the Croun." But, in fact, David's lavish expenditure, whatever it may have drawn from the legitimate resources of the Crown, was mainly furnished by his exactions from the people in the parishes and seizure of the entire national Church and robbery of her clerical servants.

It is vain to ask if he did any private injustice. Of course he did, in such a sweeping confiscation. Culdees resisted, but they could only protest. If they would retain a place in the Church, they had to accept it under the new organization, and abjure their own. In some places their order was disintegrated gradually, a law being enacted that when one of their number died his place should be filled by a canon of the Catholic Church; in others they were allowed to retain their own order, but under such limitations as to reduce them to insignificancy; and in others they were at once abolished by an act of extinction.

Of David's arbitrary way of treating the owners of the property he seized evidence remains in his own hand's work. One example will suffice. In a charter conveying the Culdee abbacy of Lochleven to St. Andrews for establishing a priory of Augustinian canons there, King David declares that he has given and granted to the canons of St. Andrews the island of Lochleven, that they might establish canonical order there; and the *Keledei* who shall be found there, if they consent to live as regulars, shall be permitted to remain in society with and subject to the others; but should any of them be disposed to offer resistance, his will and pleasure is that such should be expelled from the island.[1] Some colleges of Culdees submitted to that helpless dependency where they had once been principal, and, suffering successive diminutions of duties and importance, prolonged a half-alive existence for a century—some for more than two centuries. It was cruel injustice to the memory of the blessed and glorious days of Scottish evangelism to deprive that ministry of everything that made it valuable, and to keep its weakness on exhibition.

That long and lingering death was spared Iona. In 1203, Pope Innocent III. took the island under his protection and filled her cells with Benedictine monks.

What the sentiment of the Scottish people was we can only conjecture, for the records of

[1] Skene, ii. 388.

Scotland now passed into hands which exercised a retrospective care in manipulating those of the past as well as in tingeing with their own colors the facts of current history. But what were the feelings of the Celtic people toward their more than half-Saxon rulers is put beyond a doubt by the repeated insurrections to drive them and their successors from the throne.

Within the same twelfth century the Irish Church was also subordinated to the great dictator of religious profession. In 1171, Henry II. entered upon the conquest of Ireland, which resulted in bringing that country under English and papal dominion. In 1282, Wales was finally subdued, and the last resistance to English power in South Britain brought to a end. The papacy now spread its wings over all the formerly unfettered churches of the British Isles.

The ancient Scottish Church may be presumed to have been worse than the Romish, or better; but all pretension that it was the same is indubitably in error, seeing that a national revolution was needed to make it conform, and the effect of conformity was extinction.

Yet it must be said for the king that he undoubtedly believed himself in the right. He had been educated religiously, under the influence of a mother and a sister both devoted

Roman Catholics, and of intelligence and of consistency of life to recommend their faith. During his long residence in England he had been impressed with the regularity and imperial weight of power evinced by the Church of which the pope was the head. On the other hand, the Scottish Church appeared to be in a state of decay, without any common centre of authority or source of protection. In one quarter and another he saw it the prey of a rapacious layman, who, under the name of abbot, turned its property to his own use, leaving to his prior and a dozen Culdees some remnants of the income and all the work of the ministry.

To strengthen a feeble Church, to provide for the ordinances of religion among the people, and to turn the property so alienated into its right channel again, was certainly a good work for a king. But the whole religious construction needed to be renovated, built up anew from the foundation. Must it not also be built with sound material? In the king's mind of course there was no question. The Roman Church was the only true Church. To put it into the place of the feeble Scottish Church was a duty to the nation and to God. And whatever was needed to effect that end was right. Nor is it to be denied that the union of Scotland with the Catholic Church was at that time, and for the next hundred and fifty years, of unspeakable benefit to her progress in civilization and general national prosperity.

Scotland came into the Catholic Church at the beginning of those changes in church building which created the Gothic style of architecture. Her religious revolution, in the first half of the twelfth century, made an extraordinary demand—in fact, more than could be immediately met—for new buildings. All the parishes, with few exceptions, had to be provided for. The new bishoprics claimed cathedrals, and the bishops palaces consistent with their dignity. The multitude of monastic colonies had to be supplied with their appropriate accommodations. All this could not be done at once. Of course necessity took precedence of elegance. As far as existing Scottish buildings could answer the purpose they were converted to it, but all new structures were copied from those of their kind in England.

At that period the architectural style prevalent in England was the Romanesque, characterized by its round arches, its roofed towers, its correspondent sobriety of decoration and balance of sentiment between that of aspiration and repose. It could not fail to be transported with the spiritual structure into Scotland. Cathedrals and abbeys took longer time to finish, and some of them were not begun until many years after the death of David I., and when finished exhibited features of successive varieties of architectural progress. But the parish churches, a first necessity, where they did not retain the humbler character of the old Scottish, were probably all constructed after the Romanesque. "By far the greater number of ancient parish churches of which fragments still exist" are of that style.[1]

As many of the finest ecclesiastical buildings in Scotland reached their completeness in the latter part of the twelfth century and at different dates in the thirteenth, they presented more or less the graceful and stately outlines of successive varieties of the Gothic, then in England rising toward its maturity of beauty, which it reached in the fourteenth century. Unfortunately for Scotland, her progress in that art was abruptly suspended by the long and devastating war of independence, and ages of industry were needed to replenish the coffers of the builder. King Robert I., when victory had established him upon the throne, showed a disposition to repair the losses of the Church to the utmost of his power. He was present at the consecration of the cathedral of St. Andrews in 1318, and endowed it with the gift of a hundred marks a year, and toward the rebuilding of Melrose, laid in ruins by English invasion, he set apart "all the feudal casualties and crown issues of Teviotdale

[1] Dr. Campbell's *St. Giles Lecture*.

until they should amount to two thousand pounds sterling—a sum equal to more than fifty thousand pounds in the present day,"[1] and on his deathbed urged that it should faithfully be paid. The proceeds do not seem to have realized the king's expectations. The work went on slowly. Meanwhile, a richer variety of Gothic came in vogue in time to honor the more advanced part of the abbey with some of its most beautiful creations.

Thence, onward to the Reformation, Scotland in her architecture and other arts preferred the example of France.

At the religious revolution, the country must have been in a highly prosperous condition to afford such sumptuous institutions as it was now called upon to sustain. For the Church itself there must have been abundant provision—that is, for all the parish churches and parish priests. But when princely hierarchs had also to be maintained, the drain upon the parishes was greatly increased. And when a large proportion of the parochial income had also to go into the endowment of monasteries, or was otherwise disposed of, the burden became oppressive. From the first, the sons of St. Margaret had adopted the practice of conferring the revenues of parishes upon monastic houses. It increased as the twelfth century went on, and into the follow-

[1] *Quarterly Rev.*, June, 1849, p. 140.

ing. "In the reign of William the Lion thirty-three parish churches were bestowed on the abbey of Arbroath. Dunfermline had as many; Paisley, thirty; Holyrood, twenty-seven; Melrose, Kelso and Lindores, nearly similar numbers. The revenues of bishoprics were increased from the same source. In the early part of King William's reign the bishopric of Glasgow possessed twenty-five churches, and several more were afterward acquired by it." "Seven hundred Scottish parishes—probably two-thirds of the whole number—were vicarages; that is to say, the greater tithes of corn, etc. went to the monks and bishops, while the vicar, who performed the parochial duties, got only the lesser tithes or a very small money stipend." After dividing their earnings with the bishop and the great distant house of monks, the parishioners and their vicar must, many a time, have found the residue a scanty support. "The underpaid curate was despised for his poverty, which disabled him from worthily ministering to the varied wants of his parishioners, while those emoluments which would have provided a comfortable subsistence for a resident clergyman were carried off to the distant monastery or to the bishop's palace."[1]

Had those burdens accumulated by an insensible process of growth out of fundamental

[1] Dr. Campbell's *St. Giles Lect.*

principles admitted by the public to be right, as they had grown in most countries on the Continent, they might have been borne meekly as a necessity of Christian life. In Scotland the people had learned the demands of the gospel in another way—a way which had no leading in that direction. Romanism in its full maturity, both secular and regular, was stamped down upon them, without preparation for it, by purely absolute authority. They did not submit without a struggle, repeated struggles, but the royal arm proved the stronger. The really reconciling element, however, seems to have been the parish. Already in their own Church some tendency toward a parochial division of Christian work had begun to appear in certain quarters, and the completeness of the plan seems to have fallen in with the development of a native idea. Moreover, of all the work under Romanism parish work was that in which the Scottish clergy could most freely engage, and probably by them, in the first instance, were the parishes chiefly supplied. Reconciled thereby, the people were gradually brought to submit to other things, the value of which was not equally clear to them.

In less than one hundred years after the death of King David, another reinforcement was made to the host of monastic orders in an influx of Dominican and Franciscan friars. Organized for service in itinerant preaching, those orders could find no proper occasion for their presence where the secular clergy were faithful to duty. Whether in the thirteenth century that occasion existed in Scotland or not, we find it stated that there, as elsewhere, although they may at first have done good, yet upon the whole their influence proved injurious by creating dissension among the clergy and alienation between the people and their pastors.

CHAPTER V.

PAPAL SCOTLAND.—NATIONAL CONSOLIDATION.

KING DAVID I., saint by suffrage of admirers, but without canonization, left his kingdom enlarged by the firm annexation of Moray on the north, and of all the south mainland to the line of the Solway, the Cheviot mountains and the lower Tweed, but with the national resources at the disposal of the Crown greatly diminished. His tenure of Northumbria and that part of Cumbria south of the Solway did not constitute them provinces of Scotland. They were surrendered after his death. His earldom of Huntingdon was subsequently confirmed to his successor, on condition of paying homage to the king of England for it. But his extensive possessions in England, obtained with his wife, passed at her death into the hands of her son by a former marriage.

David's only son, Henry, with the consent of Stephen, king of England, was made earl of Northumbria. Henry dying before his father, in 1152, the succession to the throne of Scotland fell to his eldest son, Malcolm, not quite twelve years of age. By royal appointment the earl of Fife, chief of the seven native earls of Scotland, acted the part of guardian, and, securing the allegiance of his peers, crowned the young king without the intervention of a regency (1153). The policy was prudent. A war from the side of the Celtic population was already moving under Somerled, king of Argyll. It was successfully encountered, but not brought to an end until after five years (1159).[1] It was followed next year by a rebellion within the kingdom, led by six of the seven native earls. They failed in their attempt, and the king received them again into favor. In the same year he reduced Galloway finally to subjection, and the restlessness of Moray was terminated by scattering its native inhabitants elsewhere, and filling their places with more peaceful subjects—no doubt largely Saxons and Normans. Four years afterward (1164) another invasion was made by Somerled of Argyll, which was brought to an end by the death of its leader.

At the end of twelve years Malcolm IV. died, and was succeeded by his brother William, called the Lion. The district of Ross was now annexed to the kingdom. Another rebellion of the Celtic population put forward, as

[1] Skene, i., ch. ix.

candidate for the throne, a Celtic leader, Donald Ban Macwilliam, a descendant of Duncan, oldest son of Malcolm III. by his first wife, a Norwegian. It was followed by an insurrection in Galloway, and another in Stratherne, which carried its attacks into Lothian, and afterward joined the insurgents in Galloway. But there Reginald, the royalist leader, who had already worsted his domestic enemies, encountered and repelled them. Caithness was taken by force out of the hands of the Norwegian earl, and annexed more intimately to the kingdom of Scotland. And an insurrection of the people of Ross, repressed in the last years of William's reign, brought that province also into more complete subjection.

Occasion was given to some of these disorders by William's misfortunes abroad. In the beginning of his reign, grieved for the loss of Northumberland by Malcolm, he demanded from the king of England its restitution. That being refused, he attempted to recover it by arms. The Yorkshire barons, marching to meet the invading army, by accident captured the Scottish king. They sent him to their king, Henry II., then in France,[1] and Henry shut him up in the stronghold of Falaise. There he was retained until December, 1174, when he was set free under a treaty

[1] Buchanan, i. 294.

whereby he submitted to hold Scotland as a feudal dependency of the English crown, for which he was to do homage as absolute as that of any other vassal of England. As pledge for the fulfillment of these conditions he was constrained to yield five of the strongest places in Scotland—viz. Edinburgh, Stirling, Berwick, Jedburgh and Roxburgh—to be held by English troops.

This exorbitant ransom was, fifteen years afterward (1189), completely remitted and the English garrisons withdrawn by Richard I., Cœur de Lion, among the first acts of his reign, who instead of it accepted the sum of ten thousand marks, more valuable to him, in his contemplated crusade, than an empty homage. In her troubles under King John, England saw a Scottish army once more upon her borders for recovery of the contested provinces. Nothing was effected. William died (1214), leaving the unsettled controversy to his son, Alexander II. It was closed in 1237 by the king of England conferring upon the king of Scotland certain lands in Cumberland and Northumberland, to be held in feudal tenure. But the peace effected thereby was brief. In 1222 commissioners were appointed on both sides to determine a boundary-line between the kingdoms. After two separate trials they failed to agree.

Alexander II. had reigned barely a year when

the two Celtic parties of Donald Ban Macwilliam and Malcolm Macbeth united to recover the throne. But a new Celtic party now arose in favor of the reigning house. Its head, Ferquard MacIntagart, was descended from the abbot of the old Scottish monastery of Applecross, and heir of its large possessions, which had not yet come into the kingdom as now constituted. With his own means MacIntagart reduced the rebellion and presented the heads of its leaders to the king. In that act the northern part of what was then Argyll, being the inheritance of MacIntagart, was peacefully annexed.

Southern Argyll still belonged to the family of Somerled. Alexander marched into it at the head of an army. The people, having no leader in whom they had confidence, submitted without resistance. Thus was the possession of the mainland completed.

By these conquests on the north and west the dominion of Norway had been to the same extent diminished. It was now the purpose of the Scottish kings to regain the long-alienated isles. Proposals were made to Hakon, king of Norway, to surrender them. Hakon refused, on the ground that his right to them had been conceded by Malcolm III. and afterward by Edgar. Alexander proposed to purchase them. Hakon declined the offer. Alexander then undertook to recover them by force of arms, but had only commenced operations on the island of Kerreray when he died, July 8, 1249. His son, Alexander III., on the fifth day afterward, was crowned at Scone, although not quite eight years old.

Celtic opposition, since the example of MacIntagart, had been yielding to the apparently irresistible course of events. It was now formally surrendered. At the coronation of Alexander III., after the king had received the homage of the feudal baronage of the kingdom, Saxon and Norman, as well as that of the seven earls, a Highland *senachie* advanced, and, hailing him king of Alban, recited his pedigree, through a long line of Gaelic kings, from the founder of the race—a formal Celtic acknowledgment of the new king as belonging to the true Scottish line. Next year the bones of Queen Margaret were, in presence of the king, the seven earls and seven bishops, solemnly taken up and deposited in a shrine set with gold and precious stones. At last the Scoto-Saxon family had received a voluntary recognition from the Celtic people, to whose preferences, in religion or otherwise, they had never paid much regard. But that royal line had ceased to be Celtic in its spirit, and in successive generations had partaken increasingly of Saxon blood. In the case of Alexander II.

and Alexander III. it became allied to the Norman, and in the death of the latter became extinct.

Among the southern Hebrides and on the coast of Lorn the Scottish monarchy began in the hands of the Dalriad Scots. But while in prosecution of gains on the mainland it had been advancing eastward, northward and southward, Norwegian arms had been allowed to take possession of its original seat of power. In 1249 an attempt to compel the earl of Argyll to transfer to Scotland the homage which he paid for certain isles to Norway gave occasion to the campaign of Alexander II., in which he died. The earl of Ross also and others were charged by the Norsemen with hostilely invading their island dominion. Much anxiety was created among them thereby. In the failure of negotiations, Hakon, king of Norway, resolved upon a naval expedition for the protection of his distant subjects and the chastisement of their invaders.

In the summer of 1263 the armament was complete, the largest and best-equipped that had ever sailed from the land of the Vikings. Committing the general government to the hands of his son, the heroic old king, who had ruled that warlike people forty-and-six years, put himself at the head of the expedition. Proceeding first to Orkney, the principal seat of Norwegian rule for the northern isles, as Man was for the southern, his operations were thence addressed to the coasts of the Scottish mainland. The attack fell like a tempest from the Atlantic, sweeping all along as far south as Ayrshire, and penetrating in some places to a great distance inland. About the end of September the main body of the fleet, to the number of one hundred and sixty ships, rounded the Mull of Kintyre and assumed a position in the firth of Clyde. Negotiations were attempted on the part of the Scots. They were willing to acknowledge the Norwegian as king of all the islands outside of Kintyre. But Hakon demanded also those within, the possession of which would have given him command of the firth, and thereby entrance to the very heart of Scotland. It could not be conceded, and Hakon would be content with nothing less. While they delayed the weather became stormy, and some of the Norwegian ships were stranded near the village of Largs. Hakon sent troops to assist in bringing them off; they were encountered by Scottish forces. Both sides were hastily reinforced, and the conflict became a battle which proved disastrous to the Norwegians. The storm continued and increased. The great armament was scattered, and many of the ships were destroyed. Hakon withdrew the shattered fleet to Orkney. So serious was his loss that the hope of repairing it could not be entertained. Utterly broken in spirit, the old sea-king shrank from facing his people of Norway. He lingered in Orkney under great despondency, and seeking consolation or forgetfulness in the duties of religion, and in listening to the Bible, to lives of the saints, and adventures of his heroic predecessors, the old Norwegian kings. He died on the 12th of December the same year.

With the battle of Largs terminated the long career of Scandinavian aggression on the west coast of Scotland. Three years afterward (1266) a treaty was formed whereby the Hebrides and the Isle of Man were transferred to the full sovereignty of the Scottish crown, for which the sum of one thousand marks was to be paid and the yearly rent of one hundred marks. Orkney and Shetland remained Norwegian until 1469, when they were pledged by Christian I., king of Denmark, Sweden and Norway, as security for his daughter's dowry when married to the king of Scotland. The dowry never was paid, and the islands never returned to their Scandinavian allegiance. They were subsequently constituted a county of the Scottish kingdom and annexed as a diocese to the Scottish Church.

After the death of Alexander III., the Isle of Man was placed by its inhabitants under the protection of Edward I. of England, and created an English diocese as that of Sodor and Man.

Excepting the invasion by Hakon, the reign of Alexander III. was little disturbed by military events, and was one of great national prosperity. The family relations in which the king stood to the royal house of England were faithfully respected, and the peace with Norway was fortified in 1281 by the marriage of Alexander's daughter to the crown-prince Eric.

CHAPTER VI.

SCOTLAND SUBMITS TO BE A ROMISH PROVINCE.

AMONG the effects of that revolution which extinguished the old British, Irish and Scottish churches was the union of all the churches of the British kingdoms under spiritual allegiance to Rome—an important element of power to England, who had been the agent in effecting it, and whose religion was thereby established over all. In the case of Ireland and Wales it was connected with military subjugation; in Scotland it was the work of English influence engrafted on the native royal stock; but there also it led the way to English pretensions to superiority. Those pretensions appeared first among the high ecclesiastics.

With the introduction of so many English clergy into Scotland the archbishops of Canterbury and York began to claim jurisdiction over ecclesiastical affairs in that kingdom. The archbishop of York especially urged with great persistency his metropolitan rights over all the territory north of the Humber, and that it belonged to him to appoint even the principal bishop of St.

Andrews. The Scottish king manfully resisted. He could not fail to see that if a subject of the English king were allowed those claims, the English king himself would follow with claims still more exorbitant. In the conflict which ensued the metropolitan honors of St. Andrews were long deferred.

In the treaty of Falaise—that instrument by which William the Lion purchased his personal freedom at the expense of a formal surrender of his kingdom's independence—an attempt was made to subordinate also the Church of Scotland to that of England. But a complete Catholic hierarchy now existed in the former, and, the more effectually to repel the persistent obtrusion, recourse was had to papal authority. The pope made his first interference in the affairs of his new province by protecting it.

At Northampton a papal legate held an ecclesiastical conference in presence of King Henry, the king of Scotland, with the bishop of St. Andrews and five other Scottish bishops, being also present. The Scottish prelates were there called upon to submit to the terms of the treaty and take their place as subordinate to the English Church. They denied the right to any such supremacy. And when the archbishop of York asserted his claim over Glasgow and Galloway, Jocelyn, bishop of Glasgow, took the ground that he was under the immediate authority of the pope. After the conference, the Scottish bishops sent agents to Rome, who obtained a papal bull fully vindicating the position of Scotland as a separate province of the Romish Church, and forbidding all interference with it. Thus, to escape the aggressions of one foreign power the little kingdom acknowledged the jurisdiction of another, for the pope protected her from English metropolitanism by declaring her a province of his own empire. Sleepless watchfulness was needed to maintain the national standing.

About the same time the cardinal legate, Vivian Tomasi, arrived in England. He also visited Ireland, Scotland and the Isle of Man. The new relations effected or contemplated with those countries rendered some personal observation of them expedient on the part of the papal court. In Scotland the legate held a council. Of its transactions little is known, except its limitation of the immunities and revenues of the Cistercian monks.[1] Its principal effect, perhaps, was that of further familiarizing the people with papal authority, and making a demonstration of interest in them.

The weight of the pontifical hand was also invoked in a domestic episcopal dispute. A vacancy having occurred in the see of St. Andrews (1178), the chapter forthwith elect-

[1] Burton, ii. 5.

ed their own candidate, John Scot. But the king, whose prerogative was thus slighted, had designed Hugh, his own chaplain, for the place, and actually put him in possession of its temporalities. John appealed to the pope, and obtained a decision in his favor. But the king held the endowments, and banished John from the country. Again the pope was called on to interfere. The archbishop of York and the bishop of Durham were vested with powers to decide the case, and commenced action in the spirit of former assumptions. But at that juncture the pope, Alexander III., died, and his successor preferred to settle the matter by a decision of his own. A compromise was effected. Hugh was put into full possession of St. Andrews, and John was content with the bishopric of Dunkeld.[1]

Not many additions were made to the monastic institutions of David I. in the next four succeeding reigns; but one such merits attention. The great abbey of Arbroath, erected in 1178 by William the Lion, was endowed with uncommon munificence, and devoted to the memory of the recently-made saint Thomas à Becket—an act of royal compliment to Rome, in whose interest Thomas lost his life; and something of the contrary to the king of England, who had received the scourge upon

[1] Burton, ii. 6.

his bare shoulders for the death of that same St. Thomas.

The papacy was then at the summit of its power. The hand which could inflict an ignominious punishment upon the founder of the line of the Plantagenets was able to protect its servants, and to punish their enemies of humbler rank. A case of that kind occurred in Scotland within the same reign. In the war for Caithness the king of Scots, having proved to some extent successful, created his new territory a bishopric. Not long afterward Harold, the Norwegian earl of Orkney, arrived with forces to recover the lost province. In storming a castle which he took, slaying almost all who were in it, the bishop fell a prisoner into his hands. Lombard, a layman, informed Pope Innocent III. that he was himself "compelled by some of the earl's soldiery to cut out the bishop's tongue." For that savage crime the pope condemned the earl "to walk about conspicuously in his own territories fifteen days with bare feet and only clothing enough for decency, his tongue being so tied as to hang from his mouth, while he suffered the active discipline of the rod. He was then within a month to set forth to Jerusalem, and there serve the cross for three years." The far-away Orkney earl succeeded in evading the penance. He had the sea for his friend. But the event sustained with papal sanction the forces of William the Lion in that quarter when he appeared for the final annexation of Caithness.[1]

The English king, adding to his feudal pretensions the assumption of dominion over a Church ruled by bishops who were created such by his own subjects, proposed to collect a tax from the new benefices of the neighboring kingdom. The pope again interposed and forbade him, on the ground that such exaction from the domains of a foreign prince was unprecedented.

But the pope meanwhile was counting up a debt of revenue from Scotland in his own favor. And, as occasion seemed to demand, he drew upon it. When Innocent IV. in 1254 wished to persuade Henry III. to undertake a crusade, he offered him the twentieth of all the benefices in Scotland as a gift out of what belonged to the papal treasury. The king and clergy united in this case to evade both pretensions. They raised the money themselves, and, as the plea was a crusade, laid it out upon one of their own. A small crusading expedition left Scotland under the earls of Carrick and Athole. Whatever came of them, none returned.

But papal exaction was not always to be evaded. Money was the motive-power of the engine to which Scotland was now attached, and it must be collected. A valuation

[1] Burton, ii. 11.

of church property had to be made to determine the amount of the tax, and a system of legislation constituted to make its payment obligatory. A partial estimate of the value of church livings had been made "as early at least as the reign of William the Lion."

In 1225, Pope Honorius III., in consideration of their remote locality, and having no metropolitan to preside over them, empowered the clergy of Scotland to hold national councils, without special papal call or presence of a legate, "for carrying out the decrees of general councils and other purposes of discipline." Such councils were composed of all the bishops, abbots and priors, to whom subsequently "were added representatives of the capitular, conventual and collegiate clergy." They met once a year, for three days if necessary, and opened their sessions with a sermon preached by each of the bishops in turn. "One of the bishops was chosen for a year as conservator of the canons or statutes of the council, with power to enforce them. The conservator also summoned the council, and presided in it, or, in his absence, the oldest bishop. Two doctors of the civil law attended as representatives of the sovereign."[1]

In such councils, between 1237 and 1286, a code of ecclesiastical canons was drawn up,

[1] Dr. Campbell, *St. Giles Lecture.*

whereby the laws of the Church of Scotland were made conformable to those of Rome.

"There were also synods of the clergy of each diocese, presided over by their own bishop."[1]

In 1267 the papal legate, Ottobon Fiesci, accredited to England, proposed to carry his authority to hold a council thence into Scotland. He was not permitted, apparently, lest it might be construed into an admission of dependency. He then called the Scottish bishops, with delegates from the lower clergy, to meet him at a council in England. Only a few were sent, and those few to protest against any action affecting Scotland taken by a council in England.[2] He further persisted in sending them certain acts, which he informed them were to be observed by the clergy. But the king and the bishops agreed in rejecting them, saying that "they would acknowledge no statutes but such as proceeded from the pope or a general council."

Again, in 1275, another papal legate, Boiamond de Vicci, arrived from Rome with a commission to estimate the value of benefices, and to assess and collect the tenths accordingly. He proceeded by calling before him successively all the beneficed persons in the kingdom, and causing them, upon oath, to state

[1] Dr. Campbell, *St. Giles Lecture.*   [2] Burton, ii. 39.

the value of the endowments upon which they were taxed. The list thus made up served for the then present collection, and became a law for ecclesiastical taxing until the Reformation.[1]

[1] Burton, ii. 38.

CHAPTER VII.

EXTINCTION OF THE SCOTO-SAXON DYNASTY.

ON the night of the 12th of March, 1286, King Alexander III., riding with a small escort along the coast of Fife near Kinghorn, was thrown from his horse over a promontory and killed. The only surviving member of his family was the infant daughter of the deceased queen of Norway. A convention of the estates assembled at Scone and elected a regency to govern in her name. It was proposed by Edward I., king of England, to form a contract of marriage between her and his son Edward; and for that he obtained a dispensation from the pope, because the parties were within the degrees of kindred prohibited by the canon law. The proposal was accepted by the regency, and the hope entertained that the peace of the two countries, then existing, was to be continued by another bond of affinity between their royal houses. But all was defeated by a final stroke of that fatality which waited upon the family of Alexander III. The young queen died at Orkney, on her way to Scotland, at the age of seven years (1290).

The lineage of William the Lion was now extinct, and the nearest heirs to the throne were the descendants of his brother David, earl of Huntingdon, youngest son of Henry of Northumberland. But David had left no sons, and the question of succession was found not easy to settle. Several candidates put forth their claims. The nearest were two Norman noblemen, Robert Bruce, son of David's second daughter, and John Baliol, grandson of his oldest daughter. Lineally considered, Baliol was the nearer. But fifty years before, Alexander II.,[1] while yet without children, had provided that, if he died childless, Bruce should succeed him, as being then the only male descendant of his uncle. Bruce was now, in 1290, a man advanced in years, and meanwhile a grandson had been born to Earl David's oldest daughter. That grandson was John Baliol. Both were sustained by numerous adherents. Edward, king of England, was requested to act as arbiter, and availed himself of the occasion to promote the designs of his own ambition. His judgment in favor of Baliol was no doubt just in itself, but it was given upon condition that Baliol should acknowledge the king of England as lord superior of Scotland, and submit to him in all things belonging to that relation. In complying with that condition,

[1] Burton, ii. 12.

however, Baliol did nothing worse than all the other nine candidates, Bruce not excepted, had professed themselves willing to do. They were all of them Normans paternally, having no more patriotism than belonged to the place of their residence and possessions. Most of them had estates also in England, for which they paid homage to Edward, and which, of course, they were unwilling to forfeit. At the same time, it must be said of Bruce that he was the head of a family which came into the country among the very first of his race, and his interests were identified with those of Scotland, while Baliol had still most of his estates in France. The collusion between the candidates and the arbiter was in the interest of their common Norman descent. In their descent from Earl David there was but little Scottish blood among them, even from their mothers' side.

Baliol was crowned on the 30th of November, 1292. For him it was an unfortunate award. Popular detestation of the assumed English superiority, together with the jealousy of his disappointed rivals, rendered his reign very uncomfortable; and the humiliation of having to plead, in cases of appeal from his own court, before that of his feudal superior, became so grievous that before three years had elapsed he yielded to the national demand, and

consented to an alliance with France against
Edward, and to an invasion of England during
Edward's French campaign of 1295, and finally
sent a renunciation of his vassalage. When
that last step was taken Edward had returned
from France, and was in Scotland with a large
army. Baliol was forthwith deposed and sent
into England. After a few years he was permitted to retire to his estates in France.

The king of England now determined to abolish the Scottish monarchy and annex the kingdom to his own. The oath of allegiance was
demanded for himself. All the strong places
of the country were garrisoned with English,
and upon his return to London, in 1296, he carried with him, among other valuables, the celebrated Stone of Destiny upon which the kings
of Scotland were crowned,[1] believing that he
had reduced Scotland to submission and held
her fortunes for the future in his hands.

Bruce, the rival of Baliol, died in 1295. More
than twenty years before, his son, of the same
name, in a journey through the west, traveled
into Carrick. The countess of Carrick, in the
line of the Celtic lords of Galloway, and widow
of the earl of Carrick, who perished in the crusade, was enjoying the pleasures of the chase.
Accidentally meeting the young knight, whose

[1] This stone is now in the seat of the chair in Westminster Abbey on which the British monarchs are crowned.

name and lineage were certainly not unknown to her, she invited him to join the party. He politely declined. The countess, calling her attendants, ordered the arrest of the trespasser, and, herself laying hold upon his bridle, with a gentle violence conducted him a prisoner to her castle of Turnberry. The captivity proved far from grievous. In course of time, certain feudal scruples being overcome, the young Robert Bruce became the earl of Carrick. His son Robert was accordingly born to the same inheritance, and, on his mother's side, of the native Scottish race. At the beginning of the national troubles he was too young to take any part in them. His father never entered the arena of ambition.[1]

Upon the removal of Baliol the immediate candidate for the crown was Comyn of Badenoch, a Norman, who, in addition to his own claims, being the near connection of Baliol, inherited also his. But every claim of the kind was now set aside by the act of the king of England in assuming to govern Scotland as a subject province.

In that lowest depth of the national misfortune, though the nobility and their adherents submitted to what seemed inevitable fate, the commonalty never succumbed. They found a fitting leader in one of their own rank, Wil-

[1] Robertson's *Scotland, her Early Kings*, ii. 109.

liam Wallace, a country gentleman, who, by his success and daring and well-planned skirmishes with the enemy, soon collected around him a large body of followers and formed them into an efficient army. Before the end of the year 1297, Wallace had defeated the English in the field, reduced their garrisons and driven their forces beyond the border. He was constituted guardian of Scotland.

But the nobility were jealous, and refused to act under his authority or to take their orders from him in the army. The king of England returned in the succeeding summer. Wallace, deserted by the men of rank, who ought to have sustained him, and by the bodies of troops whom they withdrew, was overwhelmed by numbers, and the brave remnant of his forces scattered. Finding that he could no longer be of service to his country at home, he retired to the Continent, where he endeavored to promote her interest in Paris, and perhaps also in Rome.[1] He had already established friendly relations with France through his agent, Bishop Lamberton.

When Wallace withdrew, the guardianship was continued in the persons of Comyn of Badenoch and John de Soulis; and, however obscure and however oppressed, there was still a government which the Scottish people might

[1] Burton, ii. 202-208.

consider their own. But at the same time English rule was set up and enforced by English troops over the whole land, and to it did the nobility again formally submit.

Subsequently to 1298 active hostilities were suspended for a few years by negotiations between France and Scotland on one side, and England and the Low Countries on the other. The Scots were well represented at Paris, and also at Rome. Pope Boniface VIII. asserted the justice of their cause. In 1298 he sent to King Edward a letter of admonition on the subject, and soon afterward followed it up with a bull charging him with violating the rights and liberties of the Church and kingdom of Scotland, exposing the erroneous nature of his claims, and asserting for Scotland the rank of a free monarchy, owing allegiance to the Romish see alone. On that ground the pope, as pastor of all Christians and arbiter of right and wrong among the nations, interposed for protection of the injured country. The offending king was invited, if he had anything to say in defence of himself, to plead his cause before the papal court.[1]

The bull was sent to the archbishop of Canterbury, who was to put it into the hands of the king. But the king was then away in the north, concerned with further operations

[1] Baronius (Raynaldi contin.), Luca ed., vol. xxiii. p. 267.

against Scotland. The journey after him was full of danger and made with long delays, and before the archbishop could reach Carlisle the king had already entered Scotland at the head of another destructive invasion. When, finally, the papal epistle reached its destination, still greater delay was created by the king's preparation of his plea, in which he employed many assistants, and which was designed perhaps to excite the feelings of Englishmen against Romish aggression, more than to satisfy the pope, whose right to interfere was denied. The plea finally constructed was of the most extraordinary description, tracing the English monarchy in its growth from the days of Eli and Samuel, when it was founded by a certain Brutus, who came from Troy, and, taking possession of Britain, forthwith divided it among his three sons, giving England to Locrin, the oldest, Scotland to Albanac, and Wales to Camber. It was also stated that the invariable practice in Troy was that the oldest son and his descendants should rule the younger and their descendants; and that, farther down in the history, the great King Arthur appointed one of his followers, called Anselm, to rule over Scotland; and for that, Anselm did feudal homage to Arthur as his lord superior. Upon this learned foundation the royal defendant built his argument up to the point on which he himself stood, and sent it to Rome in May, 1301, when he was mustering men and material for another invasion of the country in question.[1] The papal admonition effected nothing toward restraining aggression, but it fortified the Scottish clergy and people in the righteousness of their cause. The highest authority under heaven, as they conceived, had spoken in its defence. Thus encouraged, the nation put forth its best efforts for the preservation of its life, and to expose at home and abroad the injustice of the English pretension. Wallace also, it appears, returned from the Continent, and animated as far as lay in his power the resistance to oppression.[2]

Within the same years Philip of France, as well as Edward, fell under censure of the pope, and succeeded in setting at naught the papal admonitions. Finally, the better to facilitate the progress of their negotiations with each other, the two great kings abandoned their respective allies.

Edward, thus relieved from his embarrassments on the Continent, resolved to extinguish for ever the spirit of Scottish independence. In the spring of 1303 he led the largest and best equipped army he ever mustered in a third campaign to the north. He swept almost the whole length of the land. All opposition

[1] Burton, ii. 208-214.   [2] Knight, xxvii.

seemed to be put down before him. The guardians submitted. In their stead he created a new government. There was now to be but one king and one great council for the whole island. Scotland was to be ruled by a lieutenant and council appointed by the Crown. All the subordinate departments were accordingly organized anew.[1]

The guardians and others concerned in opposition to his former arrangements, the victor, in the good humor of success, punished lightly, but made an exception of Wallace. The popular hero, now betrayed into the hands of his enemy, was carried to London, and on the 23d of August, 1305, put to death with inexcusable barbarity.

John of Bretagne entered upon his administration as lieutenant, and to appearance Scottish independence was extinguished. But the long-continued war had added bitterness to patriotic persistency in the Scottish mind, and engendered a degree of hatred to everything English, which had not existed before. Later severities had also enlisted that part of the Norman population who now inherited the feelings of Scotsmen, and Comyn of Badenoch was looked to by them as the national leader. But a truer and more national leader than he —one who really united in himself the Nor-

[1] Burton, ii. 229-231.

man and Celtic elements of the nation—appeared at that juncture.

Robert Bruce, son of the Countess Margery of Carrick, and on his father's death (in 1305) earl of Carrick, and grandson of the rival of Baliol for the throne, was then living in favor with the English king. One day early in the month of February, 1306, it was remarked that he had disappeared from court. A few days later he presented himself in the neighborhood of his paternal estates in Dumfriesshire.[1] Falling in with Comyn in the church of the Minorites at Dumfries, an altercation ensued, in which he stabbed Comyn with his dagger—an act followed up by one of his attendants, Kirkpatrick, with more fatal wounds. For that act, perpetrated in a church, whereby sacrilege was added to murder, Bruce was soon absolved by Wiseheart, bishop of Glasgow; but papal excommunication followed, and papal indignation continued many years to be leveled against him.[2] On the 27th of March he was crowned at Scone. But misfortune attended his first enterprise in arms. Among the western mountains and islands he found hiding-places, and on the lonely isle of Rathlin, off the coast of Ireland, spent most of the succeeding winter. With the spring he once more appeared in the field.

The escape of Bruce, the enthusiasm awak-

[1] Lingard, iii. 275.　　　[2] *Ecc. Chron. of Scot.*, ii. 486.

ened by his appearance in Scotland and his coronation, provoked the king of England to the utmost. Although now old and feeble, he resolutely pushed forward with the alacrity of youth preparations for a fourth campaign against Scotland, designed to take vengeance for the death of Comyn. Putting his son Edward, prince of Wales, at its head, he followed on as the infirmities of disease permitted, but lived only to come in sight of Scotland, and died at Burgh-on-the-Sands, July 7, 1307. His successor, Edward II., was actuated by less passion. After proceeding a few marches farther, and finding no army to encounter, he returned to England.

Another incursion of the same kind followed three years afterward, and a third next year, with the same result. Still, it was the purpose of the English king to maintain his dominion in Scotland. John of Bretagne was succeeded as royal lieutenant by Aymer de Valence, earl of Pembroke, and he by others. But one garrison after another was falling, while the strength of the resistance continually increased.

With prudence and cautious enterprise Bruce pursued his advantages, defeating hostile Highland chieftains, driving English troops out of Scottish strongholds, and retaliating invasion upon the land of his enemy. In the spring of 1314 his brother, Edward Bruce, besieging

Stirling, pressed the garrison to the condition of surrender if not relieved by the 24th of June. A large and magnificently equipped English army crossed the border a week before that date. Should it succeed in relieving Stirling, it would then be in condition to go anywhere over Scotland and undo all Bruce's work of years. Such was the stake for which the battle was fought, in sight of Stirling Castle, at Bannockburn on the 24th of June, 1314. The English forces were driven from the country. The independence of Scotland was secured, with a native monarch once more seated on her throne—a monarch not of pure Celtic blood, but representing in his own person all the three great ethnic stocks, Celtic, Saxon and Norman, to which by that time her population also belonged.

CHAPTER VIII.

SCOTLAND'S RELATIONS TO THE PAPACY DURING THE WAR.

THESE events occurred when the papacy was at the summit of its strength. Malcolm Canmore was contemporary with Hildebrand, Pope Gregory VII.; William the Lion with Innocent III.; the Scottish war of independence began in the pontificate of Boniface VIII.; and the coronation of Bruce took place in the year after the removal from Rome to Avignon—the beginning of papal decline.

The subjugation and annexation of the British churches in Scotland, Ireland and Wales added to the glory of the papacy when in its prime. Through all that period, until the death of Boniface, the popes treated Scotland with favor, pursuing a policy designed to attach the nation to their cause. Recognizing her as a monarchy owing ecclesiastical allegiance immediately to Rome, they assumed to be her protectors from English aggression. Upon the coronation of Alexander III., Henry II. of England applied to Innocent IV. to forbid the sacred sanction of anointing, but received in reply a courteous refusal. Yet so little had previous popes to do with the inauguration of Scottish kings that anointing was a new ceremony on that occasion. Nor was it then thought in Scotland to be essential, nor that the omission of it could in any degree invalidate the solemnity. King Robert Bruce was not held to be the less a king that no papal legate had poured upon his head the consecrated oil.

When Alexander III. died the country had enjoyed a long period of tranquillity. For border raids ordinarily disturbed only the border counties, and the expedition of Hakon was a hasty dash which ravaged the western coasts, but did no lasting injury. In the course of that long peace the nation made great progress in the culture of the soil, a matter in which some houses of monks set a good example, as well as in the practice of various industrial arts and in commerce. All the monasteries were seats of education as far as pertained to their own pursuits. In them were the schools for the clergy. No university was yet established in the land. But for Scottish youth, desirous of pursuing their studies to greater length than the monastery course, Balliol College was founded at Oxford, about the middle of the reign of Alexander III. (1268), by the Lady Devorgill of Galloway. In many of the towns also there were schools for secular education, some of which attained an honorable reputation. Nor had the old habits of popular religious instruction by the Scottish clergy been abandoned. Wealth had accumulated, and seems to have been more equably distributed than in England, or perhaps in any other country at that time. The workers of the soil were intelligent and comfortably provided for. From the beginning of the war of independence, the common people were well acquainted with the interests at stake, and had their own judgments about them, unbiased by those of either the nobility or the hierarchy. It was in the latter half of the thirteenth century that the Roman Catholic Church enjoyed the fullest confidence of the people of Scotland, and seems to have deserved it.

In the arbitration, the prelates, at first, took part with King Edward. Neither they nor the nobles made any opposition to his claim of being overlord. From the commons, however, a response was made which he disliked and withheld from publication. Denial of his right or some remonstrance against it came first from them. The Norman leaders, both lay and ecclesiastic, were willing to submit. Many of them were liegemen of Edward for part of their estates and honors, and might as well be for all. Such, at least, seems to have been their common feeling at first. Frazer, bishop of St. Andrews, being of a Norman family, attached himself to the cause of Baliol, which at his coronation was that of Edward, and when Baliol was dethroned, went abroad in his interest, and died there.

The native Scottish clergy were opposed to the English pretensions entirely, and in that agreed with their people. With a view to extinguish that influence, working so steadily and powerfully against him, Edward resolved to fill all vacancies, among the parochial and other lower places in the Church, with Englishmen. In 1297 he sent orders to his lieutenant, Fitz-Allan, to that effect. The prelates could not fail to foresee that, in the prosecution of such a policy, their order must become alienated from the people—must forfeit the popular confidence, and be viewed, by those whom it was their office to guide in spiritual things, as a mere political agency of a foreign power designed to oppress them. Prelatic places, it is true, had at an earlier time been created and filled with foreigners, but that had been the work of Scottish kings; and those dignitaries did not come into immediate contact with the common people, but sought their security in conciliation of the native working clergy, which, in the main, they seemed to have effected. But now the breaking of that link between the prelates and the people threatened a danger to the whole structure.

A change took place next year, when William Lamberton came to the see of St. Andrews, if his coming to it was not a fruit of the change, in the uprising of the commonalty. He was indebted for his promotion greatly to the influence of William Wallace. And the rise of Wallace was the rise of the common people. His victories were their protest, their declaration of independence, which made itself heard and respected. From that date the higher clergy as well as the lower stood by the national cause.

Lamberton's first years in office were spent abroad, and Wallace, after his withdrawal from the guardianship, appears to have joined him in representing the cause of their country at Paris, and probably also at Rome. He certainly got credentials from King Philip to the French "representatives at the court of Rome, recommending to them his good friend William le Walois, of Scotland, knight, and desiring them to do what in them lay to expedite the business he had to transact at the court of Rome."[1] But Scotland had also her publicly commissioned servants there, among whom was William, archdeacon of Lothian, and her interests were well attended to. The papal officers

[1] Burton, ii. 202.

concerned evinced a thorough acquaintance with the state of the case for Scotland as opposed to the pretensions of the king of England.[1] The papal admonitions, as already mentioned, received little honor from him to whom they were addressed, but they proved of the utmost import in reanimating the confidence of the oppressed people, and determining and uniting the policy of the Scottish clergy. The unhesitating decision of Pope Boniface VIII. gave assurance to both lay and ecclesiastic in the holiness of the national cause. To its interests the prelates thence onward remained sincerely attached to the end—sincerely, but not all of them with consistent profession. Some of the bishops and others in conspicuous places bent readily before the storm of invasion, and rose erect when it had passed. On their part, as well as on that of many laymen, there were frequent alternations of allegiance—taking the oath to Edward when he came, and breaking it when he went away. Bishop Lamberton himself thus changed sides five times. Wiseheart of Glasgow took the oath six times, violating it in every interval, and at last went off to assist Bruce with all his might. The war of independence was a long and heroic contest, but was not promotive of religion or morality.

[1] Raynaldus, contin. of Baronius, vol. xxiii., p. 267, Luca ed.

It was Lamberton and Wiseheart, with David, bishop of Moray, who presided at the coronation of Robert Bruce. The ceremony was completed by the countess Matilda of Buchan, in place of her brother, chief of the clan M'Duff, then in an English prison, whose hereditary duty it was to place the crown upon the king's head. For that act Lamberton and Wiseheart were confined to prison, from which they were released upon Edward's death. For the countess a cage was prepared in the castle of Berwick, in which she was confined four years. At the end of that time she was removed to less severe confinement, for three years more, in the Carmelite convent of Berwick. Nigel, a younger brother of the Bruce, and some of his adherents were taken by the usurper and executed.[1] The part acted by the pope until the arrival of Bruce did much to fortify the influence of his office among Scotsmen, and inspired them with a higher degree of veneration for his person.

The war of independence lasted long, and ere it closed a change had passed upon the spirit of both parties in it, as well as upon the condition of the papacy. Edward II., after his rout at Bannockburn, was no doubt earnestly desirous of peace, but refused to recognize the national independence of Scotland, or to treat

[1] Lingard, *Hist. of England*, iii. 280.

the king whom she had crowned with the honor due to his rank. Bruce proposed a final settlement of peace, but when he found Edward resolved to refuse him the title which acknowledged the independence of his country, he broke off the negotiations. The warfare changed into repeated invasions of England, not for conquest, but to compel a recognition of Scottish independence.

The papal residence was now at Avignon in France, to which it had been removed, by constraint of Philip the Fair, in 1305, and Scotland had for some time no representative there. Lamberton was in his old age, and devoting his remaining strength to the interests of the Church at home, especially in repairing the injuries which church property had suffered in the war, and in completing his cathedral of St. Andrews. He also built many new churches and episcopal residences in various places. At the consecration of the completed cathedral, July 5, 1318, King Robert was present, and added an endowment of one hundred marks annually out of gratitude "for the illustrious victory which St. Andrew had afforded him at Bannockburn." Lamberton continued, nevertheless, to take part in the efforts for securing peace with England. He died in 1328.[1] Before that date his country had again been well

[1] *Ecclesiastical Chronicle of Scotland*, i. 186.

represented at the papal court, and was recovering favor there.

The Scottish king was under excommunication for sacrilege, in having slain Comyn in a church. Interest was also made at the papal court to procure the issuing of denunciatory writs against the people who had rejected English rule, and persisted in so doing under a sacrilegious leader. But the people stood inflexibly by their beloved king, and paid no respect to any measure designed to degrade him. The national clergy of every rank, being now of the same mind, would not put the papal mandates in force.

The population of Scotland had been both sifted and welded in the course of the war. "The first note of contest banished every English priest, monk and friar from the northern realm," and its termination was followed by the departure of the great Anglo-Norman lords who held possessions in both kingdoms;[1] while all who felt their interests identified with the country, and their affections enlisted in it, whether of British, Scottish, Saxon or Norman descent, were fused into one nationality. Under the effects of a law passed during the war (1318), as well as from the necessities of the case, owners of property in both countries had to part with their estates in one or the other.[2] So we lose sight of the distinc-

[1] *Quarterly Rev.*, June, 1849, p. 138. [2] Burton, ii. 306.

tions Pict, Scot, Norse, Saxon, Briton and Norman, except in family genealogies. A common love of the land of their birth, which they had unitedly defended from oppression under a leader whom they all admired, himself both Celt and Teuton, and by exploits in war of which they all were proud, had resulted in making them all alike Scotsmen, bound together in a bond of enthusiastic patriotism and mutual respect. Only one remnant of ethnic division held its place in the difference between Highlanders and Lowlanders, which continues to this day.

Papal opposition turned against Scotland at that period, chiefly between 1306 and 1324. Although, by the patriotism of the native clergy, of little or no inconvenience at home, it was a serious obstacle in the way of all dealings with foreign nations. In France and the Netherlands it was suffered to interfere very little with business; but elsewhere the English government made use of it to injure commerce, and procure denial of respectful treatment for those whom they everywhere held up as an excommunicated people, the followers of a sacrilegious and excommunicated leader.

A full end to the war was not reached until the acknowledgment of independence was secured. Scotsmen and their king alike knew that there would be serious loss in stopping short of that. They must vindicate their standing among nations, and leave no ground for a future usurper to build upon. And now the pope, as well as the king of England, had to be persuaded.

As Edward II. refused to treat with them on the footing of national equality, they continued the war by invading his kingdom. His northern counties were laid waste year after year, while he was utterly unable to protect them. The pope was persuaded to interfere. He issued a bull of peace, ordering both sides to cease from fighting for two years. It was addressed to "our dearest son in Christ, the illustrious Edward, king of England, and our beloved son, the noble Robert de Bruce, conducting himself as king of Scotland." Two cardinals also arrived in England in the autumn of that year (1317). Both kingdoms were concerned in the business they came to transact. Into Scotland they did not go themselves, but sent two messengers, who, as they were not permitted to address Bruce with the title of king, could accomplish nothing. Their visit proved valuable only to history by the account which they wrote of the popular feeling on the question of the time. A sealed despatch was presented by them, addressed to Robert Bruce, governing in Scotland. The king declined to open it, except by consent of

Parliament, but that could not be immediately obtained. He was not the only Robert Bruce who might have something to do in the government of the country. For his own part, he was king. He also refused to comply with their demand to lay down his arms until his own rank, and therein the independence of his kingdom, was fully recognized. The messengers, moreover, as the result of their own observations, reported their opinion that, even if the king had been willing to waive the informality, the Parliament would not have consented.

A daring monk, Adam Newton, undertook to publish the bull in Scotland. He found the king preparing for the siege of Berwick, and his success proving no better than that of the messengers, he applied for permission to go among the Scottish clergy and execute his mission. That was not granted. The feelings of the clergy were well known to be so fully enlisted in the national cause that no papal writ adverse to its interest could be legally served in the land. The monk then requested to be sent back to Berwick under a safe-conduct. But that could not be done, for he had seen the preparations for the siege. In trying to find his way back by himself he fell among robbers, and all his documents were taken from him.[1]

Papal fulminations against Scotland were fre-

---

[1] Burton, ii. 277, 278; Lingard, iii. 314–316.

quent in those days. A new bull, adding to previous offences the indignity done to the papal messengers, was sent to the cardinals with urgent instructions to enforce it, with " the personal excommunication of Bruce."[1] But that mandate also, through the faithful patriotism of the national clergy, was found impracticable.

The war with England went on. Berwick was taken. The English tried to retake it, but could not. Raids into England were repeated with desolating effect. The papal peace was not regarded. Many people in the northern counties of England began to think seriously of breaking away from their relations with a government which failed to protect them, and of seeking a connection with the northern kingdom. It seemed high time that such warfare should come to an end. A truce of two years was agreed upon between the parties, in hope that it might lead to a satisfactory settlement. It began on 21st of December, 1319.

The Scots also took occasion to renew their dutiful relations to the pope. For, although his repeated denunciations had hitherto done them no harm at home, the attitude in which they were put by the head of the Church was not a desirable one in those days, and might, on occasion of adversity, be calamitous. It prevented

---

[1] Burton, ii. 277, 278; Lingard, iii. 314-316.

other states from extending to them the ordinary international courtesies and privileges. In a Parliament held at Arbroath in April, 1320, a solemn address to the pope was adopted explanatory of the wrongs under which they had suffered and the reasonableness of their present demands. In the most respectful terms the state of the case was clearly and forcibly laid before His Holiness, who was brought to admonish and exhort the king of England to suffer the Scots to live at peace under their own government, "in their own remote and obscure corner of the world." On their part they expressed their willingness to agree with the king of England in everything necessary to procure peace, as far as not compromising their own nationality. Although the document is not in the name of any ecclesiastic, but purely of laymen, "the barons, free tenants and whole community of Scotland," it expresses entire and cordial allegiance to the papal see.[1]

The statement had some effect. Denunciations ceased, though those issued were not forthwith revoked. An admonitory bull was addressed to the king of England in July of the same year. But the result of negotiations was not what Scotland demanded, and when the truce expired the war recommenced. Edward, having settled certain domestic troubles,

[1] Burton, ii. 283-287.

conceived himself now in condition to humble this obstinate people. In August, 1322, he led a numerous army across the border, and marched northward as far as the firth of Forth. But it was through a wilderness. The people had deserted their humble homes, carried off all their goods, driven away their cattle and betaken themselves to the mountains. The invaders were defeated by absolute famine. On their retreat the Scottish army appeared in their rear, pursuing and harassing them far into their own country.

Edward was again constrained to negotiate. A truce for thirteen years was agreed upon at Berwick on June 7, 1323. Bruce was allowed to take the title of king, but Edward would not give it. This was not satisfactory, but was accepted for the time being.

In order to a better result the head of the Church must be propitiated. It was in the pontificate of John XXII. King Robert despatched his nephew, Randolph, earl of Moray, to Avignon to plead his cause with the pope. Randolph conducted his embassy with delicacy and judgment. In January of the next year the pope wrote a long letter to the king of England, explaining how, by conversation with the Scottish nobleman, his knowledge of the case had been enlarged, and that he had consented to address future "letters to Bruce by the title of king," recommending also to Edward the desirableness of peace between the two countries. Edward's reply was an angry remonstrance. But Randolph, having secured the favor of the pope, had also, before returning home, effected a highly important treaty with France.

When Edward III. in 1327 succeeded his father on the throne, he undertook to repel the Scots, who, seeing nothing done toward the establishment of a permanent peace, had renewed the war. For that purpose he led a large and expensive army to the north. But the inexperienced lad, who was afterward to be hero of Creci, was as nothing in the hands of Douglas and Randolph, men in the prime of life and of military experience. They beguiled him from place to place, reduced his army without fighting a battle, and then marched away home, leaving him to disband his discomfited host in a singularly mortifying way.

Anything was better than this. To be defeated so often was bad enough, but to be made sport of in the field, and worried into disaster by the mere strategy of their enemies, and under their ridicule, was unendurable. Better admit their titles, and for trial of prowess await a more propitious time. An English Parliament was held at York in January of the next year to consider the question. Its action was followed by a treaty concluded at Edinburgh March 17, and ratified by the Parliament of England at Northampton in April, yielding Scottish recognition in its full extent. "All documents in possession of the king of England containing stipulations inconsistent with the independence of Scotland were declared void," and were to be given up to the king of Scots. The king of England was to use his good services in the withdrawal of all proceedings in the papal court prejudicial to King Robert or his dominion. The Scots were not to aid the Irish in case they should rebel, nor were the English to aid the inhabitants of the Scottish islands in rebellion against the king of Scots; and Scotland was to pay twenty thousand pounds, apparently for losses inflicted in the late raids upon England.[1]

The work of the Bruce was at last complete. His native land, rescued from oppression, her internal order regulated by many wise enactments, her population united and her character fortified in self-reliance by long-continued discipline and success—so firmly united as to stand unshaken even under excommunication and repeated papal denunciations—and with her independent sovereignty fully recognized, had closed her protracted struggle successfully.

King Robert, reconciled with the Church of

[1] Burton, ii. 303, 304.

Rome five years before his death, beheld also the re-establishing of entire concord between the papacy and the church authorities of his kingdom. It was also his wish to lead or take part in a crusade for the Christian cause against the Saracen. But his labors had been so persistently demanded by affairs at home that he had never been free to undertake the foreign enterprise. And before the treaty of Northampton had given him release he was already broken in health by the inroads of an incurable disease. He died at Cardross, near Dumbarton, on the 7th of June, 1329. Lord James of Douglas, one of his most faithful and trusted companions-in-arms, and doubtless designed to be one of his knights in the crusade, actually undertook it with a few brave followers the next year. The king's heart, according to his own request, was carried with them in a silver casket. The papal bull of absolution "for extracting the heart from the body" and its removal by Douglas, in terms of his master's injunction, declares the purpose "that it might be borne in war against the Saracens" in Spain. The crusades in Palestine had come to an end.

In the service of Alphonso, king of Leon and Castile, at war with Osmyn of Granada, the crusader chose the lists in which to consecrate his latest heroism. In a certain battle, when the Christians were hard pressed and threatened with defeat, he threw the casket into the midst of the enemy, shouting, "Onward as thou wert wont, thou noble heart! Douglas will follow thee." Victory must have driven the enemy from the field. For it is added that the body of Douglas was found, and with it the casket. Both were taken home, Lord James to be consigned to the resting-place of his fathers; the heart of the Bruce to sacred keeping in Melrose Abbey.[1]

[1] Burton, ii. 308; Weiner, *Vetera Monumenta*, 251.

CHAPTER IX.

PAPAL RELATIONS OF SCOTLAND UNDER RESTORED INDEPENDENCE.

SCARCELY was King Robert laid in the grave when the Norman nobility of England, who had formerly held lands in Scotland and had lost them in the war, made a push for their recovery. First, they attempted to gain their lost estates by civil process, but it soon appeared that nothing could be done in that way. The claimants then resolved to unite their interests with those of Edward, son of John Baliol, who now pretended to the throne of Scotland. Like themselves, he was perfectly willing to accept the king of England as lord superior. And why not? None of them were really Scotsmen. The circumstances were of fortune. Scotland was at peace, relying upon the settlement of Northampton, and her king was a child. Randolph, the regent, had just died (July, 1332), and his place was occupied by an inferior mind, Duncan, earl of Mar. The adventurers, putting Edward Baliol at their head and raising a small army, took ship and landed on the coast of Fife. Fortunate enough to overcome the Scottish forces under command of the regent, who was slain in the battle, they forthwith hastened to take the city of Perth, and repelled another Scottish force which pursued them. Among the Scots they found friends—men of their own class— ready to be Scots or English as served their interests best. Confident in victory, they crowned their leader (Sept. 24, 1332), and went on to organize a new government under the feudal superiority of England.

Meanwhile, Edward III. of England brought his army to the north and called a Parliament at York. The question proposed was, What degree of subordination should now be enforced upon Scotland? While Parliament was debating the two Edwards made a secret compact of their own, whereby Scotland was to become a fief of the English crown; and each bound himself to aid the other "with all his power against every domestic enemy." And these conditions were "to have been ratified by their respective Parliaments."

But meanwhile the new regent of Scotland, Andrew Murray, one of the heroes of the liberation army in the days of King Robert, took expeditious and effective means to rally the nation to its allegiance. In a few weeks the stunning effect of the surprise had passed over.

The Scottish army was organized anew. Baliol, in Annandale, was receiving the submission of the nobility in the south, and through secret agents concocting his treaty with the king of England. Archibald Douglas, a brother of the deceased Lord James, at the head of a Scottish force fell upon his army in the night, and threw it into confusion and rout. Baliol leaped from his bed half naked, mounted a horse without a saddle, and fled full speed by the nearest way across the border into England (Dec. 16, 1332). His enterprise had lasted in all about four months. It began like a flash of lightning, and ended like a bubble.[1]

The Scots followed up their advantage by a raid into England, which gave occasion to the English to charge them with violating the treaty of Northampton. King Edward retaliated by openly supporting Baliol with a strong force, laying siege to Berwick and putting the pretender in command. The Scots, in attempting to protect the place, suffered the disastrous defeat of Halidon Hill (1333). Baliol was again set up as king, of course only as a vassal of Edward III., to whom he also ceded all of the kingdom south of the Forth and east of a line from Linlithgow to Dumfries; that is, the Saxon part of the south. Loyal Scotsmen were enraged and adhered the more zealously to their

[1] Buchanan, b. ix., king 99th; Burton, ii. 316.

national cause. Upon the death of Murray a new regent was appointed, and again, through a long course of internal war, the foreign interest lost ground. Baliol could feel safe only in the lands he had ceded to England, as long as they were held by English troops. When the ambition of Edward III. found a more promising field in France (1338), Baliol abandoned Scotland, never to return (1339). In 1341 the heir of the Bruce, David II., returned from France, whither he had been taken for his education, and although only seventeen years of age assumed the government.

Subsequently, the matured military skill of Edward III. and of his brilliant son, the Black Prince, which otherwise might have overpowered Scotland, was occupied with long-protracted wars in France, in which Scotland was concerned only by the conditions of her treaty with the latter country. An invasion of England, undertaken in that cause in 1346, when Edward was in France, was defeated at the battle of Neville's Cross, in which David II. was taken prisoner. With some of his nobles he was carried to London and committed to the Tower. Again the government of his kingdom was administered by the abler hands of the regent steward. A truce made by Edward with France included Scotland, and continued by renewals until 1354.

David was ransomed, and returned to his throne in 1357. His reign was feeble and unpatriotic, and failed of doing permanent harm only because in his long absences the wise and moderate steward filled his place, and when he was at home the estates held a firm check upon his designs, which seem to have been far from obstinate. When he died (Feb. 22, 1370) Robert Allan, or Fitz Allan, his sister's son, and high steward of Scotland, succeeded, according to the arrangement made by king and Parliament more than fifty years before. So long had the office of steward been retained in his family that its title had become his surname, and so well had he exercised the powers of royalty as regent that nothing save the title and honors of king remained to be added to what he had already worn.

The reign of Robert II., first of the Stewart dynasty, corresponded with the last seven years of the reign of Edward III. and those of Richard II. to 1390. It was followed by that of his son John, which continued until 1406. But such was the disfavor in which the name John was held, from hatred to the elder Baliol, that John Stewart at his coronation took the name of his father and great-grandfather, and counts as Robert III. on the list of Scottish kings.

It was from the reign of Robert Bruce, and through those of his son and grandson, that the sentiments and customs of chivalry entered most deeply into the character of English and Scottish warfare, as depicted by Froissart and illustrated by the adventures of Douglas and Randolph, of Edward III. and the Black Prince, in the earlier part of the period, and of the Douglases and Percys toward the end of it.

The records of the Roman Catholic Church in Scotland during these reigns are of no spiritual import whatever. Concerned solely with successions of ecclesiastical dignitaries, with facts of their temporal interests, their ambitions, jealousies, quarrels, honors, revenues, scarcely can an allusion to the state of religion be gathered from their pages. We read of bishops building cathedrals and managing affairs of state, but rarely of preaching the gospel.[1] Of the parish work no mention is made at all.

For England, the last two-thirds of the fourteenth century was a period of great distinction, from her victories in France and Spain, but still more from the rise of her native literature, and the dawn of the Reformation in religion. It was the time of Chaucer and Wycliff. In Scotland there was a similar literary progress. It had been preceded by the learning of Michael Scot, of Thomas of Ercildoun and John of Dunse, the last of whom died in

[1] *Ecc. Chron. in the fourteenth century.*

1308. John Barbour, author of the celebrated poem on the adventures of the Bruce, and John of Fordun, earliest of the general historians of Scotland, lived at the same time with Chaucer and Wycliff. Barbour and Fordun, however, unlike their English contemporaries, seem to have entertained no disposition toward a religious reformation.

From causes already recounted, papal authority, declining in some other quarters, in the fourteenth century, increased in Scotland. To counteract the intrusion of England the king and the higher clergy favored immediate relations with Rome. The papal animosity, from 1306 to 1324, was a perfectly rational exception on both sides. Bruce had been guilty of what the Church could not regard as other than a crime of the highest magnitude. A right-minded pope could not fail to brand it with the severest censure, nor to continue what penalty his office was capable of inflicting, as long as it was unabsolved. Aggravating misrepresentations, made persistently by the king of England touching the whole Scottish nation, prolonged untruthfully that state of the case, and must have justified the popes of those years in their own eyes while keeping the ban upon the followers of a sacrilegious chief. On the other hand, the king and people of Scotland, involved in a struggle for existence, the desperate pitting of the skill and endurance of a few against surpassing numbers of equal valor and sometimes not inferior skill, left no breathing-time for explanations. Before time could be given to satisfy the censor of the true state of the case, life must be secured. Every man competent to such negotiation was needed at home. As soon as such a man could be spared he was delegated, in the person of Thomas Randolph, to counteract the slanders accumulated at the papal court. The subsequent rescripts of John XXII. testified to his restored favor. To the same pontiff King Robert Bruce, in his last illness, sent messengers to request "that the bishop of St. Andrews, who had been in use to invest the Scottish kings with the ensigns of royalty, might thenceforth be authorized by the pope to crown and anoint them." The request was granted, and, in 1331, David Bruce was the first Scottish sovereign crowned with papal solemnities.[1]

The bull of John XXII. granting to Bishop Bane and his successors in St. Andrews the right to anoint the kings of Scotland, orders also that at their coronation the kings shall take their "corporal oath that they will *bonâ fide* study to exterminate from their kingdom, and all other places subject to their authority, all such heretics as are denounced by the

[1] *Ecc. Chron. of Scot.*, i. 190.

Church; and they will not presume to injure or diminish the rights of the Church, but rather preserve them untouched."[1]

Upon Edward Baliol's invasion, Bishop Bane fled into Flanders, where he died at Bruges, September 22, 1332. On that occasion Edward III. wrote to the pope, desiring him to consecrate an Englishman for St. Andrews, and recommended his own treasurer, Robert, archdeacon of Berks. The pope took no notice of the application, But Edward's letter is extant.[2] To be safe on both sides, some plea was found by the court at Avignon for withholding consecration of a bishop for St. Andrews, until, at the end of nine years, the king of France united with the king of Scotland in soliciting the promotion for William Landel, who entered upon office in 1341. "During that vacancy Edward, king of England, seized the estate of the bishopric, without regarding the title which his vassal Edward Baliol might have had to it."[3] Thus the highest places in both Church and State were acknowledged to be indebted to the pope for their most solemn sanction.

Scotland was, upon the whole, a favored province of the papal empire, and enjoyed, at some important junctures, its invaluable protection, and regarded it with loyal attachment.

[1] *Ecc. Chron. of Scot.*, i. 192.   [2] Ibid., 195.   [3] Ibid.

Countries in which a relation to the Church of Rome had grown up spontaneously from the earliest times had also their hereditary episcopacy of native growth, with hereditary privileges. In Scotland the episcopal system was introduced by royal policy from abroad. The first diocesan bishops were foreigners, and for support took refuge in the foreign powers from which they came. Over against that, the king and native placemen sought protection from the pope. When, in the course of time, all placemen were native, the national Church stood related to the Roman immediately and without reserve.

In the old British and Columban churches *the first duty of the clergy was instruction.* Nor afterward, under the papal rule, was that duty entirely neglected in the parishes. It is stated by Burton that in almost all periods of the history of Scotland whatever documents deal with the social condition of the people reveal also a machinery for *education*, always abundant when compared with any traces of art or other elements of civilization. The genealogy of education in that country must be carried down from its earliest Christian churches. The doctrines and facts of Scripture formed the popular instruction of the old British and Irish churches, from which the Scottish was descended. At the same time, it can hardly be doubted that parochial instruction was greatly impaired, if not broken down, in some places in the long and desolating wars which followed the death of Alexander III.

No movement for reformation, like that headed by Wycliff in England, appears among the Scottish clergy of the fourteenth century. Yet among the common people, especially in the West, and some of the parish clergy a demand of that nature was very likely operating quietly as an inheritance from earlier times, preparing the way for that dissent of the so-called Lollards of Kyle which broke out in the succeeding century.[1] As late as the accession of James Bane to the bishopric of St. Andrews (1328) the Culdee society of that church was still in existence and asserted its right to elect the bishop.[2] If such was the case at the very head of the Romish organization for the kingdom, it is not unlikely that among out-of-the-way parishes in the West, where the old Church had its original strongholds, more of its earlier spirit may have remained. The revolution to Romanism, so far as the laity and parochial clergy were concerned, pertained only to system of government and ecclesiastical allegiance. If these were satisfactory, it was a matter of little moment to the rulers how pious or well-informed were the country parishes and their

[1] Intro. to Knox's *Hist.* [2] *Ecc. Chron.* i. 189.

priests. And yet, from a sentence in the rescript touching the coronation of David II., the pope appears to have had a suspicion of such freedom being, in some quarters, indulged too far.

CHAPTER X.

PROGRESS OF EDUCATION.—RISE OF THE SCOTTISH UNIVERSITIES.

JAMES, the only surviving son of Robert III., left Scotland in the year 1405, on his way to France, where it was designed that he should complete his education. When off Flamborough Head, the ship in which he sailed was captured by an English squadron, although the two countries were then at peace, and he was carried to London and confined in the Tower. At the end of two years he was removed to Nottingham Castle, from which (in 1413) he was taken back to the Tower of London, and ere the close of that year transferred to Windsor Castle. Carried to France by Henry V. on one of his expeditions, he was again remanded to Windsor Castle, and there remained to the end of his long imprisonment.

King Robert III. died in April, 1406. His brother, the duke of Albany, became regent, and at his death, in 1418, the same office passed into the hands of his son, no earnest effort apparently having been made for the liberation of the young king, in whose name the government was conducted.

As the ambition of English kings in regard to Scotland was only to have it annexed to their own dominion, they had no motive to treat with harshness a captive king whom they might hope to win over. To furnish him with all means of education which the times possessed was perfectly consistent with the purpose for which he was retained in custody. James made good use of all. In his long durance of eighteen years he became the best-educated prince of his time. In literature, in philosophy and law, in music and poetry, he excelled. Nor was he prohibited the practice of such manly exercises as were consistent with the nature of the constraint under which he was held. The poem called the " King's Quair," in which he sings of his calamities and of his love for a lady casually seen from the window of his prison, is, without any allowance for the royal rank of the author, the finest poem of its time in the English language. Nor did he fail, after the death of his uncle, the duke of Albany, to make his influence felt in the politics of Scotland. From Henry V. he received the most respectful treatment that could be extended to a captive.

After Henry's death, and the misfortunes of the English in France began, it was expedient to come to better terms with Scotland. James, by proposal of the English council, was released upon ransom or pay for his maintenance, and on condition of a truce of seven years between the two countries, and that he should forbid his subjects to enter the French service.[1] When, before his return, it was thought desirable that he should be allied in marriage with the English royal family, it was found that the heroine of the "King's Quair," to whom his heart was already devoted, was no other than the Lady Jane Beaufort, daughter of the earl of Somerset and cousin of Henry V. With his queen and a splendid escort James took his way northward. He was met by a royal company on the border of Scotland, and crowned at Scone on the 21st of May, 1424.

During the long time of the regency, the usurpations of a rapacious and haughty nobility had encroached oppressively upon both the commons and the Crown. James put forth every effort to establish an equal balance of rights, to assert the royal authority over the land and to improve the condition of the people. At the same time, he lived in a simple, accessible way, seeking intelligence of the wants of all classes, and open to the presentation of all grievances. With the unguarded openness of a brave man he trusted too far to the intrinsic merits of his government,

[1] Lingard, v. 61; Burton, ii. 397.

believing that its public benefits would recommend it. The selfish malignity of a few, who deemed themselves aggrieved by those measures of public advantage, found therefore but little obstacle in its way. A body of assassins broke into the monastery at Perth, where he was temporarily residing, and slew him in the midst of his family. It was on the evening of the 10th of February, 1436. National indignation was fiercely expressed in the long and loud condemnation of the murderers, and in the elaborate punishments inflicted on them.

The reign of James I. constitutes an epoch in the history of Scottish legislation, education and literature. The plans of the king were sustained by the Church, which fully appreciated the value of improvements falling in with a progress of her own. Legislation was the principal field of the king's own efforts. He called frequent Parliaments, and kept them busy.[1] Effects proceeded thence to all other departments of national culture, and James's own example of high education and literary accomplishment recommended to popular favor pursuits which otherwise were gaining ground in public esteem.

In Scotland education was, in the first instance and for many centuries, entirely the work of the Church, and literary men were

[1] Burton, ii. 399.

churchmen. King James I. was the earliest author of any note among laymen. For ministers of religion ability to read and write the Latin language was required, and a competent knowledge of the Latin version of the Holy Scriptures, in addition to all that they were expected to impart to the people. For that purpose had the Columbite colleges been continued, until supplanted by the Romish monasteries. These latter, in the thirteenth century, were actuated by an all-pervading zeal for knowledge and intellectual training. By the opening of the fourteenth century a stage had, in some countries, been reached preparing the way for the culture of the modern tongues. In Scotland the war of independence greatly retarded that progress. That it was not entirely stopped was due to the Church, in her old hereditary capacity of instructor, maintaining a degree of popular intelligence. Although the rise of a native literature was not at first so abundant as in England, it was more purely national. The works of Barbour and Wynton are concerned with purely Scottish themes. With the exception of the "King's Quair," such also are the poems attributed to James I. What is called the English language grew up simultaneously in England and the Lowlands of Scotland.

In the liberalizing tendency which affected

the church schools generally in the fourteenth century, Scotland, though behind, came in for a share before the century closed; but in the next century her literary rank became conspicuous, even above that of her southern neighbor.

There are no statistics of education "sufficient to afford an idea of the number of schools in the country," or the subjects taught in each, down even to the Reformation. "But in documents much older than the war of independence the school and the schoolmaster are familiar objects of reference." They occur in connection with business of the religious houses. The schools consisted of two classes —parish schools and the monastic schools devoted to preparation for clerical office, the first care being to provide public instruction in practical religion. Separate institutions for secular education were the growth of a later time. In the fifteenth century mention occurs of schools attached to the borough corporations, which were called grammar schools, in which instruction was continued as far as a good practical knowledge of Latin. An act of Parliament passed in 1496 enacted that through all the kingdom the eldest sons and heirs of barons and freeholders should be continued at the grammar school "until they be completely founded and have perfect Latin," and after that to attend the schools of art and law three years. Compliance with that statute was to be enforced by a fine of twenty pounds upon failure.

Education *for the people* has always in Scotland taken precedence of education for the few.

The earliest Scottish university was founded at St. Andrews in 1410 by Bishop Wardlaw, and received the sanction of Pope Benedict XIII. in 1413.

During the papal schism, when from 1378 there were two rival lines of popes, one at Rome and the other at Avignon, and from 1409 a third at Pisa or Bologna, Scotland adhered consistently to the pope at Avignon. It was the Avignonese pope who gave his sanction to the University of St. Andrews. But next year the Council of Constance met, which deposed all three popes and elected another—namely, Martin V., who was to be sole pope. Benedict XIII., unwilling to submit, retained his papal court and as many adherents as he could persuade, until his death. The action of the council was communicated to Scotland by the abbot of Pontiniac, who had audience given him in a large assembly of the clergy at Perth. On that occasion Benedict was also represented by one Harding, a Franciscan monk, who made a long address upon the theme, "My son, do nothing without advisement; so shall it not repent thee after the deed," in which he labored to prove the informality of the council and that none were under obligation to comply with its decrees, and that Benedict XIII. was still entitled to the allegiance of the Christian world. To that plea answer was made by John Fogo, a monk of Melrose, who from the text, "Withdraw yourselves from every brother who walketh disorderly," refuted Harding's arguments, and showed that the supporter of him, who pretended to be pope in opposition to the council, was a disturber of the peace of the Church. The assembly resolved to accept the action of the council, and Scotland once more fell into line with the adherents of the pope of Rome.

The Church of Scotland, which for five hundred years held little or no connection with Rome, had now, through the course of events already recounted, before the opening of the fifteenth century become one of the most closely dependent upon it. Rome had been propitiated as an ally against England; the metropolitan pretensions of York had been encountered with the arms of papal authority; Scottish sovereignty had been recognized by the pope, and its recognition enjoined by him upon the king of England; and papal favor, though not always consistent, had been sought in the dangerous conflict with a near and stronger power.

In the fifteenth century the attitude of England became less threatening; both countries were too much occupied with internal troubles to have much strength to spare for harassing each other. The long minorities of James II., James III. and James IV., with the brevity of their personal reigns, gave occasion to an exaggerated growth of power in some of the great aristocratic families of Scotland, the Douglases, Hamiltons, Dunbars and others, among whom it was a matter of no common difficulty for the monarch to maintain his ascendency. Englishmen were wholly engaged with their wars in France, and afterward with those of York and Lancaster among themselves, and the succeeding policy of Henry VII. of England was wisely pacific. The frequent conflicts between northern and southern inhabitants of the border were only local and predatory raids. Through most of the century the Scottish hierarchy, absorbed in its own rivalries and ambitions, took little concern to scrutinize the opinions of obscure people. Not that heresy was deemed harmless—it was punished with the severest penalty when discovered—but in the press of more imminently threatening dangers and more exacting interests it no doubt often escaped attention. Dissenters existed in both countries without much public notice being taken of them; and yet not all with impunity.

The highest places in the Church of Scotland were now in the gift of the king and the pope, while their large revenues rendered them objects of ambition for the nobility. Wealth, possession of power, and impunity in luxurious indulgence were producing effects which, in course of time, became scandalous. Bishops whose temporal interests were but slightly affected by discharge of duty, and very much by hierarchical policy, were tempted to neglect the care of souls, to look after their own revenues and pleasures. In such cases, the men put into parishes as pastors were such as suited the worldly views of those who appointed them. The moral character of the clergy, upon the whole, degenerated. It became worldly, and religious service formal. Preaching ceased to be considered the duty of a pastor. It was not expected of a bishop. Spirituality abandoned the routine of services which made no demand on either mind or heart.

In that state of general ecclesiastical unfaithfulness, there were still traditions of a better time, and rumors came of reforms being attempted elsewhere. Among the best informed of the parishioners some were found to sympathize with the English and Bohemian dissenters. In the year 1408, James Resby, an Englishman and follower of Wycliff, was arrested in Scotland for teaching doctrines contrary to those of the Catholic Church. He was charged by Lawrence of Lindores, president of a council of the clergy, as guilty of forty heretical opinions. Only two have been recorded— namely, that the pope was not the vicar of God, and that no man could be rightly esteemed pope if he was of a wicked life. For those opinions he was burned to death at Perth, under authority of the regent, the duke of Albany.

Other critics of prevailing doctrines and clerical practices arose; nor is it to be presumed that every such dissenter came under the notice of a bishop or informer. The writer who records the execution of Resby states also that "the opinions and books of Wycliff are entertained by several Lollards in Scotland, but in extreme secrecy," and that "they seldom or never are restored to the bosom of the faith." One whose name is not mentioned was burned for heresy at Glasgow in 1422; and Paul Craw, the more conspicuous for being a foreigner, was condemned for heretical opinions touching the sacrament of the Lord's Supper, the adoration of saints and auricular confession, and burned at St. Andrews in 1432.

With the progress of education the advocates of dissenting opinions increased in number, for an important distinction existed between the neglected instructions of the pastorate and those of the expanding colleges and universities. As education in the latter was provided free, or at a trifling expense, its influence extended to high and low. It was, moreover, the avenue to promotion. Learning was in those days a very common object of ambition among young men of all ranks. The hierarchy, who were most bitterly opposed to reform, were in many cases founders or munificent patrons of schools. The same bishop who laid the foundations of St. Andrews also committed Resby and Craw to the flames. To resist the higher education was more than any bishop's reputation could stand, and yet in promoting it they were unawares constructing weapons for use against the absoluteness of their own authority.

The colleges and universities of Scotland increased in number. St. Andrews University, established in 1410, was sustained by the addition of St. Salvador's College about 1455, by that of St. Leonard's in 1512, and by that of St. Mary's in 1537. The University of Glasgow was commenced by Bishop Turnbull in 1450, with authority of Pope Nicholas V., after the model of that at Bologna. The old College of Aberdeen was in 1494 erected into a university on the model of that of Paris by Bishop Elphinstone, with the papal sanction of Alexander VI.

The royal patronage of James I. was judiciously extended to the same cause. At St. Andrews he not only encouraged the "professors by his presence at their lectures, but also gave order that no person should be preferred to any benefice unless it was testified by the professors that he had made a reasonable progress in learning; and for that effect he kept a roll of the best qualified from which to fill places that happened to fall void. Such he thought to be the surest way for banishing ignorance from the Church." He also frequently admonished churchmen in place to "live as they professed, and not to shame the bountifulness of princes by abusing their donations in riot and luxury."

St. Andrews, after ages of pre-eminence as an actual primacy, was at last, in 1472, by the due formality of a papal bull issued by Sixtus IV., erected into an archbishopric, and all the rest of the bishops in Scotland, twelve in number, ordained to be subject thereto. The latter provision was too explicit, and called out a strong opposition from other bishops. The difference was settled when Glasgow (in 1488) was also honored with archiepiscopal dignity, with Galloway, Argyll and the isles as subordinate sees, while the primacy was reserved for St. Andrews. In the latter case, the papal action was taken on the ground of Scottish national sovereignty, and to cut off the pretensions of English metropolitans.

Among the people of the west country, where once the old British and Columbite ministry had been most highly revered and their churches had been longest sustained, a party arose who strongly dissented from many of the doctrines of their Romish priests. Along the coast of Ayrshire, in the district of Kyle and Cunningham, they seem to have been most numerous. Very naturally, they were confounded by the public of their time with the followers of Wycliff, who were themselves confounded with the Lollards of the Netherlands, and those early Scottish Reformers were accordingly called the Lollards of Kyle. They had proceeded to the length of agreeing upon certain principles, and of drawing up a list of articles on which they held that the Church needed reformation, when in 1494 they were brought to the knowledge of the archbishop of Glasgow. Their articles, as preserved by their opponents, and extracted from the register of Glasgow, were in number thirty-four, of which some of the more important were—

1. That images ought not to be made nor worshiped.

2. That the relics of saints ought not to be adored.

4. That Christ gave the power of binding

and loosing to Peter only, and not to his successors.

5. That Christ ordained no priests to consecrate.

6. That after the consecration in the mass there remaineth bread, and the natural body of Christ is not there.

8. That Christ did abrogate the power of secular princes.

9. That every faithful man and woman is a priest.

12. That the pope deceiveth the people with his bulls and indulgences.

13. That the mass profiteth not the souls that are in purgatory.

17. That the pope exalts himself above God and against God.

18. That the pope cannot remit the pains of purgatory.

20. That the excommunication of the Church is not to be feared.

22. That priests may have wives, according to the constitution of the law.

26. That the pope cannot forgive sins.

31. That to worship the sacraments of the Church is idolatry.

For distributing those articles no less than thirty persons were cited to appear before the council. The charge was brought against them by the archbishop of Glasgow. Fortunately for them, the king himself, James IV., presided, and was favorably impressed with the statements made by their speakers, and no little amused with the ready and pithy way in which they met the arguments of the archbishop. They were dismissed with an admonition to beware of new doctrines and to content themselves with the faith of the Church.[1]

[1] Knox, Intro. *Ecc. Chron.*, ii. 513.

CHAPTER XI.

CLOSING SUMMARY.

THE Christian Church in Scotland, from the earliest hint of its existence in the third century until the dawn of the sixteenth, passed through four stages of existence. In the first it was a missionary enterprise, in which the principal personages were such men as Ninian and Patrick and Columba and Aidan, who, at the head each of his company of followers, planted themselves on the border of some heathen district and labored for its conversion. The system which they carried out was that of religious schools, all on the same plan. These schools were set up in places convenient for their converts or for the heathen, for whose conversion they were designed, and were devoted to educating clergy and sending them out to build up congregations or to minister in them. The pastors thus appointed were held to be related specially to the college which educated and appointed them, and unless sent out to form another station, or choosing to be voluntary anchorets, the college was their home; and all the colleges adhered to the same common doctrine and plan of government.

It was a peculiar plan. It was not presbyterian, for although the heads of the colleges were presbyters, as also were many of the brethren, yet each college acted, in some respects, with a separate authority. The parochial distribution of presbyters was undeveloped. They ministered according to clans and septs of clans, and the college to which they belonged was their government. No presbyterial meetings, no synodal meetings, no general assembly of all, had any existence. Their regular consultations were those of the brethren in a college. Iona or Lindisfarne or Abernethey sends out her licentiates by authority resident in herself, and to her do they continue to look for moral and ecclesiastical support.

It was not episcopal, for the chief authority was not in a bishop, but in the society of brethren who constituted the college, and the superior was the presbyter head of the fraternity. No place existed for a bishop. The country was not divided into dioceses. And if a wandering bishop appeared in any of the colleges, he was respected as of higher ecclesiastical rank, but they had nothing for him to do, which could not be as well done in his absence.

Upon the establishment of that system over the whole country, with its colleges at Iona,

Dunkeld, Abernethey, Melrose and elsewhere, a second stage began, in which the missionary feature gave way to pastoral routine, and the system became the national Church establishment of the Scots and Picts. Among the Picts an imperfect attempt to substitute the Romish secular system from England was only partial and temporary. The Church which adapted itself to clans and families, instead of to parishes and dioceses, was perhaps thought to be best suited to the social condition of the country. Absence of the ordinary stringent monastic vows left the brethren free to hold property and to marry. Perhaps few comparatively availed themselves of the freedom, but a goodly number did. In cases where the superior was a married man, his revenue was sometimes retained by his son, who, without being a clergyman, inherited also his father's rank and title as abbot.[1]

It was in that state of things that the Culdees arose, a society of clerical reformers to enforce stricter observance of the collegiate method.

A third stage of the record opens in the reign of Malcolm Canmore and his Saxon queen—a revolution continued by their sons —whereby the Romish system, both secular and regular, was enforced by royal authority

[1] Joseph Robertson, in *Quart. Rev.*, vol. 85, art. iv. 117.

upon the nation, and the native Scottish Church extinguished.

A fourth stage was gradually reached in the course of ecclesiastical aggression from England, to escape which the Scots sought refuge in the pope. His protection was granted, and, as far as concerned the Church, was effective. A papal tax was submitted to, and Scotland became papal. Notwithstanding an interruption during the war of independence, that favor continued, and was cultivated as a protection against a nearer and very obtrusive power. Thus it came to pass that, before the end of the fourteenth century, Scottish ecclesiasticism was more directly and completely conformable to the papacy than that of the churches of France or England, which had been part of the papal empire from a much earlier date.

Through the fifteenth century an inverse process went on, whereby the easy security of the exotic ecclesiasticism declined into indulgence, and, on the other side, the increase of education led to more discriminate observation of existing practices and a more common knowledge of the Bible. It might be called the period of the rise of the universities, from the erection of that of St. Andrews until the controversy of the Reformation became a national question—one destined to control every other for the next one hundred and fifty years.

The change toward emancipation from the papal yoke was slow, and by successive steps, and had proceeded to a great length before men perceived to what a revolution things were tending. For a long time that growing spirit of revolt was not against the papacy. The popes, upon the whole, had been very friendly to Scotland. It was against doctrines and practices in the national Catholic Church that protests arose—against senseless, unscriptural doctrines, the immoral lives of the clergy, especially of the higher clergy, and their oppressive treatment of the people. Putting to death those who made public such protest no doubt deterred many from professing the same opinions, but it also called attention to them and challenged examination of them. Then arose questions as to the personal character of some of the popes, which toward the end of the century was so notorious as to be an offence to all Europe. It began to be denied that a wicked man could be made the head of the Chnrch on earth by any forms of consecration.

A further step led to denial of the papal claim to be vicar of God, and to power of pardoning sin. In its first stages, that progress appeared not in the action of any reforming priest, but among the better educated laymen. In the last years of the fifteenth century, it was evinced in the Lollards of Kyle, and by action of the estates of the realm, in remonstrating against papal intrusion and pretension to distribute all church patronage in the land, and in denouncing persons who backed up those pretensions by going to Rome to secure presentation to benefices, and those who carried litigation to Rome, and thereby recognized the papal court as higher than that of the nation. Those who had cases there were ordered to bring them home to be settled by the law courts of the land.

Yet during the same time, by the erection of St. Andrews and Glasgow into archbishoprics, and their disputes and appeal to Rome, papal intervention in Scottish affairs was for a time increased. Possession of great revenue by churchmen, sustained in place by a strong foreign power, and influence wielded by them in the monarchical politics of the times, secured the ascendency of the papal system for two generations longer, without in the least degree retrieving its impaired popularity. Power to repress the utterance of dissentient opinions failed to prevent people from entertaining them, while successive utterances became bolder and fuller in denunciation of prevailing error and immorality, until finally redress was demanded and obtained.

Scotland, for a long time favorably impressed with the benefits of Romanism, and cherishing it as a friend, upon better knowledge of it and fuller experience of its fruits lost her respect for it, and, as those fruits developed in the pastorates of her Church and the morals of her higher clergy, found it at last to be intolerable. To return to her old collegiate or monastic plan was neither desirable nor practicable; a missionary form of the Church was no longer adequate to the demands of the nation. A more complete theology and greater experience in church affairs dictated a better method of discipline and a fuller creed. The compacted civil union of all that is now Scotland, and the steady settlement of her increased population, called for a similar unity and comprehensiveness of the governing system in the Church, with territorial distribution of the clergy.

How these topics arose for discussion, what answers were proposed, what was adopted as authority for arbitration, with the inevitable war of logic and of arms, and what conclusion was reached, will fall into another part of this narrative.

BOOK THIRD.

CAUSES WHICH LED TO THE REFORMATION.

CHAPTER I.

DECLINE OF CLERICAL PIETY.

GAVIN DOUGLAS, at the age of twenty-two, was made rector of Hawick, and evinced his qualifications for the office by a Scottish translation of Ovid's "Remedy for Love." Among churchmen of rank one of the best, in literary merit second to not more than one of his contemporaries, for sobriety of deportment, he stood conspicuous in an age of violence. The events of his life present perhaps as unbiased a picture of the motives prevailing among the hierarchy, and of the way in which benefices were conferred in those days, as can now be obtained.

Royal perfidy and murder had broken the old line of Douglas, but the younger branch of Angus inherited its honors and popular favor. Already it had reached the summit of its greatness in the hands of Archibald, the great earl of Angus, commonly spoken of by the nickname of "Bell-the-Cat." Hamiltons, under the leadership of the earl of Arran, had risen also to a degree of wealth and political influence scarcely inferior to the Douglases; Stewarts of the royal line and its affiliated clans, with Gordons of Huntly, Hepburns of Bothwell, Campbells of Argyll, and other stems of the aristocracy, sought to subordinate the richest places in the Church, as appanages for cadets of their own houses.

Papal patronage had long been making progress and limiting that of the Crown and the nobility. Laws had been passed to resist it, and although not always enforced, because of the conflict of parties, were a strong defensive armor when the native interests were agreed.

Repeated and long minorities in the royal line had given occasion for greatly disproportioned increase of power in a few baronial families, whose ambitions came in conflict, and the pope profited by their dissensions.

The most honorable benefice in the Church was the archbishopric of St. Andrews, now the authoritatively constituted primacy of all Scotland. Next to that was Glasgow, then Dunkeld and the other diocesan episcopates, the great abbacies of Aberbrothock, Lochleven, and so forth. These places were desirable no less for emolument than for honor.

It was in the eighth year of the reign of James IV. (1496) that Gavin Douglas received his first benefice. Soon afterward he was promoted to the place of provost in the cathedral church of St. Giles in Edinburgh, which, being in the gift of the Crown, he took possession of without opposition. In subsequent preferments the weight of his family was greatly to his disadvantage, bringing the force of various opposing interests against him. The third son of the great Earl Archibald Douglas of Angus, he was born in 1474, or early next year, and was designed from boyhood for the Church—more, it would seem, from his literary turn of mind than for any depth of religious feeling evinced by him. His education, the best then to be obtained in Scotland, was completed in Paris.

When James IV. made his invasion of England in 1513, the great earl strongly remonstrated against it. His remonstrance failed. But although, because of his advanced age, he himself remained behind, his two oldest sons, George and William, followed their impulsive king, and, together with about two hundred gentlemen of the Douglas name, fell by his side in the battle of Flodden. The earl retired to the religious house of St. Mains in Galloway, and died soon after, leaving a grandson of his own name to inherit the estates and honors of the house of Angus. Among the slain on that disastrous field were found clergymen of the highest rank in the Church of Scotland. One of these was the archbishop of St. Andrews, a natural son of the king—of course a youth—who had held for several years, in addition to that honorable see, the abbacies of Dunfermline and Aberbrothock, with the priory of Coldingham. All these places, left vacant by his death, became objects of cupidity to some of the greedy families of rank.

Queen Margaret, in a letter to Leo X., strongly urged the merits of Gavin Douglas as a suitable person to be secured in possession of Aberbrothock, to which he was already assigned, and soon afterward nominated him also to the primacy. Presuming that the royal nomination would not be disputed, he forthwith occupied the castle of St. Andrews. But John Hepburn, of the noble family of Bothwell, and already prior of the cathedral, was elected by the canons. The pope, who (notwithstanding the national laws to the contrary) continued to assert his right to dispose of all benefices, mediately or immediately, granted his sanction to Andrew Forman, a nephew, it is said, of Alexander, Lord Home. At that time, Forman was bishop of Bourges, a benefice in the Gallican Church, conferred upon him for his services to France in promoting the march of James IV. into England. Leo X., now having a nephew to provide for, persuaded Forman to resign that bishopric, in view of promotion to the primacy in Scotland.

Hepburn, having possession of the ecclesiastical buildings and sustained by his friends, raised a military force, and expelled the adherents of Douglas and garrisoned the castle. The young earl of Angus interposed with two hundred cavalry, but his uncle declined the unseemly contest, and withdrew his claim. Hepburn, for a time, ruled in St. Andrews by strength of arms. And Forman, with his papal bull, was helpless, because no man dared to publish it. At last, his kinsman, Lord Home, came to his aid with ten thousand of his Border followers, subdued the opposition, and caused the papal gift to be proclaimed in Edinburgh with great solemnity. For this service the brother of Lord Home was to receive the priory of Coldingham. But the end of the quarrel was not until after Hepburn had presented his plea at the court of Rome, and the arrival of the duke of Albany from France.

Before the end of the first year of her widowhood, the queen married the earl of Angus, nephew of Gavin Douglas. Doubtful, as some were at first, of the wisdom of constituting her regent, on account of the advantage it might open to her brother, Henry VIII. of England, to interfere in Scottish affairs, still more was it questioned now, when it put the most dangerous rival of the royal dynasty in its very place of power. The estates began to think of measures to prevent the evils apprehended from that quarter. The duke of Albany, younger brother of James III., had long been resident in France, where he enjoyed the friendship of Louis XI., with extensive possessions and princely honors. Immediately after the battle of Flodden, the opinion had been advanced that he was the proper person to act as regent. Now that opinion became the policy of the nation. But His Grace was unwilling to leave France, where he had become completely naturalized. He delayed, and did not arrive in Scotland until the 18th of May, 1515. The war for the primacy was still unsettled. Under his management the parties submitted to a compromise, facilitated by the distribution of other rich benefices, which in that juncture had become available.

Forman was left in possession of St. Andrews and of the abbacies of Dunfermline and Aberbrothock. The latter, taken by Gavin Douglas, was for a time to be conceded to Beaton, archbishop of Glasgow. Coldingham went to the brother of Lord Home. John Hepburn, prior of St. Andrews, was to receive from the archbishop a pension of three thousand crowns a year. To his brother, James Hepburn, was assigned the rich bishopric of Murray. Alexander Gordon, cousin to the earl of Huntly, was made bishop of Aberdeen. James Ogilvy, a kinsman of Lord Ogilvy, was appointed abbot of Dryburgh; and George

Dundas, of the noble family of that name, received as a layman the "commendation" of Torphichen. And so the prizes were distributed among the honorable candidates.

In all this nothing fell to the lot of Gavin Douglas, who had early withdrawn from the squabble. But neither did he escape the conflict of arms. Four months before the arrival of the duke of Albany the bishop of Dunkeld died; and the queen again recommended her husband's uncle to a vacant see. In this instance she succeeded in obtaining, it is thought through influence of her brother, the king of England, a papal bull in favor of her candidate. But here, also, a competitor preoccupied the field. The earl of Athole had persuaded the canons of Dunkeld to "postulate" his brother, Andrew Stewart, who had not yet been advanced to sub-deacon's orders. Douglas was resisted, and accused of procuring a bull from Rome, and thereby violating the laws of the realm. He was found guilty and committed to prison. It was the same cause which in Forman's case had not only passed unchallenged, but had been solemnly published in the capital of the kingdom. But the enemies of the Douglases were now in power. After about a year, during which Stewart drew the revenues of the see, an arrangement was entered into whereby Douglas obtained his freedom, and by the intercession of Beaton, archbishop of Glasgow, with the duke of Albany, his claim to the bishopric of Dunkeld was secured.

All the obstacles, however, were not yet removed. For although, at Dunkeld, most of both the clergy and the laity received their new bishop with favor, the episcopal palace was still occupied by the retainers of Stewart, who also seized by force the tower of the cathedral, and obstructed the performance of divine service. Stewart himself arrived with a force of armed men, and commenced firing upon the bishop's party where they sat in council. Lord Ogilvy, and others with him, prepared for battle, and by mustering from the neighboring districts, in the course of the next day, had a formidable body of fighting men assembled. Stewart, perceiving himself to be outnumbered, withdrew to the woods. But some of his party held their ground until the cathedral was taken by force. Nor did they surrender the palace before the matter was settled by interference of the regent, for the bishop refused to carry violence to the shedding of blood. It was finally agreed that Stewart should give up his pretensions to the bishopric, but retain the rents he had levied, together with two subordinate benefices, on which he was to pay a certain tax. For that agreement the regent obtained the papal sanction.

In the whole of this history not a thought of the interests of the Church or for the people concerned is evinced—not a care for the kingdom of Christ, not a shadow of the gospel. It is a mere record of shameless greed, the working of that simple plan,

> "That they should take who have the power,
> And they should keep who can."

Certain places in the Church were worth so much money; certain formalities were needed to qualify a man to hold one of them, and with a view to that end certain persons submitted to the formalities. Nor in the presence of such conspicuous examples can there be a doubt that many humbler places were disposed of in the same manner. Even a man of such peaceful disposition as Gavin Douglas, devoted to literary pursuits, and ready to withdraw from unchristian quarreling, could not get possession of what was conferred by authority, undisputed in that time, without the use of violence. It was much that he avoided bloodshed.

CHAPTER II.

CLERICAL MORALITY.

GREED of money, actuating the hierarchy of Scotland to such a degree and in such a shameless way, was a constant provocation to remember that it was a system of foreign origin, and that its interest in the country centred in its gains. Intelligent men could not fail to know that it was introduced, at no very distant date, in the hands of foreign bishops, abbots and monks, whose places were created for them by suppression of the native Church government, and subordination of the native clergy. None could fail to know that it held allegiance to a foreign ecclesiarch, or to perceive that Scotsmen, who occupied its places of emolument, were alienated thereby from the interests of their humbler countrymen. Its highest dignities were still so recent that men then living could remember when they were constituted. Much fault was found with it among the people from whom its revenues were drawn. It was felt to be a growing evil, and the more oppressive that utterly unworthy men held its highest and most lucrative benefices. Sir David Lindsay, who on so many points gave expression to the popular sentiment, one day approached the king when surrounded by a numerous train of nobility, and declared himself a candidate for an office which had lately become vacant. "I have," said he, "servit Your Grace lang, and luik to be rewardid, as others are; and now your maister taylor, at the pleasure of God, is departit, wherefore I would desire of Your Grace to bestow this little benefite upon me." The king replied that he was amazed at such an application from a person who could neither shape nor sew. "Sir," rejoined the poet, "that maks nae matter, for you have given bishoprics and benefices to mony standing here about you, and yet they can neither teach nor preach; and why may not I as weill be your taylor, thocht I can nouther shape nor sew, seeing teaching and preaching are nae less requisite to their vocation than shaping and sewing to ane taylor?"

Teaching and preaching, however, had ceased to be any part of the work done by bishops; they had ceased to consider it their duty. By the parish priest it was also generally neglected, left to the occasional visits of mendicant monks. The people of all ranks were destitute of religious instruction, except in as far as they collected for themselves.

But that was far from all the evil nestling in

the system and making its effects known before the public. To put men into the ministry without ministerial qualifications was bad enough, but when many of them were also without piety, or positively immoral, it became scandalous. What religious influence can be expected of godless men living in luxury and furnished with the means of gratifying every desire?

Rome, moreover, had added to the Decalogue, and thereby greatly added to the number of sins. Forbidding their priests to marry had almost, in relation to them, abolished the seventh commandment—so far, at least, that marriage inevitably excluded a man from the priesthood, concubinage not necessarily. The effects were, in the fifteenth century, widely spread over Western Christendom. On this subject the conduct of certain bishops and archbishops of the Scottish Church was notorious. The evidence to the fact, only too plain and abundant, is much of it of a nature unfit for republication and is so undisputed as not to need repetition. So common was that kind of immorality that it had ceased to be regarded with shame. In some cases no concealment was attempted. Beaton, cardinal and archbishop of St. Andrews, was open in his amours, and succeeded in marrying his oldest daughter, with great and almost regal state, to a son of Earl

Crawford. Hepburn, bishop of Murray, was equally shameless, but with a coarseness of bravado against which the cardinal was guarded by his culture and better taste. Even the decorous Gavin Douglas, bishop of Dunkeld, "did not die childless."

With such examples in the primacy and in the episcopal palaces, similar conduct in the lower clergy was sure of impunity; and contemporaneous literature corroborates the voice of common fame. From the fourteenth century to the sixteenth few themes occur in the works of poets and authors of popular tales more frequently than the immorality of the clergy. Nor is it necessary, in order to justify the common censure, to assume that all priests were bad men. The bad might not have been a majority of the whole, but even if a relatively small number were openly guilty and went unpunished, very plainly the whole were either corrupted in opinion, or intimidated by what they deemed the greater power of the guilty. It is not a certain conclusion that the laity will be bad if their priests are bad; but, with the bad conduct of the priesthood before their eyes, those who are viciously disposed will feel emboldened in vice, a lower standard of morality will be maintained, and persons of wavering virtue will the more readily yield to temptation.

In the days of James IV., when the opposing currents of events were hastening to their respective conclusions, when intelligence was increasing toward a movement for reformation, and the proclivity of corruption reaching a degree which could no longer be endured, a goodly number of authors, of both verse and prose, appeared in Scotland. Their works are contemporaneous testimonies to the progress in both directions. The satire of some, who themselves were not strong enough to resist the downward stream, is the most telling testimony of all.

William Dunbar, the chief of early Scottish poets, and without an equal until the rise of Burns, though he gave no evidence of belonging to the reforming party, at least penetrated and exposed the conduct of the other. He was a native of Lothian, born about the middle of the fifteenth century, flourished in the time of James IV., and died within a few years after the battle of Flodden. In his early days he was a novice of the Franciscan order, and in the Franciscan garb had traveled and preached in the principal towns of England from Berwick to Calais, and beyond the sea among the people of Picardy. He declares that in such capacity his mode of life constrained him to practice many a pious fraud from which no holy water could cleanse him. Later in life he enjoyed much admiration, but little emolument, at the court of James IV. He would have accepted a benefice in the Church, and thought it a hardship that none was offered. His licentious poems do not seem to have occurred to him as an obstacle in the way to promotion. With the sharp scalpel of satirical wit he laid open to public contempt vices which it does not appear that he had himself the fortitude to resist. But if he could not heal the evils in which he was involved, he laid them bare before the eyes of men who had the remedy to apply.

As a matter of course, when unchastity was common many other sins abounded. No sin ever reigns alone. Among the evils which prevailed were violence, rapine and disregard of life, against which, in many parts of the country, there was very imperfect protection. Profane swearing was notoriously common over the whole island, and especially was the profanity of Scotsmen proverbial among foreigners. What in our day is meant by swearing like a trooper was then to swear like a Scot. Guilty as all classes were, the clergy took the lead. Testimony remains in literature. The writings of Bishop Douglas are liberally interspersed with profane oaths. As the spirit of the Reformation gained ground, it was deemed proper for Parliament to interfere. An act was passed in 1551 forbidding the practice.

"A 'prelate of kirk,' earl or lord was to be fined in twelve pence for the first offence, committed within the next three months; different penalties were apportioned for different ranks during the first year; and for the fourth offence, committed after the expiration of that period, a prelate, earl or lord was to be banished or imprisoned for the space of a year and a day." Of what class did that majority consist which thus attempted to restrain the lords and bishops from profane swearing?

For men who were sensible of the turpitude of vice to hate the system which was training their country in such iniquity and disgrace hardly needed Christian faith. It was within the reach of a decent morality. National ambition, desire to have the country respected among her neighbors, the moral safety of families, the protection and comfort of society, demanded a reformation.

Things already mentioned were operating to produce alienation between the clergy and laity of Scotland, giving the impression to the laity that the clergy were not reliable guides where they were legally constituted the sole guides, and that their interests were not the best interests of the people. But there were other causes tending to the same end more directly. It was impossible to respect profligacy, especially in men whose office implied godliness, or grasping covetousness and ambition on the part of men claiming to be successors of the apostles.

But there was a stronger feeling than contempt engendered by the conduct of the hierarchy in Scotland. Had their moral character been immaculate, there was in their treatment of the laity, high and low, a hardness repulsive of all affection.

The canon law had grown up in the hands of ecclesiastics and for their benefit. The people had no part in its preparation, and knew it only as it was applied to their disadvantage. In Scotland such relations were established between it and the civil law that the one sustained the other. The screws of compulsion could thereby be turned down upon reluctating subjects, who often felt that they were wronged without the possibility of redress. When the king or regent was favorable to the hierarchy, it was easy to find a plea for forfeiture of estates in whole or in part. The property of the nobility and well-to-do commoners had long been gradually sliding into the hands of the clergy. By the beginning of the sixteenth century the larger part of the landed estates of the kingdom belonged to the Church. James IV. resisted these aggressions, but his successor, though entertaining little love for the bishops about him, yielded to them, and to enrich them distressed the nobility with "forfeitures and penalties." It is said that James Beaton, archbishop of St. Andrews, had prepared for him a long list of properties to be forfeited as circumstances might prove favorable. The report may be true or not; that it was accepted as credible proves what the public of that time had learned to believe, and so believing were accumulating hatred against the class of whom it was believed. To marry the illegitimate children of some of those wealthy churchmen could not have been a very satisfactory way of making reprisals. A more sweeping plan began to take possession of the minds of not a few. The artifices of what was to them inscrutable craft many began to think of encountering with open force.

Canon law entered in many ways into the dealings of priest and people to embarrass the security and comfort of society. One fertile source of such evil was the wide range of relationship within which marriage could not be contracted. Persons descended from a common ancestry to as far back as a great-great-grandfather or great-great-grandmother were within the prohibited bounds, and that whether the connecting link was one of consanguinity or formed by the spiritual relation of godfather or godmother. If at any point within that series of generations it could be shown that one pair had been so united, unless corrected by a papal dispensation it would invalidate the legitimacy of all descended from them. By this means were brought into the church courts all questions of legitimate birth and of hereditary inheritance.

In a population so small as that of Scotland, with a clan system pervading so much of it, persons not versed in that kind of lore might very ignorantly and innocently wed within the prohibited eight degrees, and among the nobility to avoid it must have required no little circumspection. As the Church or some churchman was, in many cases of disputed succession, the adverse claimant, such mistakes contributed to increase the ecclesiastical wealth at the expense of the laity, and to the alienation of their good-will. This extravagant law had also its immoral consequences. Persons wishing to marry within the prohibited degrees would sometimes obtain a papal dispensation for the purpose, thereby making the moral character of the act depend upon the decision of the pope. Others—and such cases were not unfrequent, it seems—would contract marriage with the intention of procuring the papal dispensation afterward, but upon experience of a few months or years prefer to separate without applying for it, or continue to live together on such terms that they might separate at any time. And even when the parties stood to all appearance outside of the sacred circle, but in the course of their married life tired of each other, it proved in many instances to be no difficult matter to discover some link of kinship, natural or spiritual, to invalidate their union and justify them in considering it null. The better class of churchmen and of laymen lamented these evils. An archbishop of St. Andrews, in a letter of information for the pope, recounts them with regret, but neither he nor the pope seems to have thought of a remedy.

Excommunication, the highest of ecclesiastical punishments, depriving a man of social and civil as well as church privileges, had latterly been too frequently inflicted, in most countries of Western Europe, to retain its earlier terrors. In Scotland, from the working together of civil and canon law, it had become disgracefully common, and yet sufficiently in force to be an instrument of great legal severity. Under the name of "cursing" it had come to be "the preliminary step of a warrant for arrest and imprisonment, and for the impounding and seizure of goods. Hence, 'letters of cursing' were as much the usual order in debit-and-credit transactions as any common writ of later times for seizing the person and distraining the goods." In the case of persons unable to pay tithes, or other church dues, the cursing was felt to be especially offensive. Tithes exacted in kind continued to increase in value, while the land tithed stood in a different relation to its owners and cultivators. In many cases much had been laid out on its improvement, and the fruit of other men's labors had greatly augmented the value of the proportion furnished by it for those to whom it owed nothing. Distraining was felt to be singularly offensive in that case, especially to the small landowners and farmers, whose own parsimonious industry perhaps had just brought their property to the condition of supporting their families. But the tithes were exacted from those to whom they were most oppressive, like other debts, by the ecclesiastical process of cursing. Excommunication of a poor man for his poverty was grievous enough, but when inflicted as the first step in a process of distressing for debt, it was of a nature to kindle a fire of indignation against those from whom it proceeded.

Besides tithes, there were other church dues and perquisites of clerical place, some of which, falling upon families in times of affliction, pressed with an aggravated cruelty. Such were the priest's perquisites upon the occasion of death in a family, when the vicar claimed for his services, real or constructive, certain compensation. In the family of a farmer this entitled him to one of the cows, and what was called the "upmost cloth" or outer garment of the departed; nor does it seem to have been usual to remit the claim if the clothing of the family was already too scant or if the one cow was all the poor man had. Many people were reduced, by repeated exactions, from a humble independence to absolute beggary, while the wealth and luxury of the exactors were daily increasing. Can it be doubted that the ecclesiastical cursings had their responses dark and deep in thousands of agonized hearts all over the land?

Such were facts which, when exposed by the most popular writers of the age, found no denial. In this respect the writings of Sir David Lindsay are of much historical value. Extensively popular, read among all classes, they abound in censure of prevailing vice and of abuses in both Church and State. The clergy are not spared, but the theme of satire was not denied. It was admitted that such things ought to be corrected, but no correction by the authorities was ever made.

Moreover, this draining of the people was enriching a class of men who held themselves to be the subjects of a foreign potentate, at whose court they plead in preference to that of their native monarch. Was it surprising that the people should detest the whole system and seek to expel it from their country? The more education advanced among them, and the fuller their knowledge of the existing state of things, the more rational their hatred became. Were they zealots because they desired freedom from such unbearable servitude? Then "zealot" must have a nobler meaning than we have given it credit for.

Sir David Lindsay was a courtier from his youth—one of the most accomplished men of his time, of gay and lively temperament, of ready wit and great affluence of thought, which, if not deep, was always clear. His scholarship and correct moral character recommended him as a proper companion for the young king; and after James V. arrived at actual sovereignty he received the office of chief herald for Scotland, under the title of "Lion king at arms." In that capacity he was connected with various embassies to the court of the emperor, to that of the king of France and to that of Denmark. Lindsay, although observing the Catholic worship and reverencing its authorities, when conformable to their own recognized principles, was a fearless exposer of malpractices. What the people in their private thoughts felt to be wrong, Lindsay subjected to ridicule in songs, tales and dramas, which carried exposure of it all over the land. People enjoyed his rhymes and laughed at his wit, but were roused to indignation by his unveiling of their wrongs. Of all agencies going to effect a common understanding among intelligent people on the subject of their respective grievances, and thereby bringing about a nationality of sentiment in detestation of that bondage of separate individuals and families into one common burst of hatred against the common evil, the greatest were the poems of David Lindsay. That persecution did not cut him off was due to the fact that he confined his criticism to abuses which no authority denied or presumed to defend. He was not, however, inconsistent with himself, and when the reforming purpose had, in course of things, created a party in the politics of the country, he took a place in its ranks, willing to follow men better qualified to be leaders. His death occurred shortly before 1558. Although he did not live to see the triumph of the Reformation, his work played an important part among the causes which led to it.

CHAPTER III.

TRUTH AND ERROR.

THERE is no power among men equal to *a doctrine clearly apprehended and firmly believed.* It gives aim and concentrated purpose to the individual mind, and combines as one man the multitude actuated by it. Call it by what name you may—a scheme if among merchants; a policy among statesmen; an idea or system among philosophers; or a faith in religion—a DOCTRINE is the most cogent of all things in human affairs.

What great act was ever performed without such a stimulus? What nation ever rose above insignificance without it? There have been men, as there have been nations, who have never apprehended any doctrine firmly enough to be impelled to any sacrifice for it; but they are, and always have been, of that flabby, undecided character which, if it has done little good in the world, has indulged in an abundance of evil. Doctrine is morally the bony frame of human character. A man without a doctrine is a pliant piece of clay, unreliable and doubtful.

He may be a man whose purpose is to behave himself properly in a general way, or may carry his lack of aim so far as to have no attachment to any principle; but he is not the man to be relied upon in a time of need, nor to leave any mark of himself for good. To leave deep enough impressions of evil needs neither doctrine nor discipline.

Conviction of the truth of a doctrine is sometimes reached by mere habit of mind in hearing it taught and recommended as the only right thing, and sometimes by finding the various parts of which it consists fitting neatly into one another and making a consistent whole. Many of our common beliefs have no better foundation. On either of these grounds men are capable of believing—honestly believing— doctrines which, when compared with the real outside world, are found to be utterly untenable. It is quite possible in either of these two ways to believe firmly in great error, and to defend it with all the zeal and concentrated energy of a national or party policy. A doctrine merely consistent in its own constituent parts and inculcated by systematic teaching, and resisting comparison with things outside of its own circle, may hold its ground indefinitely and wield the controlling and fortifying power of truth. But when, instead of being a mere fabric built of assumptions of the mind, it is the fruit of a full and fair comparison of all things properly concerned in it, a power is constituted which nothing can shake as long as the knowledge of it is maintained.

Upon doctrine, and some sound doctrine, was the religion of Scotland founded as it stood in the fifteenth century. But much of it also had no better foundation than tradition and inner concinnity; and the most chimerical doctrines were the most persistently forced upon the public faith. All of them were capable of a plausible proof, but so long had it been the custom to take their truth for granted that the clergy were provoked by any requirement for proof. As long as the clergy were the stronger it was easier to prohibit inquiry than to furnish evidence.

The doctrine that a piece of bread could be changed into the Lord Jesus Christ by a few words of a priest was certainly startling to common sense where common sense was free. A little education and thinking did that service. With some timidity, no doubt, was that step taken by most people in the first instance. When common sense began to assert her view of the case, the next care was to know what Scripture said about it. And when the discovery was made that Scripture and common sense were on the same side, it became impossible to believe a doctrine which contradicted both. The only remaining argument by which to maintain it was that of force. If men could not be reasoned into belief, they might be intimidated into compliance.

That although all men are wicked, yet all who are in the Catholic Church will be saved some time, through the merits of the Saviour, is entirely consistent with both Scripture and good sense. But what it was to be in the Catholic Church admitted of discussion, and the time when to be saved left a terrible gap open. That gap was bridged over, in the fifteenth century as in many foregoing centuries, in an ingenious mechanical way, thus: Christ saves all Catholics from eternal punishment, but each one of them must meet the account for his own actual sins, and suffer the penalty in this life or in the intermediate state. That suffering may be of any conceivable duration before the day of judgment. Fortunately, there had been some men and women so holy as to have credit for more good works than they needed for their own salvation. Upon death they went straight to heaven, and their surplus goodness was there collected in a common treasury, a sort of bank of deposit, which was safely locked that none of it might escape uselessly. The key of that treasury of merit was put into the hands of the pope, and to him belonged the right to draw from it at pleasure for his own use or the use of others. By applying to imperfectly sanctified souls as much of that hoarded merit as was needed to make up their deficit, they could be at once prepared to ascend to heaven, even from the flames of purgatory. Or a limited amount of the treasure could be conferred upon a living sinner to do away with a corresponding amount of sin. The pope had only to draw his check upon the bank of heaven in favor of the person who applied for it, and the paper would be honored by St. Peter. A very neatly-jointed doctrine was that, complete and harmonious in itself—a perfect beauty of construction. To men who never concerned themselves to look into the solidity of its foundations, or the truth of its several parts, it was entirely credible—as easy to believe in as the Bank of England.

But there was an addition made to it, in the sixteenth century, perfectly consistent with the symmetry of the rest, which brought it too closely into practical comparison with affairs of the business world: that was the reasonable condition that the pope should receive some compensation for his trouble. Consistently, he ought to have been content with a percentage of the treasure he was dealing in; but he preferred earthly cash, and sent out his agents to sell his bonds for what they would bring—an inexpedient measure, forcing the whole doctrine into the sphere of ordinary business, and upon the common sense of the public, where common sense was at home. The factitious character of the papal proceeding in the case could not escape the detection of minds moderately well educated, and free enough to think their own thoughts. To examine the doctrine from that point of view was to disintegrate it, and to call every element of it into question. Some of those elements were assumed above the sphere of common sense. It became necessary to find out if they were contained in the Scriptures. Upon seeking for them in vain in that quarter, belief in them vanished and the whole structure ceased to be credible.

While the public mind was extensively occupied with such inquiries, a great impulse was given to the publication of the Bible, and to the translation of it into various languages. In Scotland the translation made by Wycliff was as accessible as in England, and books presenting the substance of Scripture doctrine, facts and truth in a popular manner were widely published. Some of Sir David Lindsay's poems were of that nature. The conviction was becoming more common also that Holy Scripture was the only rule of faith and of practical religion.

While this process was going on among the

laity in general and a few of the clergy, the greater number of the latter went on in the old way, creating their god, holding him up for adoration, and then eating him, pardoning sins and taking their pay for it, and so on, as if no light had been breaking in about them. Respect began to withdraw from their practices. People treated the errors, which they saw through, according to their disposition and mental enlightenment. Some ridiculed them; others indignantly censured the then existing system of religion as one of impudent falsehood; while others reasoned against it out of Scripture, proving that wherein the Church differed from Scripture it was in the wrong.

The clergy, who made no denial of the commonness of immorality among men of their order, nor defence of the abuses whereof they were charged, had their own way of explaining and defending their doctrines. To the really believing Catholic priest the internal consistency of his doctrines was sufficient satisfaction, because the Church was the authority for the truth of all its ingredients. His mind was not free to go beyond the supreme decision of the Church. Scripture, to his mind, meant only what the Church determined it to mean. The Church was to him the interpreter of Scripture. Beyond that traditional interpretation he could not go. He might read the Bible as well as others, but in reading it his mind was overawed by a greater and supreme authority. Accordingly, there were Catholics who believed the doctrines and practices of the Church as honestly as many disbelieved them.

The parties were soon arrayed around two great centres respectively, the traditional judgments of the Church on one side, and Scripture, as addressing the individual judgment, on the other. The controversy became one of doctrine. Priests could hear their faults reproved, and content themselves with promising measures of amendment, but to attack their doctrines was fatally to damage the whole system to which they belonged. Moreover, on this question the parties did not occupy a common ground of controversy. Though both accepting Scripture, it was in an entirely different way. The priests admitted no other but church interpretation, but they could not impress that upon men who felt the force of the grammatical and logical interpretation. What, then, was to be done to stop the progress of increasing dissent? In reality, the hierarchy were reduced to the last argument of force, if they were to make any resistance at all. Some good, well-meaning men among them did attempt other means. Instruction for the people, in such doctrines of the Catholic Church, in such a way as seemed most likely to win back to her fold those who had not too far gone astray, was provided in the Aberdeen Breviary and Archbishop Hamilton's Catechism, but not until too late—not until the nation had been hopelessly alienated by severities of persecution never to be forgotten, not until Reformation instruction had gone far beyond the capacity of Catholic lessons.

Touching other matters, criticism, ridicule, indignation, even hatred, might assail the hierarchy without provoking more than a warning, perhaps might be appeased with an apology; but on the subject of doctrine the conflict was deadly. No penalty was deemed adequate to the guilt of heresy but the appalling death by fire, which represented the punishment of the damned.

CHAPTER IV.

JOHN MAJOR.

IN the year 1523, John Major, who had been for several years a professor in the University of Glasgow, was transferred to St. Andrews. It was his fortune to be concerned in educating and giving particular bent to the minds of certain youth who were to be leaders in the great coming revolution. In his classes at Glasgow he had seen John Knox, and in those at St. Andrews he met George Buchanan. Their indebtedness to him was subsequently acknowledged by both. Patrick Hamilton, Henry Balnavis, and others who defended the same cause, came also under his influence. Whether Knox followed his teacher to St. Andrews or not, he was soon after associated in study with the illustrious group connected with that university.

John Major was one of those men whose personal influence far exceeds the value of any contribution made by them to the sum of human knowledge or wisdom. It is a gift of Nature not to be lightly esteemed—that by which impressiveness is given to commonplace learning and to wisdom and virtue, the inheritance of ages. It is a power. There are men whose affluence of thought is practically boundless, and whose originality is ever turning up new aspects of things, who yet, in their own lifetime, never secure an average respect for their opinions or their persons. They walk among common men with so little mark of their greatness about them that every one feels himself in some respects, and especially as a common-sense man, their superior. Yet the world will read what they write, or listen with the most interested attention to their reported sayings, or behold the material fruits of their genius with admiration, and when they have personally disappeared for ever the place they have left grows bigger in the eyes of succeeding generations. Such men are like preachers with a poor delivery. The sermon is well prepared, it is even superior in richness of instruction, but the preacher seems to take little interest in it, seems to think that there is nothing of importance in it; and his hearers take it at his own estimate. Or they are like a good book in the hands of a helpless publisher, who prints it, and stows it away, to let it take its chance; enterprising research may find it some time. On the other hand, the world is largely indebted to men who have the power of delivery —men who can set themselves and their instructions in such a light that the world will recognize them for what they are. The multitude of mankind are not discoverers, and need to be impressed with its value before they can think anything worth looking into. It is well that there are some men of that impressive personality which propitiates respect. They are not sources of thought; they are invaluable reservoirs of force. The man who takes the sermon which was smothered in birth by its author, and with it thrills the hearts of all who hear him, has inspired it with the new life of his own personality.

John Major was certainly a power in his day. Without any great reach of thought or originating capacity or attractions of literary style, he made an impression upon the youth who attended his instructions, and established for himself the weight of an authority in church matters, even over men of greater originality than himself. Having lectured in Paris, as well as in the highest seats of learning in Scotland, his reputation became quite extended. His published commentaries on Scripture, or on the celebrated Books of Sentences, may be of little or no practical value; the topics on which he loves to dilate may be, in some cases, utterly useless, and the style in which he writes, dry and barren; his history of Scotland may have nothing to recommend it, either in original research or literary attractions; and yet that is not enough to justify us in discrediting the effects he is said to have produced. Those effects were of a kind which go to make up a great part of the character of a successful teacher, who has necessarily more to do with already known truth than with original discovery; more to do with making things clear to the understanding than attractive to the fancy; more to do with instilling into the young mind that which will help to put it on a par with the already educated, than with exploring new fields of science or research; more to do with the tongue than the pen. He was a faithful Catholic, and an advocate of papalism, who defended some of its absurdest tenets with arguments on which only a servile superstition could lean. He had been trained in the scholastic theology, and adhered scrupulously to its minute and shallow method of reasoning; and readers of his works testify that their drudgery has been but scantily repaid with a grain of truth now and then from pages of rubbish. And yet when some of those grains amounted to doctines learned in the school where Gerson and D'Ailly had taught, they could not be without weight upon the minds of youth ardently pursuing knowledge in the beginning of the sixteenth century.

Major was born in the neighborhood of North Berwick in the year 1469. He studied at Oxford and Cambridge, but for longer time in Paris, where he also began his career as a lecturer. After holding a professorship in Glasgow for a few years, he returned to Paris, but came back to Glasgow to accept the situation of principal and professor of theology in the university there. In 1523 he removed to the chair of philosophy and theology in St. Andrews, where he was still residing in 1547. The greater part of his education had been received in France, the country which had been among the first and the loudest in demanding a regular and authoritative reformation of ecclesiastical abuses, and where the reforms of the Council of Basel were still in force. It needed little originality for a pupil of Gallicanism in those days to apprehend the doctrine that a general council was superior to a pope, and competent to bring him to trial, subject him to censure or depose him from office. The new professor at St. Andrews also denied the temporal supremacy of the pope, and that he had any right to set up and put down princes. Ecclesiastical censures, even papal excommunication, he declared to be of no force, unless pronounced for sufficient reasons. Tithes in the Christian Church, he taught, were not of divine but human appointment. He hesitated not to censure the extravagance and vices of the papal and episcopal style of living, and the evils undeniable among the monkish orders, and " advised the reduction of monasteries." Still more radical was the doctrine he held concerning the civil ruler—that a king, though superior to any one of his subjects, is not superior to them as a whole, in their capacity as a nation—that if he rules to the injury of his people he may be lawfully controlled by them, deposed or prosecuted to capital punishment.

On none of these points was Major an originating teacher; but the position which he occupied at Glasgow, and afterward at St. Andrews, and his own personal character, conferred upon them a great weight of importance in the eyes of those to whom they were addressed, and to whom they were really novel. Some of them proved to be seeds planted in soil where they were subsequently to develop into a growth which the teacher perhaps never anticipated. They were only related to religion, but the promulgation of them in Scotland, at that juncture, suggested or sustained opinions and expectations without which the Reformation could not have been effected.

Statesmen and impoverished nobility had long been looking with jealous eyes upon the wealth and power of churchmen, which they saw increasing at their own expense. Ideas of reprisals had crossed their minds, but a ground of justification, by which a party could sustain itself, was lacking. The ecclesiastical laws were dangerous to brave, and they were yoked with those of the realm. The civil authorities had sometimes been constrained to bow before them. Now, here comes a great doctor in theology, laden with the learning of the universities of England and France, who teaches that the Church has no right to subordinate the civil government; that even the pope is amenable to a council, and may be deposed if guilty of great sin; that the corruption prevailing among bishops and monks is very great, and that of the monastic orders, at least, is such that it might be a righteous act to diminish the number of their houses. Such doctrine, distributed by various channels, found docile listeners among men exasperated by long-contiued aggressions from the clerical side. It prepared the way for many worldly men to join the growing Reformation interest—men who looked only to the transfer of power and property. It prepared political or family parties to regard the change of religion favorably, in the light of policy.

But, above all else that it effected, the teaching of the learned professor started a few of his own zealous pupils, at the head of whom were George Buchanan and John Knox, on a course of thinking destined to sift the rights of all powers and potentates of earth, and even to try the spirits whether they were of God.

CHAPTER V.

PATRICK HAMILTON.

MANY things combined to urge forward the Reformation in Scotland. It was not singly prompted by religious motives, not singly by moral considerations, nor by oppression, nor by jealousy of foreign influence and alienation of native resources; politics also entered, as inevitably they will in all national affairs, and the cupidity of covetous men, eager to avail themselves of all changes to advance their own gains. Yet, after all, the hinge of the whole controversy was Christian doctrine. But for that, it would never have reached to a revolution. Evils encrusted upon the church system might have been removed without breaking down the system, and might have left it in a better condition to hold its own. But the life of the system, and all that could give it reverence in the eyes of intelligent adherents, was doctrine. If that should prove corrupt, no reform of anything else could save it. To contend for that was to do battle for existence. It was that which evoked the apprehensions and hatred of the hierarchy. To attack doctrine was to incur the most terrible of penalties. For that had Resby, Craw and others in Scotland, and a great number in England, perished in the flames.

Those early martyrs for the Reformation, unsustained by numbers, disappeared in darkness. By the multitude they were regarded as the worst of criminals, and the instructed few were discouraged by their fate—discouraged from putting forth effort publicly in the cause. A change, notwithstanding, was going on, and in the first quarter of the sixteenth century it advanced with accelerating rapidity.

So far, executions for religion's sake had been few in Scotland as compared with those of England and France. The long endurance of the Scottish people had procured them a reputation for adherence to the Romish faith. But endurance awaited only satisfactory conviction. Printed translations of the Scriptures began with the year 1526, by the cheapness of their price, to bring the admitted standard of religion within reach of all who could read the common tongue of England and the Scottish Lowlands. Books written in Latin by the continental Reformers began also to arrive from Germany, producing their immediate effects upon the better educated. Great numbers, high and low, were found prepared to receive the new instruction with avidity. The feeling after truth, which had for at least three generations been extending from the well-educated to the less-educated laity by means of popular tales, poems, songs, dramas and private conversation, eagerly grasped at any portion of the Holy Scriptures offered in the spoken tongue, while trained thinkers consulted with anxiety the doctrinal statements of Reformed theologians of other lands. The party opposed to reform were aware of the danger to their cause from that quarter. Parliament, July 17, 1525, passed an act prohibiting the importation of the books of Luther or of his disciples into Scotland, which, it was claimed, had hitherto been always "clene of all sic filth and vice"—not quite so clean, however, as the act presumed, as had appeared, at a date long prior to Luther's appearance, in the articles and association of the Lollards of Kyle; while at the very date of the act John Major, on the north side of the Forth, was announcing, in the hearing of young and appreciative auditors, certain doctrines of popular freedom and sovereignty which, although not expressly religious, needed only to be carried consistently into practice to shake the foundations of the existing religious government at its centre, and subject its minister, the civil arm, to the will of the people. One of those young contemporaries was soon afterward on his way to Germany to listen to the great Saxon Reformer in his own lecture-room.

Patrick Hamilton, of the noble family of that name, a nephew of the earl of Arran by his father, and of the duke of Albany by his mother, and through both related to the royal family, was born in 1504. Designed by his parents for the Church, he was endowed with the abbacy of Ferne while yet a child. His education was certainly of the best order belonging to the times. By some of the means of instruction then multiplying in the land, before he was twenty-two years old he had acquired intelligence of the work going on in Germany. In company with three attendants he undertook a journey to Wittenberg. Luther and Melanchthon were greatly pleased with him, and when, after studying with them for a time, he left them, recommended him to the university recently established at Marburg by Philip, landgrave of Hesse. At the head of that institution was Francis Lambert, a Reformed theologian from Avignon, in whom Hamilton found a warm friend and a faithful instructor.[1] While diligently enlarging his knowledge of Reformed doctrine and of Holy Scripture he was smitten with a zealous desire to explain the way of salvation to his countrymen. Not ignorant of the danger which awaited such an enterprise, and

[1] *Lambert d'Avignon*, par Louis Ruffet, prof. à Genève.

which Lambert also set before him, he resolved that, for the end in view, it must be encountered. Attended by only one of the companions who had left Scotland with him, he returned in the latter part of 1527.

Young Hamilton's preaching was with fervor and tenderness, setting forth the doctrines of the gospel. Nor did he shrink from exposing the errors of the Romish Church and the vices which had crept into the practices of the clergy. Many recognized and accepted the truth which he preached, while they loved him for his gentle and courteous deportment toward all sorts of people. Entirely free from violence, he was full of warmth in proclaiming the message of salvation. The treatise which he wrote to expound the articles of religion popularly shows remarkable clearness of thinking, and skill in putting truth in a brief and forcible way, in a spirit of tenderness. Knox valued it so highly that he copied the whole of it into his history.

A very brief time was allowed him for the work of preaching. The clergy of St. Andrews were alarmed. He was enticed to visit their city. When he arrived, a friar, Alexander Campbell, was appointed to visit and hold conversation with him. Campbell, professing to have a leaning to the same way of thinking, succeeded in obtaining a knowledge of the different points of his belief, admitting for his own part, what no one ventured fully to deny, that in many things the state of the Church needed to be reformed. Hamilton was left without suspicion of danger until he was apprehended by night, taken from his bed and carried prisoner to the castle. Next day he was charged before the primate with holding and preaching heresy. A long list of doctrines were presented to him, on which he was called to express his belief. The first seven he held to be undoubtedly true, and was willing to subscribe. The rest, he said, were disputable, but such as he could not condemn without having better reason than he had yet heard.

The whole list was then committed to the judgment of a council consisting of the rector and the heads of the Black and Grey Friars and two lawyers. After a day or two, these men rendered a report in which they condemned the whole list of articles as heretical and contrary to the faith of the Church. Sentence was accordingly pronounced against Patrick Hamilton, giving him over to the secular power to suffer the penalty of heresy.

The seven points which he fully professed to believe, and for which he suffered, were—

1. Man hath no free will.

2. A man is only justified by faith in Christ.

3. A man, so long as he liveth, is not without sin.

4. He is not worthy to be called a Christian who believeth not that he is in grace.

5. A good man doeth good works; good works do not make a good man.

6. An evil man bringeth forth evil works; evil works, being faithfully repented of, do not make an evil man.

7. Faith, hope and charity be so linked together that one of them cannot be without another, in one man, in this life.

To us of the present day it is amazing that the holding of such opinions should ever have justified, in the minds of any men, capital punishment, and that of the most appalling kind.

On that occasion the primate, James Beaton, was assisted by the archbishop of Glasgow, three bishops, six heads of monastic houses and eight other ecclesiastics, who all set their signatures to the sentence. To give it the greater weight, all persons who were of any estimation in the university were required to subscribe it. The act was an act of the Catholic Church of Scotland through her highest authorities.

On the same day Hamilton was condemned by the civil judge, and in the afternoon led out to execution. The process was hastened, to prevent interference on the part of the king, who was then absent on a pilgrimage. The place of execution was in the public street before the gate of St. Salvator's College. When he arrived there, Hamilton, with a gentle deliberation, put off his gown, bonnet, coat and some other articles of apparel, and gave them to his servant, saying, "These will not profit in the fire, but they will profit thee. After this, of me thou canst receive no commoditie, except from the example of my death, which, I pray thee, beare in mind; for albeit it be bitter to the flesh and feirefull before men, yett it is the entrance into eternall life, which none shall possesse that deny Christ Jesus before this wicked generation."

While being tied to the stake, about which a great quantity of combustible material was piled, he kept his eyes steadily turned toward heaven. The attendants were awkward in kindling the fire. While they delayed he addressed some words to the spectators, but was interrupted by the monks, especially by Friar Campbell, calling to him to recant and to pray to the Virgin Mary. He answered by saying to Campbell that he knew he was not a heretic, and that it was the truth of God for which he suffered, and appealing to the judgment-seat of Christ. When the fire at last was kindled he was heard to say in a clear voice, "How long, O Lord, shall darkness oppress this realm? How long wilt thou suffer this tyranny of men?" He then closed with the words,

"Lord Jesus, receive my spirit." His body was quickly consumed, for the fire was strong.

Great feeling was evinced by the spectators, and many did not fear to say that they believed Hamilton to be an innocent man and a martyr for Christ. People also remarked afterward that Friar Alexander Campbell never was the same man after that day, but became moody, "fell into a fit of frenzy," and died wretchedly within less than a year.

It was a mistaken policy, on the part of the hierarchy, that atrocious execution. The conspicuousness of the victim, instead of carrying intimidation abroad, which they counted on, excited the more extensive inquiry. Over the length and breadth of Scotland flashed the startling question, "Why was Patrick Hamilton burned?" An intelligent and satisfactory answer could not be given without a statement of some Reformed doctrine. The most powerful sermon Patrick Hamilton was destined to preach was his own burning in the streets of St. Andrews.

CHAPTER VI.

CARDINAL BEATON.

AMONG the many tongues set in motion by the burning of Patrick Hamilton, not a few were heard in St. Andrews itself, and some were those of clergymen. To speak freely of heresy and withhold condemnation of it, or to express sympathy with those who suffered for it, was dangerous. But among men who thought alike, and felt that they could trust each other, a certain freedom of utterance was indulged, and that in some places where it might least have been expected. In St. Leonard's College, under the example of its principal, Gavin Logie, students discussed the doctrines of Reformers with a lack of disapproval which brought suspicion upon themselves, and gave rise to the saying, about one who might allow a sentence of questionable orthodoxy to escape him, that he had been "drinking at St. Leonard's Well." The opinions thus privately agitated in St. Andrews were, in the course of a few years, scattered over the country wherever those young men resided, and took to themselves inevitable publicity.

Five years later, Gavin Logie, like some others, found it expedient to escape beyond the bounds of Scotland.

A similar spirit made its way among the monks of the Dominican and Franciscan orders in St. Andrews, and, by connivance of the sub-prior, John Winram, among the novices of the abbey. Some of the friars began, before the year of Hamiliton's execution was over, to "preach publicly against the pride and idle life of the bishops, and against the abuses of the whole ecclesiastical state." But the bishops were also aroused, and suspiciously watchful. Censure of their practices, which once would have been dismissed with a jest, was now regarded as indicative of a deeper design or of lurking heresy. It henceforth became dangerous to expose the vices of the clergy. Although death could be lawfully inflicted only for heretical doctrine, it might be possible to make out a charge of heresy against a man from his assaults upon clerical character, which would be sustained by an ecclesiastical tribunal.

One Friar William preached at Dundee a sermon in which he exposed the licentiousness of bishops—perhaps not more severely than had been done before, but they were not now disposed to bear it. The bishop of Brechin had his retainers in hand, who fell upon the monk and beat him as being a heretic. Friar William went to St. Andrews and consulted John Major on the subject of his sermon. The learned professor assured him that his doctrine was all right, and might well be defended. The friar resolved to repeat the sermon at head-quarters, and had notice given to that effect. So, in the great church of St. Andrews, before a large audience, including several of the ecclesiastical dignitaries, he rediscussed the clergy and their desecration of the most holy things, as of excommunication—or, as it was called, "cursing"—and of miracles, with a rough humor which subjected them to ridicule.

Once more he ventured on the theme, and took for his text "The Abbot of Unreason." The real prelates of their day, he told the people, were as regardless of divine law as that farcical hero of their own revels; and he took occasion to relate some very indelicate stories about prelates then alive. He withheld proper names, but some of the parties happened to be well known. That treatment of the subject proved too serious for laughter, and the preacher, to save his life, fled into England; yet Friar William was no Protestant, as was subsequently proved by his imprisonment under Henry VIII. for papalism.

A more dignified opposition to prevailing errors was made by Alexander Seton, a highly respected monk of the Dominican order, or

Black Friars. Through the whole of Lent, succeeding the execution of Hamilton, he preached on the Ten Commandments, exposing not only actual vice, but the errors of doctrine which led to or justified it. He insisted especially "that the law of God is the only rule of righteousness; that if God's law be not violated, no sin is committed; that it is not in man's power to satisfy for sin; that the forgiveness of sin is not otherwise purchased than by unfeigned repentance, true faith apprehending the mercy of God in Christ." Of purgatory, pilgrimages, prayers to saints and priestly pardon, or indulgences, he made no mention. Opposition was arrayed against him. One of the same monastic order was, during his absence from St. Andrews, set up to counteract his preaching. He returned to defend his ground, but was reported to the archbishop, who sent for him and took him to task for saying that a bishop should be a preacher, and that bishops who did not preach were dumb dogs. Seton replied that his reporters had misrepresented him—that the sayings referred to were not his, but contained in passages he had quoted from Isaiah and St. Paul. The archbishop was annoyed by feeling that he had exposed his own ignorance of Scripture, but perceived that the ground he had chosen could not sustain him in a prosecution. Seton was dismissed. But being also confessor to the king, Seton discovered soon that the countenance of His Majesty was changed toward him and withdrew to Berwick, whence he wrote a full explanation to the king. Receiving no answer to his letter, he went on to London, where he became chaplain to the duke of Suffolk, and in that capacity continued until his death.

About the same time Henry Forest, a young man of the order of Bennet and Collet, had been heard to say that Patrick Hamilton had died a martyr. A friar was appointed to confess him, to whom he acknowledged that he thought "Master Patrick a good man, and that the articles for which he was condemned might well be defended." This confession, being revealed to the archbishop, was deemed sufficient evidence against him. He was forthwith condemned as a heretic. While they were consulting about the place of execution, where it would be most conspicuous and strike terror into the greatest number, John Lindsay, a plain layman, advised that if they burned any more people they should burn them in a cellar; "For," said he, "the smoke of Master Patrick Hamilton had infected all on whom it blew."

Among those arrested about that time for heresy we find a brother and a sister of Hamilton. But both escaped, through favor of the king toward them as kindred.

The intensity of persecution relaxed for a few years after the death of Henry Forest, caused partly by the intestine wars between several great families, and finally between the king and Douglas, earl of Angus, in which the earl was, after a long defence, worsted and driven into exile.

In Scotland the number of victims was far short of what it was in some countries on the Continent, or in England, in the reign of Mary; but in the twelve years succeeding 1528 it was great enough to appall and exasperate a nation to which such executions had hitherto been little known. They resulted in heaping popular detestation upon those who conducted them, and on the Church which they were designed to defend. But the principal object of censure and abhorrence was the primate, by whose signature the whole array of those cruelties was sanctioned. And yet James Beaton was a man who in circumstances less unfavorable might have earned the praise of wisdom and humanity. Descended of an ancient Norman family deriving its name from the town of Bethune in Artois, and whose residence in Scotland dated back at least as far as the thirteenth century, he enjoyed every facility of education which the country could afford. In youth he evinced great natural talents, and his career proved to be one of remarkable success. Having entered the University of St. Andrews in 1487, he received his master's degree in 1492. In 1497 he was presented to the chantry of Caithness; in 1503 he was made provost of the collegiate church of Bothwell and prior of Whithorn; in 1504 he was made abbot of Dunfermline; in 1505 he was lord treasurer of Scotland; in 1508 he was made bishop of Galloway; within a year, promoted to the metropolitanate of Glasgow, he resigned the office of treasurer; in 1513 he was chancellor of the kingdom, and secured to himself the rich abbacies of Arbroath and Kilwinning; and in 1522, on the death of Andrew Forman, he was elevated to the primacy in St. Andrews, which he retained until his death. On succeeding to the primacy he resigned the commendatory of Arbroath in favor of his nephew, David Beaton, reserving to himself half of its revenue. Dunfermline and Kilwinning he retained.

The execution of Patrick Hamilton was an act in which he was certainly the principal mover, and for which he was highly commended by Catholic theologians. A letter from the theological faculty of Louvain exalted it with the highest praise. If human approbation could have satisfied his conscience, he had all that he valued most among his fellow-men. But he does not seem to have been satisfied.

For, after the mortifying interview with Alexander Seton and the death of Henry Forest, it appears that he never was forward in seeking out or instituting proceedings against heretics, though he sanctioned the conduct of others more zealous in proceeding against them. In the place he occupied perhaps he could not consistently do less, however he may have felt about his own former atrocities. The more impetuous Catholics thought he had become lax and not very solicitous about the Church, how its affairs might prosper.

Archbishop Beaton has been credited on both sides with being "a very prudent man." Others, using less complimentary language, represented him as crafty—"a fox," who among furious political parties, Scottish and English, so sagaciously "fled from hole to hole that he could not be apprehended." The remark implies that he had also his hardships and many enemies. And the hands of some of those enemies he did not always succeed in eluding. The Reformers disliked him, but they were not yet organized sufficiently to constitute a dangerous party.

In the responsible place which he held at a time when dissatisfaction with the Catholic Church was beginning to break out in public protest, James Beaton, if not cruel and intolerant by nature—of which his contemporaries,

even leading Reformers, do not accuse him—
was unfortunate in the tasks demanded of him,
and in the men with whom he was associated
and who acted in his name. By his death, in
1539, the ecclesiastical sovereignty came into
the hands of one about whose character there
is no question, and who never gave any sign
that charity could construe into a scruple of
conscience.

By the calamity at Flodden a sudden revolution was wrought in the government of Scotland. In one day the country lost her king,
with the leaders of her councils, and a new generation of nobility came into power. The heir
of the throne was a child of one year old, and
in Parliament the places of the old members
were filled with comparative youth. Queen
Margaret was looked to as the proper regent
in the minority of her son. But in less than a
year she married, and thereby changed her relations to the kingdom. Her new husband was
the young nobleman who, by the death of his father at Flodden, succeeded his grandfather as the
earl of Angus. Jealousies at once arose. That
a Douglas should by marriage seize on the powers of regency could not be quietly tolerated by
the rivals of that family. A motion was made
in Parliament to transfer the regency to Alexander Stewart, the duke of Albany, uncle of
the young king's father. Albany, then living in

France in the enjoyment of great wealth and honor as high admiral of the kingdom, came to Scotland with much reluctance, discharged the duties of regent a little over a year, and returned to his adopted country. He left a French gentleman, De la Bastie, in high place to see to his interests during his absence. But Parliament appointed as colleagues in the regency the two archbishops, with the earls of Angus, Huntly, Arran and Argyll.

Albany, by his French affectations, his alien manners and airs of superiority, had disgusted the Scottish people, both noble and common. The conduct of the men whom he had brought with him, with whom he had garrisoned three of the strongest places in the kingdom, and by some of whom he preferred to be attended, intensified that feeling. During his absence some dispute, leading to fighting and bloodshed, took place toward the English border. De la Bastie went with a small number of followers to reduce it. The parties turned against him as a foreign intruder. He took to flight, but in a marsh was overtaken and killed. No person was legally tried for the violence.

The duke did not return to Scotland until after the lapse of five years. His unpopularity was greater than before, and was beginning to extend to the country of his preference. A check was put upon that tendency by a false step of Henry VIII. of England, who issued a threatening demand to the Scots to send Albany back to France or he would make war upon them. For the time they felt constrained to rally round the unpopular regent to maintain their own dignity. Raising a large and well-equipped army, they marched to the border to encounter the expected invasion. Henry, however, was not prepared for war. The "insulting demand" was withdrawn, and the cloud blew over.

The duke of Albany soon after went back to France of his own wish. But hostilities again broke out on the English border. Albany returned with a French fleet and a few thousand troops. It was well for France to keep the arms of England employed in that quarter. He landed in September, 1523. The campaign was conducted feebly, and in May of the next year he left his native land, never to return. His foreign followers went with him.

One effect of this unwilling and interrupted administration was to strengthen, both directly and indirectly, a party which was gradually forming itself in favor of friendly relations with England. But for the headlong and foolish measures of Henry VIII., which sometimes defeated what he most ardently desired, that party might have prospered better than it did. But between his impetuous blundering and the artful policy of France, sustained by the clergy, to keep hold of the Scottish alliance, as a flank movement upon England, two conflicting parties agitated the politics of the northern kingdom. Family quarrels intensified and complicated the disorder. Some of the nobility betook themselves to England and some to France. Queen Margaret had separated from her husband, who had also gone abroad. The government for a few months was in the hands of churchmen, and a duel of artifice took place between Beaton on the side of the French interest, and Wolsey to secure and promote that of England in Scottish politics. After many devices to get the "fox of St. Andrews" out of his hole, he was finally clutched and put away in prison to keep him harmless—too late, however, to suit the designs of his adversary. For just then another plot was on foot.

Certain Scottish noblemen, who had no taste for either French or English dictation, conceived that, although their king was still but a boy, it would be better to set him on the throne, and sustain him by the best advisers they could secure, than to live without any certain head to the government, even in name, exposed to the plots of partisans of foreign interests. To that measure the queen-mother's approval was easily obtained, as well as that of her royal brother. Accordingly, James V.

commenced his actual reign in the month of August, 1524, at the age of twelve years. Still, of course, he was but a minor under guardianship, and the rivalry of French and English machinations, spies and agitators continued at the Scottish court.

In 1526 the king reached the age of fourteen, when by law he was free to choose his own guardians. He chose his stepfather, the earl of Angus, who had now returned to Scotland, and with him the Lords Argyll and Errol. It was understood that they were each to have charge of their royal ward for three months. Angus had his term first, but when it expired he refused to resign. Attempts were made to compel him, and battles were fought. But Douglas proved the stronger. At the end of about two years the young king planned his own escape, and with only two attendants fled from his watchful guardian. The legitimate powers of the nation sustained him. Douglas took refuge in his strong castle of Tantallon. James, now at the head of an army, besieged it, and prosecuted operations until he reduced his rebellious stepfather, who again withdrew to England.

It was in the midst of these troubles that the burning of Patrick Hamilton took place. The young king was too busy with his own affairs to have any knowledge of the case of heresy. He was on a pilgrimage to the shrine of a northern saint when it occurred, and the execution was hastened that he might not know about it until too late for prevention.

When Douglas was defeated, the king found that he had only begun the conflict with refractory chieftains. On the border many held themselves to be retainers of Douglas, and some had assumed to themselves almost the independence of sovereigns. In the Highlands, although there was no longer a Norse viceroy or a Lord of the Isles strong enough to resist the monarchy, the connection of the several chieftains with the general government had become greatly relaxed, and the peace of the whole country was at one time threatened from that quarter. The rights of the Crown had to be defended against the aggressions of aristocratic houses, which, if combined, would have outrivaled it in national power.

The jealousy of James V. toward the nobility of his kingdom was thus kept in continual activity. To reduce them to order, while he guarded the frontiers against the often-recurring threats of the king of England, occupied the most of his reign.

Meanwhile, the Protestant persuasion was making its way among people of all ranks, especially the laity. The revolution in England, whereby papalism was expelled, added greatly to the motives going to form a Scottish party in favor of friendly relations with that country. In a few years that became the policy of the Protestant party of Scotland, while the Catholic party, with the bishops at their head, became more intensely partisans of France.

James had little favor for the bishops, and was not ignorant of the ecclesiastical abuses with which every tongue was busy. But the bishops needed his support and sought his favor, and in his controversy with the nobles he could not afford to alienate the clergy also. More than once he rescued from their hands and saved life endangered by the charge of heresy, but there was a limit beyond which he could not go in that direction. He was not quite sure of the loyalty of the reforming leaders, some of whom his violence had driven to seek the protection of England. Necessity called for good terms with the clergy, and the clergy clung to the alliance with France. For real home-support it was the commons upon whom he could most safely rely, but things were not prepared for him to break through the intervening ranks and put himself at their head as a popular leader. They, moreover, were also divided, and with many of them neither France nor England was much in favor.

The credit of superior patriotism has been claimed for the bishops. It is a poor ground for such a claim that they rejected friendly relations with a neighboring state, in order to involve their country in profitless wars for the benefit of a far-distant ally, from whom some of them actually accepted honors and wealthy benefices, or that they resisted alliance with a neighbor to retain allegiance to the pope.

James V. was not a pious man. The examples with which he was best acquainted among ministers of religion were not of a nature to recommend piety. The faithful Alexander Seton, his confessor for a time, was soon undermined in influence and driven into exile, and in the family of his birth the lives of his father, his mother and uncle had little to recommend virtue except the penalties that follow vice. The access which his early companion, Lindsay, had to his convictions was chiefly the avenue of amusement. Any check put by him upon persecution was the dictate of common humanity or personal friendship. But the severities of persecution never proceeded from him.

In his marriages James was also unfortunate. The first, in 1536, was a marriage of love, to Magdalen, daughter of Francis I. of France, of whom, as having lived much under the influence of her aunt, the queen of Navarre, favor was expected for the reforming party. An early death disappointed their hopes. His second marriage, in 1538, was with Mary of Guise, daughter of the duke of Lorraine, leader of the Romanist party in France.

At that time and onward, his prime advisers were Archbishop Beaton and his accomplished but immoral nephew. In spite of himself, the king was held in bonds of their policy, which so many of the laity detested, and was kept thereby in ever-fluctuating animosity with England, with whom an increasing party of the laity wished to have peace, and his own family interests rendered it desirable to be on good terms.

By following the advice of his priestly counselors, he gratuitously made and broke a promise to meet his uncle, Henry VIII., in consultation at York, thereby incurring that monarch's just indignation. War measures followed, without real war. The Scottish army having reached the border, the principal nobility refused to invade England. James sent forward a large detachment, over which he appointed a favorite from among the commons. In surprise and indignation the whole detachment rose in a mob. In that condition they were attacked by a small English force under Lord Dacre, and scattered without a battle. James, in sickness of mortification, withdrew to his palace of Falkland, where he languished, without any apparent disease, until he died, on the 14th of December, 1542. Mary, his only surviving legitimate child, was but a week old. The country was again subjected to a long minority, and a series of conflicting regencies.

Beyond all reasonable dispute, at the death of James V. there was in the Scottish Church a party of great weight in favor of reform. They had yet no organization separate from the Church, and still were members of the establishment connected with Rome, but they reproved its errors and urged that it ought to be made conformable to the scriptural standard. It was dangerous to be a leader in such connection if weak. That not a few, for political reasons, stood forward as such, evinces their belief that the popular force to back them was strong. A weak dependant on the opinions of others, like the earl of Arran, would not have urged his claims to the regency under the colors of a party which he did not believe able to sustain him. The Parliament of 1542 set aside the other candidates, and recognized him as regent and governor of Scotland. The Reformers in his support assumed position openly before the country as a party. Some of them, recognizing him as their head, exhorted him to think for what end God had thus exalted him, from what dangers he had been delivered, and the expectations which were entertained of him. He also appointed two of their persuasion to be court-preachers, men of whom Knox speaks in terms of high praise.

Reading the Bible had so far come into practice that men began to claim it as a right, notwithstanding the law that no part of it should be read in English, nor any treatise or exposition of any part of it, on the pain of heresy. Inquiry was now freely made if it ought not to be lawful for men who did not understand Latin to use the word of salvation in the tongue which they did understand. If it was right for men who knew Latin, Greek and Hebrew to read it in those languages, why should it be wrong for men who did not know them to read it in English? The Saviour had ordered his gospel to be preached to all nations. He must have intended it to be preached to them in the languages which they understood. And if it was lawful to preach it in all languages, why should it not be lawful to read it in all languages? How otherwise could people try the spirits, according to the exhortation of the apostle?

The plea could not be set aside as unreasonable. And among those who urged it were statesmen like the elder Lord Ruthven and Henry Balnavis, and on the part of the clergy Hay, dean of Restalrig, and others. The commissioners of burghs and some of the nobility also united in requesting Parliament to enact that all should be permitted to use the translations which they then had of both the Old and New Testament, together with treatises of sound doctrine, until such times as the prelates and churchmen should furnish translations more correct. Opposition was made by the clerical members. But, overcome by the arguments, or the great majority of votes on the other side, they consented. *Reading the Scriptures was by act of Parliament made free to all*, and all acts to the contrary abolished (1542).

Immediately the Bible became a fashionable book, to be seen on almost every gentleman's table, and the New Testament was carried about in men's hands. Many also declared their gratification with being able to read openly what formerly they could enjoy only in concealment. If some made that profession who had less pleasure in it than they pretended, it only goes the further to prove the extent and force of the fashion at the time. But freedom of the Bible was a reforming measure distinctively.

Books also in refutation of the papacy and exposure of its practices, written in Scotland as well as brought from England, were read with greater freedom and by increasing numbers.

Four years later, so strong was that party and so well understood its strength, that when

Wishart was burned at St. Andrews the execution was ordered immediately under the guns of the castle, which were trained to sweep the whole ground; nor did the primate risk himself outside of his castle-walls.

By the same party, in the first years of the regency, the policy of cultivating friendly relations with England was favored. A prospective marriage of the infant queen with Edward, son of Henry VIII., was looked to as in course of time conducive to such friendly relations and to the interests of the Protestant religion in both countries. A treaty of that purport was actually made, but was defeated by the fickleness of the regent, who suddenly changed his mind and went over to the papal party, which contemplated a similar relation with the dauphin of France.

A third party, which sought its affinities with the Reformers, but really had little in common with them except preference for England rather than France, consisted of a few noblemen and gentlemen who had pledged themselves to the plans of Henry VIII. They were prisoners who had been taken at Flodden and at Solway Moss, and refugees from the severities of James V.; among whom were the earl of Angus and his brother, Sir George Douglas. After the death of James several of them returned to Scotland under a promise, exacted of them by Henry, to use their influence in his favor. Those "Assured Scots," as they were called in England, did great detriment to the Reformation, with which they had nominally some connection, reflecting upon it the charge of their own disloyalty.

Moreover, Henry VIII., in his foolishly imperious way of attempting to attach Scotland to his government by force of arms, rendered it impossible for Scotsmen to do anything for the English alliance, by any means whatever. Thus the friendship so fondly hoped for by the Reformers became impracticable on every side; for, in the estimation of the common people, far above the interests of any party were those of Scotland. The friendship of France had been well repaid by the valor and the blood of Scotsmen on many a battle-field; but when Frenchmen assumed authority in or over Scotland they were repelled without scruple. And although, for the sake of peace and the religion of their belief, a party was willing to have formed a fairly-balanced alliance with their ancient enemy, yet when it appeared that he was bent upon taking advantage of every movement of the kind to enforce his dominion over them, they could forego or suspend the purpose of their party to maintain the independence of the nation. The political strength of the reforming movement was disguised for many years by the necessity of concentrating all efforts to repel the frequently recurring violence from the side of England. But though politically in abeyance, only a very shallow inspection of the history could rest in the conclusion that the party had ceased to be of any national importance.

After the regent—a good-natured, easy, but weak and fickle man—had deserted to the Catholic party, the archbishop of St. Andrews, who stood at the head of it, retained possession of the real authority in both Church and State to the end of his days.

David Beaton, nephew to his predecessor in the see of St. Andrews, was born at Balfour, in Fifeshire, in the year 1494. Until his sixteenth year he studied at St. Andrews, and then removed to the University of Glasgow, where his uncle was archbishop. He was afterward sent to Paris, where he excelled in the departments of civil and canon law. In 1519, for his great talent and attractive manners, he was made by James V. resident for Scotland at the French court, where he managed the affairs committed to his charge with great dexterity. Even before he became a priest ecclesiastical benefices were conferred upon him. His uncle granted him the rectories of Campsie and Cambuslang, and afterward the wealthy commendatory of Arbroath, and prevailed with the pope to dispense with his assuming the monastic garb for the space of two years. Meanwhile, he enjoyed the society and gayety of Paris. Returning to Scotland in 1525, he took his seat in Parliament as abbot of Arbroath. In 1528 he was appointed lord privy seal. By that office having many opportunities of being in the company of the young king, he soon became a special favorite, and in 1533 was sent on an embassy to France, from which he did not return until after the lapse of about four years. During that interval he ingratiated himself with Francis I. and received naturalization as a French subject.

Upon the marriage of James V. with the princess Magdalen, Beaton returned to Scotland with the royal company in May, 1537. After the death of Magdalen he was sent to France to negotiate a marriage for the king with Mary of Guise. On that occasion Francis conferred upon him the bishopric of Mirepoix in the south of France, with a revenue of ten thousand livres a year, and procured for him from Pope Paul III. the dignity of cardinal, which was granted in 1538.

Cardinal Beaton returned to Scotland as escort to Mary, the betrothed of James V., whose marriage he solemnized at St. Andrews in July, 1538. In August following he was appointed assistant to his uncle, whom he succeeded in the see of St. Andrews in February of next year. A few days after his elevation he used his influence with the king to procure a gift of land for David Beaton, one of his family of illegitimate children. Perceiving the rapid spread of Protestant doctrine, especially among the nobility and higher classes, he applied to the pope and received the powers of legate *a latere* for all Scotland.

So much was he impressed with the growth of the reforming interest that he resolved to take the most stringent measures to check it. Very soon after his promotion to the primacy he called a meeting of bishops, with the archbishop of Glasgow and some of the nobility, and, presiding over them in the cathedral, represented to them the danger wherewith the Church was threatened by the increase of heretics, who had the boldness to profess their opinions even in the king's court. He denounced as one of the most active Sir John Borthwick, provost of Linlithgow, and caused him to be cited before them. As Sir John did not appear, sentence was passed against him. His property was confiscated, and as he in person could not be found—he had taken refuge in England—he was burned in effigy. Before the first month of the cardinal's primacy had closed a great number of Protestants were arrested. Five were burned to death, nine recanted and some escaped out of prison. Among the latter was the celebrated George Buchanan. From that time onward the cardinal secured the entire control of public affairs, civil and ecclesiastical. James V. never succeeded in emancipating himself from the overmastering influence of the stronger mind. When he died the attempt was made by the cardinal, on the pretence of a royal will, to prolong that domination by proclaiming himself regent, with the earls of Arran, Huntly, Murray and Argyll as assistants. But Parliament treated the will as a forgery, set the cardinal aside, and proclaimed Arran sole regent.

For a time Beaton was imprisoned in Blackness, and afterward in his own castle of St. Andrews. But when the regent became alarmed about the English treaty he set him free, forming a reconciliation with him, and immediately came under his control more completely than had the king. The regent now acted with and for the cardinal to suppress the Reformation. He dismissed his two Reformed chaplains; the act of Parliament permitting the Scriptures to be read in the vulgar tongue was repealed, and the offence made punishable with death; heretical opinions were to be rooted out, and the prelates were enjoined to make inquiry within their dioceses respecting all who dissented from Catholic practice and doctrine, and to proceed against them by law.

In these circumstances it is not surprising that the greater number of persons entertaining Protestant convictions should have made as little demonstration of themselves as possible. Even Knox, now approaching the prime of his days, was still silent, biding his time in obscurity.

BOOK FOURTH.

THE REFORMATION CONFLICT.

CHAPTER I.

GEORGE WISHART AND CARDINAL BEATON.

IT has been already stated that the spread of Reformed doctrine in Scotland was used by a class of political agitators to help forward their own designs. Making a profession of zeal for pure religion, they secured the support of a reliable influence among the people, and repaid it with the reproach due to their own evil-doings.

During the repeated invasions from England in 1544 and 1545, by which the south of Scotland was devastated and some of her finest ecclesiastical structures, Melrose, Dryburgh, Kelso, Jedburgh and others, laid in ruins, there were men who, under the plea of being Reformers, aided the enemy of their country, and willingly offered themselves for the execution of his least defensible designs. The indignation of Henry VIII. was leveled chiefly against Cardinal Beaton, by whom the treaties of alliance and intermarriage of the royal families had been defeated; and Beaton, after that victory of his policy, strengthened himself as the real governor of Scotland. The regent, if he did not in all cases act in compliance with him, proved incompetent to resist. He was strengthened by the passionate blundering of Henry VIII. The raids made along the border alienated that portion of the Scottish people who otherwise would have promoted still further effort for the English alliance, and turned their favor to Beaton as a patriotic leader.

Far from being held in popular respect, Beaton's character was notorious, his immorality undisguised and his cruelty insolent, but his opposition to the usurping claims of Henry VIII. secured him the support of the multitude, who could not know the motive of his policy. A Frenchman by naturalization, a personal friend of Francis I., and holder of a wealthy benefice in France, he acted in the interests of his adoptive country by withholding the country of his birth from enjoying a peace which would have left England free to match herself fairly with France. Beaton's patriotism was to let Scotland bleed, that France might be assisted in her war with a Protestant neighbor—to maintain alliance with a more distant Romish power to suppress the reforming party in his native land. His interests were with those who honored and enriched him—France and the papacy. One of the greatest and most accomplished men whom

Scotland has ever produced, he had been completely corrupted, both morally and politically, by his long and repeated residences among the court society of Paris. But Scotland was in danger, and her defence was the absorbing care of all loyal Scotsmen, of whatever religion, or of none. It was no time to criticise the character of one who appeared to be her staunchest friend at the head of government. For the time, Beaton was popular in Scotland.

The hatred of him entertained by Henry VIII. was fully intelligent of his purposes. Unfortunately for both countries, it was expressed in actions as stupid as they were wicked.

One of Henry's projects was to get the cardinal into his hands or to have him put to death. On the side of Scotland, a few desperate men, who chose to array themselves with the Reformers, were willing, for a satisfactory consideration, to execute that intention. The leader among them seems to have been Crighton, laird of Brunston, by whom a proposition to murder the cardinal was sent in writing to Lord Hertford by the hands of a person called Wishart. Hertford forwarded the message and messenger, together with a letter from himself, to the king, who gave the messenger an audience, approved of the plot, and promised those concerned in it his royal protection. A correspondence on the subject was continued for three years between Brunston, the earl of Cassilis and Sir Ralph Sadler. Henry would not appear in it directly, but deputed Sadler to make the arrangements and promise the reward. The conspirators, however, refused to act without the king's own authority, given under his sign manual. Accordingly, nothing was done.

During those years of war and distrust on all sides, the true reforming party of Scotland remained quiet and ventureless. But their existence could not be concealed. Arrests were made and persons executed for religion's sake by order of the cardinal. The regent caused it to be brought before Parliament, "How there is great murmour that heretics mair and mair rises and spreads within this realm, sawand damnable opinions in contrair the faith and laws of haly Kirk, acts and constitutions of this realm. Exhortand, therefore, all prelates and ordinaries, ilk ane within their own diocese and jurisdiction, to inquire upon all sic maner of persons, and to proceed against them according to the laws of haly Kirk; and my said lord governor sall be ready at all times to do therein that accords him of his office."

In 1544, the year after the regent's change of politics, George Wishart, an eminent Reformed preacher, returned from England. He had been residing at the University of Cambridge for some time. Represented by contemporaneous accounts as a man of remarkable gentleness of spirit, piety, benevolence and self-denial, he was possessed of superior learning and knowledge of the Scriptures, and was thought to be endowed with the spirit of prophecy. In Scotland he began to preach at Montrose. His manner was not violent or fiery, but earnest, tender and impressive in demonstrating and applying Scripture doctrine, and sometimes solemnly severe in rebuke of prevailing sins and errors. From Montrose he went to Dundee, where he lectured on the Epistle to the Romans, with great acceptance of all who attended. By order of the cardinal he was interrupted in that work. He made no resistance, but withdrew to the west country, where he remained a considerable time, preaching in various places, especially in and about Ayr, in the church of Gaston and at a place called the Bar. At Ayr the archbishop of Glasgow attempted to resist him by pre-occupying the church. The earl of Glencairn, hearing of it, repaired thither in haste with some friends. Other gentlemen of Kyle did likewise. When they were assembled, it was resolved by them to take possession of the church by force. Wishart would not consent to contend with the bishop for it. "Let him alane," said he, "his sermon will not meikell hurt. Let us go to the mercate-cross." They followed him to the market-cross, and there, says Knox, "he preached so notable a sermon that the very enemies themselves were confounded." Meanwhile, the good-natured Archbishop Dunbar, always averse to severe measures, preached a sermon apologetic of his own and his episcopal brethren's neglect of preaching: "They say we should preach. Why not? Better late thrive nor never thrive. Had us still for your bishop, and we shall provide better the next time."

Wishart, invited to Mauchline, went there, but was forbidden the use of the church. The gentlemen who invited him resolved to secure him the use of it, if they should have to fight for it. Wishart dissuaded them, saying, "Christ Jesus is as potent upon the fields as in the kirk; and I find that himself often preached in the desert, at the seyside and other places judged profane, than that he did in the temple at Jerusalem. It is the word of peace which the Lord sends by me. The blood of no man shall be shed this day for the preaching of it." And so, withdrawing the assembly to a little distance from the town, he ascended a stone dyke, and there preached to them, as they stood and sat about him on the moor. The day was pleasant, and the sermon was continued to more than three hours, in which, says the original reporter, "God wrought wonderfully with him."

Hearing that the plague had broken out at Dundee, and that the mortality was very great, no persuasion could withhold him from returning thither. "They are now in trouble," said he, "and need comfort. Perchance this hand of God will make them now to magnify and reverence that word which before, for the fear of men, they set at light part." He lost no time, but immediately upon arriving set to work in ministering to the sick, whom he found neglected, and preaching to all. The attendance upon his regular sermons was large, humble and docile. The effect was alarming to the hierarchy. A fanatical priest was instigated to kill him. Wishart himself detected him in time to prevent the intended crime. The assembly, who were just going out from sermon, would have inflicted summary punishment; but Wishart took the man in his arms and would suffer no one to harm him, saying, "He has done great comfort both to you and me—to wit, he has let us understand what we may fear. In time to come we will watch better."

After the plague had ceased at Dundee, Wishart revisited Montrose. While there he received an application in the name of some gentlemen of the West to meet them in Edinburgh and maintain a discussion with the bishops, in which they promised to protect him. He complied. But not finding them in Edinburgh, he took occasion to preach at some places in the neighborhood. Certain gentlemen of Lothian, who were of the Reformed persuasion, advised him that it was not expedient to remain there, and took him with them to their country residences. The Sunday following he preached in the church at Inveresk, both morning and afternoon, to a great concourse of people, among whom was Sir George Douglas, brother of Lord Angus, who openly encouraged the people by saying to them there that he "would maintain the doctrine he had heard that day, and also defend the person of the preacher, to the utmost of his power."

But other notices, it seems, had been set afloat which intimidated the people. Upon a visit to Haddington, where he expected to preach, Wishart found the audience very small, and began to perceive that machinations were on foot against him. It was while in that quarter that he became acquainted with John Knox, then living in obscurity as a private tutor to the sons of Hugh Douglas of Langnidrie. The respect for the talents and Christian character of Wishart evinced by Knox is the highest testimony which could be borne to either.

Cardinal Beaton was now in pursuit of the indefatigable preacher, and had thought the cause worth seeing after in person. He was in the neighborhood at Elphinstone. Wishart was arrested by Earl Bothwell, father of one of the name more notorious, and submitted to the cardinal's keeping. After some removals, he was taken to St. Andrews, and confined in the sea-tower of the castle or episcopal palace. The cardinal summoned a great council of the highest clergy in the land. They met in the end of February, 1546. The regent was applied to for sanction of the civil power. He refused to grant it, and informed the cardinal that he would "do well not to precipitate the man's trial until his (the regent's) coming; for, as to himself, he would not consent to his death before the cause was well examined; and if the cardinal should do otherwise, he would make protestation that the man's blood should be required at his hands."

The cardinal, confident in his powers as papal legate, replied that he "did not write to the governor as though he depended in any matter upon his authority, but out of a desire he had that the heretic's condemnation might proceed with some show of public consent, which since he could not obtain, he would himself do that which he held most fitting." Thus he assumed the whole responsibility and guilt.

George Wishart was arraigned before the cardinal and the assembled bishops and abbots on eighteen articles of heresy. He denied the jurisdiction of the court, and asserted that he was unjustly accused of some of the articles. His objections were overruled, and himself condemned to be burned as a heretic.

In this case the usual sham of handing over the condemned to the secular arm was omitted. The punishment was inflicted by order of the archbishop himself. The pile was erected in front of his own castle. Safety from interruption was secured by his own cannon, and he presided over the execution in person. George Wishart was burned to death on the 2d of March, 1546. It was a bold ecclesiastical act, under protest of the highest civil authority of the land. The perpetrator of it was satisfied that he had struck a blow at heresy, which must intimidate and deter all others disposed to preach or otherwise give publicity to its doctrines.

As long as the attempt to suppress the growth of Protestant opinions by force was persevered in, the multitude of those affected by it remained silent. The government was very plainly in a transition state, which might change in an hour. Everything depended upon the frail life of an infant. If she died, a new dynasty would come to the throne. The earl of Arran was the next heir. He had been a Protestant, and others of the Hamilton family had proved more faithful to that cause. If subjected to the advice of a strong and reliable Protestant, instead of the cardinal, he might again favor Reformation.

So many probabilities lay in the next few years of the future that good and wise men deemed it prudent to await a more favorable occasion. But some impatient spirits could not wait—men of that class who always insist upon carrying their ends at their own time and by means of their own creating.

In 1543 attacks were made by some of the populace upon monastic houses in various parts of the country. At Dundee those of both Black and Grey Friars were destroyed. Soon afterward the abbey of Lindores "was sacked by a company of good Christians, as they were called, who turned the monks out of doors." The church of Arbroath would also have been destroyed but for the intervention of Lord Ogilvy. At Edinburgh an attack of the same kind was made upon the monastery of the Black Friars, but was repelled by a promiscuous rising of the citizens.

Others were ready to lend their aid to English invasion, in hopes that, the Romish party being defeated, the nation would be free to follow a policy of the popular choice, which they fondly hoped would not be Romish. To that class belonged the earl of Angus, his brother Sir George Douglas, the earl of Cassilis, John Leslie and others. A few of them conceived of a more direct road to the end they had in view. If Cardinal Beaton were disposed of, the regent could be brought under more wholesome advice, and the principal obstacle removed out of the Reformers' way. It was well known to them that such an event would be gratifying to the king of England. Their secret negotiations with him have been already mentioned. The plan was never carried into effect.

The three years during which that disgraceful negotiation lingered contained the summit of Beaton's success. He actually ruled Scotland at the head of the papal party. Parliament complied with all his measures and enacted them as laws. The regent was in reality his second in power, generally compliant with his plans. Heresy, wherever detected in accusable form, was put down by force—constrained to recant or silenced in death. Sometimes where the charge was slight the penalty imposed was the severest. At Perth five men were put to death by hanging and a woman drowned—one of the men, because he denied that prayer to the saints is necessary to salvation; three of them, because they were guilty of eating a goose on All-Hallow evening; and the fifth, because he was found in their company. The woman was put to death because she refused to pray to the Virgin Mary, and would pray only to God in the name of Jesus Christ.

Meanwhile, George Wishart was preaching in Scotland, and his preaching was followed by great religious interest in both east and west. Some have assumed that he was the Wishart who carried the message of Brunston into England. The name Wishart was not uncommon, and such a plot as that proposed by Brunston is so strangely contradictory of all that we know of the martyr that nothing short of the most indubitable identification can satisfy us that he was the bearer of such a communication. In nothing was the martyr Wishart more signally characterized among the men of his day than by his tenderness for human suffering and shrinking from violence which might end in shedding of blood.

The burning of George Wishart profoundly stirred the feelings of all classes. The more peaceful were grieved and indignant, while the violent were stimulated to revenge. For the time being, tongues were let loose with unprecedented freedom. Impulse set caution at defiance. On some points people could censure the conduct of the cardinal without danger. He had taken the whole execution into his own hands, and brought upon the Church an obloquy which she had been always very careful to shift from herself to the civil arm. Because a man condemned that irregularity it did not follow that he was a heretic. On another point the cardinal was exposed to censure which could not be repelled as heresy: his moral conduct was notorious. Whatever gallantries he concealed, there were some which he carried on without shame and openly admitted.

The voice of condemnation was heard in many quarters, and some took the ground that, if there was no law in the land to prevent or punish the atrocities of which he was guilty, they should be stopped by the law of natural vengeance. John Leslie, brother to the earl of Rothes, and no doubt others, thought that the country had endured more than enough of this cruel and irrational despotism, and openly vowed that he would see punishment inflicted upon the man who had been guilty of it.

Meanwhile, the cardinal and his clergy were flattering themselves with having silenced heresy under their jurisdiction in the flames of him who alone had dared to preach its doctrines publicly. They were soon to be undeceived. The popularity which the cardinal once had with those who believed in his patriotism was now forfeited. Although the clergy lavished praise upon him for his defence of the Church, none among the laity, save the most extreme papalists, were found to defend him.

On the evening of the day on which Wishart was executed the cardinal caused a proclamation to be made through the city forbidding prayers to be offered for the soul of the heretic, under pain of the heaviest penalties. He had reached the summit of his pride. By the priesthood he was lauded to the skies as the true and powerful protector of the Church. They boasted that, disregarding the "governor's authority, he had of himself caused justice to be executed upon the heretic," and proved the "most worthy patron of the ecclesiastical state." Yet, proud as he was of his achievement, and perhaps most proud of having snubbed the regent, and exercised the powers which properly belonged to him, the haughty prelate seems to have been not quite sure of his own safety; for he set to work to strengthen the defences of his palace, the castle of St. Andrews, and kept it well supplied with munitions of war.

Not long after the burning of George Wishart, Cardinal Beaton went in great state to Finhaven Castle, in Angus, to be present at the marriage of his daughter Margaret to David Lindsay, heir of the earldom of Crawford, to which he afterward succeeded. The wedding was celebrated with the utmost magnificence, and the dowry of the bride was equal to that of a princess. Margaret Beaton, the illegitimate daughter of a Romish priest, became a countess and the mother of four successive generations of noblemen.

In the midst of the festivities news arrived that Henry VIII. was advancing with a great army to invade Scotland. Beaton hastened to St. Andrews to push forward the strengthening of his castle, and to rouse the nobility of the nation and organize an effective resistance, as if all the duties of government rested upon his shoulders. The alarm proved false. Not the less did he go on with the work upon the ramparts of his castle-palace.

On the 28th of May, in the evening, Norman Leslie, the son of Lord Rothes, with five followers, rode into the town of St. Andrews and put up at his usual lodgings. William Kircaldy of Grange was already there. Later in the evening, and when it was now dark, came John Leslie, the uncle of Norman, also Peter Carmichael and the gentle, modest, but resolute fanatic James Melville, and others to the number of sixteen in all—all of gentle if not noble blood.

Next morning, by daybreak, they were assembled in little groups in the neighborhood of the castle. The porter had lowered the drawbridge to admit the masons and other workmen. Norman Leslie and three of his companions entered with them and inquired for the cardinal. The porter answered without suspicion that he was not yet awake. While they were talking, James Melville, Kircaldy of Grange and others entered also. At the approach of the rest, with John Leslie at their head, the porter suspected danger and hastened to raise the drawbridge. But Leslie was too quick for him, and, having stepped on it, stayed it and leaped in. The porter was knocked on the head, his keys taken from him, and himself tumbled into the foss in a few seconds, and so silently that no alarm was given. With equal silence the workmen were led to the gate and dismissed, before they had time to exchange a word with one another or could think what was the matter. Other conspirators went to the apartments of the different gentlemen of the household, and led them in silence, one by one, to the outer wicket and dismissed them without injury. One hundred and fifty persons were thus disposed of briefly and silently by those sixteen men, resolute and self-possessed, who then, dropping the portcullis and shutting the gates, were masters of the castle.

By this time some noise awoke the cardinal. Looking out of his window, he asked, "What means that noise?" Some one answered, "Norman Leslie has taken the castle." He then ran to the postern, but finding it guarded, hurried back to his room, seized a two-handed sword and ordered his servant to bolt the door and barricade it with heavy furniture. John Leslie demanded admittance. "Who calls?" asked the cardinal.—" My name is Leslie."—

"Is it Norman?"—"My name is John."—"I will have Norman, for he is my friend."—"Content yourself with such as are here, for other shall ye get nane." With John Leslie were Melville and Carmichael. While they were attempting to force the door open Beaton called to them, "Will ye save my life?"—"It may be that we will," replied Leslie.—"Nay, but swear unto me, by God's wounds, and I shall open unto you."—"It that was said is unsaid," was the answer. Fire was now called for to burn the door. It was opened from within. "I am a priest," exclaimed the cardinal—"I am a priest; ye will not slay me." Leslie, who rushed upon him, struck him once or twice, and was followed by Peter Carmichael.

James Melville interposed. "This work and judgment of God," said he, "although it be secret, yet it ought to be done with greater gravity;" and presenting the point of his sword to the cardinal's breast, went on to say, "Repent thee of thy former wicked life, but especially of the shedding of the blood of that notable instrument of God, Master George Wishart, which, albeit that the flame of fire consumed before men, yet cries it a vengeance upon thee, and we from God are sent to revenge it. For here before God I protest that neither the hatred of thy person, the love of thy riches nor the fear of any trouble thou couldst have done to me in particular moved or moveth me to strike thee; but only because thou hast been, and remainest, an obstinate enemy to Christ Jesus and his holy evangel." Having deliberately so spoken, he passed his sword two or three times through the cardinal's body. The miserable victim's only words, as he sank down in the chair on which he was seated, were, "I am a priest, I am priest; fy! fy! all is gone!"

Great excitement had now arisen in the city, and a crowd assembled in front of the castle, demanding that the cardinal should appear. The conspirators, after some delay, finally complied with their urgency to see him by suspending the bleeding body out of a window. The crowd then quietly dispersed.

Cardinal Beaton being dead, the conspirators retained possession of his castle for their own safety. To avenge the death of a martyr they had become criminals before the law of the land. Some of them were otherwise good men, earnestly pious men, misled by erroneous ideas of natural justice, and by misapplication of certain passages in Old-Testament history. Others, of a different character, took part in the conspiracy to gratify their own outraged feelings. Beaton's private conduct had been such as to array no little of that kind of animosity against him. But all alike felt that they were involved in what the civil as well as ecclesiastical law deemed a crime of great enormity. It was thought safest to keep together and retain the protection of the castle, which was well supplied with provisions and means of defence, until the most favorable terms possible could be secured from the authorities.

Learning that state of the case, John Rough, a zealous Reformed preacher, came to St. Andrews to undertake their religious instruction. And about the same time Henry Balnavis, an eminent lawyer and statesman, with some others, joined them, until altogether they numbered not much less than a hundred and fifty.

On the other side, the regent was assailed with all urgency by the bishops to take some course for bringing speedy and condign punishment upon the murderers. He preferred the regular course of law, and issued summons for their appearance under trial. They refused to comply, and were denounced as rebels, while the ecclesiastical authorities solemnly cursed them and all who should harbor them or furnish them with aid or comfort.

For the vacant primacy the regent nominated his half-brother, John Hamilton, bishop of Dunkeld. The nomination was followed by regular election. The pope, Paul III., fearing the secession of Scotland entirely from his dominion, confirmed the election without delay, earnestly representing to the regent and the new archbishop the duty of adequately punishing the injury done to the ecclesiastical state by the slaying of Beaton.

The castle of St. Andrews stood upon the northern verge of the town, fronting toward the abbey at the opposite extremity, and upon ground a little lower than the adjoining street. Its walls on the east were washed by the sea, and on other sides looked out upon a country flat and bare. A siege conducted with the armies now in use such a structure could not have resisted for a day. But all the resources then at the command of the regent were employed against it between four and five months in vain. The besieged, by their unobstructed access to the sea, were abundantly furnished with all necessary supplies from England.

In January, 1547, the regent, apprehensive that they might be supported by an army from the same quarter, agreed to a capitulation on the following terms: First, that they should keep the castle of St. Andrews until the governor and authority of Scotland should get them a sufficient absolution from the pope for the slaughter of the cardinal. Second, that they should give pledges for the surrender of that house as soon as the absolution was delivered unto them, and that they should keep the earl of Arran, son of the regent, who was among them, as long as their pledges were kept. And third, that they, their friends, servants and others to them pertaining, should simply be remitted by the governor, and never be called in question for said slaughter, but should enjoy all commodities, spiritual and temporal, which they possessed before the committing thereof. "Articles liberal enough," says Knox, "for they never minded to keep a word of them, as the issue did declare."

The siege was raised, and until the arrival of the absolution the conspirators held the castle, and those of them not implicated in the murder went out and in without being molested.

It was during this interval that John Knox came among them, bringing with him the three lads under his tuition. "Wearied," as he writes, "of removing from place to place by reason of the persecution which came upon him," he had thought of going abroad, but the fathers of the boys whom he taught persuaded him to go to St. Andrews, that he might have the protection of the castle, and their sons the continued "benefit of his doctrine." Among the lessons which he gave was included a catechism of religious instruction, on which he examined his pupils publicly in the parish church of St. Andrews, and also reading the Gospels, which he accompanied with exposition adapted to their capacity. This was done in the chapel of the castle. Persons who happened to be present at those lessons felt themselves much profited, and the suggestion was made, and universally approved, that he should be invited to preach. He was an ordained priest, but had shrunk from service in the Romish Church, and now also declined this invitation. The congregation in the castle, after consulting together in his absence, commissioned John Rough, their pastor, to press their call upon him publicly. Rough preached a sermon on the call to the ministry, and at the close, turning to Knox, made a solemn application of the doctrine to him, and uttered the charge which he had been requested to deliver. Then turning to the congregation, he asked, "Was not this your charge unto me? And do you not approve this vocation?"—They answered, "It was, and we approve it."

Knox, overcome with emotion, made no reply, but rose and withdrew. Accepting the call as of God, he felt no comfort until he appeared, after several days, in the new capacity of a minister of the gospel. Until the response arrived from Rome he continued to assist in preaching and pastoral work in the castle, and both he and Rough occasionally preached in the city.

A certain dean, John Annan, had long troubled Rough in his ministry. Knox defended the preacher with his pen, and had beaten Dean

John from all his defences until he took refuge in the absolute authority of the Church. Knox insisted upon knowing what was the Church, by definition drawn from Scripture, and offered to prove that the Roman Church of that day "was further degenerate from the purity which was in the days of the apostles than was the Church of the Jews from the ordinance given by Moses when they consented to the innocent death of Jesus Christ." These words were spoken openly in the parish church. The people called out that they wished to hear his proof. Accordingly, he made that his theme next Sunday in the same place, taking for his text the seventh chapter of Daniel; in discussing which he carried attack upon the errors of the Catholic Church and the corruptions of the papacy in all their breadth, describing also the features of the true Church in New-Testament language.

This was heresy of a bolder type than had hitherto been heard in Scotland. It was something very different from the modest and gentle earnestness of Hamilton and Wishart. They had proclaimed the gospel with warmth and fullness, but avoided unnecessary attacks upon their enemies. This new preacher launched his denunciations against error on every hand, and hurled his arguments at the heads of its defenders with a boldness which enlisted the confidence of one party while it filled the other with dismay. With an irresistible power of logic, an uncommon command of Scripture, and a keen satirical wit and humor, he reveled in the facility of defeating all opponents. The Scottish Reformation at last beheld its leader, one of the God-made rulers of men.

The archbishop, who was not present nor yet fully inducted, wrote to the sub-prior, Winram, saying "that he wondered how he could suffer such heretical and schismatical doctrines to be taught" without opposition. Winram—partly of the Reformer's opinion, but privately—complied with the order of his superior, called a convention of both Black and Grey Friars, and cited Knox and Rough to appear before them. A list of articles was read in which they were charged with teaching heresy. The sub-prior listened to their answers, and responded with some mild objections. A Grey Friar, one Arbuckle, rushed into the discussion, but soon began to feel embarrassed under the hard and lucid arguments which encountered him, and in his desperation asserted, among other foolish things, that the apostles had not received the Holy Ghost when they wrote their Epistles. The sub-prior found it necessary to reprove his assistant and bring the conference to a close. He dismissed the preachers with a brotherly admonition "to take heed what doctrine they taught in public." That kind of debate the monks did not again invite. Such was the effect of the preaching by Knox and Rough in St. Andrews that all the occupants of the castle and many people of the town joined in partaking of the Lord's Supper after the scriptural example.

John Rough, soon after that occasion, went into England, where he continued to preach in various cities until the death of Edward VI. In the time of Mary he fled into Friesland, but, returning to England in 1557, he was arrested and burned in Smithfield.

When the papal absolution came it was found not satisfactory, and was rejected. In less than a month a French fleet arrived with a besieging army. The garrison of the castle was once more cooped up within their walls. By the end of July, 1547, they surrendered, on condition that their lives should be spared; their leading men were to be transported to France, or conveyed upon the French ships to any other country they might prefer, except Scotland.

The French captain then plundered the castle of everything worth carrying away. After he had gone, it was reduced to ruins—doomed, as a place where a cardinal had been slain. The loss of that cardinal was a calamity from which the papal cause in Scotland never recovered.

CHAPTER II.

ALLIANCE WITH FRANCE.

AFTER the capture of the castle of St. Andrews, the prisoners were taken on French galleys to Rouen. There, after some delay, orders were received distributing them all in different places of imprisonment—in Rouen, Cherbourg, Brest and Mont St. Michel, and some, among whom was John Knox, in the galleys. This disregard of the capitulation was referred to the instance of the pope and the Scottish bishops.

From Rouen the galleys sailed to Nantes, and lay all winter in the Loire. Next summer they sailed to the coast of Scotland, on the outlook for English vessels. By exposure, hard labor and cruel treatment, Knox's health was seriously impaired, and for a time his life was in danger; but he never despaired of the cause in which he suffered, nor wavered in his hope of further serving it. While sailing along the coast in sight of St. Andrews he replied to a friend, who asked him if he knew that city, "Yes, I know it well; for I see the steeple of that place where God first opened my mouth in public to his glory; and I am fully persuaded, how weak soever I now appear, that I shall not depart this life till that my tongue shall glorify his godly name in the same place." Meanwhile, in moments of relief from fever and from toil, he wrote a statement of the doctrines which he believed, and found means to have it sent to his friends at home for their instruction and the confirmation of their faith.

It was in prison also that Henry Balnavis composed that treatise on justification and the works of a justified man which was, some time afterward, prepared for the press with notes and a "recommendatory dedication" by John Knox.

In Scotland, soon after the departure of the French fleet, an English army crossed the border, and advanced, under command of the Protector Somerset, as far as the vicinity of Edinburgh. Then followed, on the 10th of September, the battle of Pinkie, that deepest and last of the disasters which humiliated the regency of Arran. The country seemed on the point of being prostrated beneath the feet of a strong and victorious enemy. But, for some unknown reason, the Protector, after destroying the church of Holyrood and other places around Edinburgh, returned to England. In February, following a victory won upon the border restored the spirits of the Scots and the expectations of their allies.

Occasion was taken of the increased animosity toward England, created by the war, to secure for France the advantages of a marriage with the queen of Scotland. A small but well-trained and well-equipped body of French auxiliaries landed at Leith in June, 1548, and proved of valuable service in helping to recover the strongholds garrisoned by the English. Soon after their arrival, the French ambassador, D'Esse, laid proposals in reference to the royal marriage before the Estates. They were jealously discussed, and a treaty was concluded in July, whereby the little maiden of Scotland was to become the wife of the heir-apparent of France, as soon as both should reach the proper age. Until then she was to reside with her mother's kindred of Lorraine. The ambassador, on his return, was to be her escort to the land of her education and her honors, and, as it proved in the end, the source of her misfortunes. To escape English cruisers on the common route, the French ships sailed out of the Forth, round the northern extremity of Scotland, and took their precious little passenger on board at Dumbarton. Mary Stuart first set foot in France at Brest on the 30th of August, 1548, when six years of age.

The Scottish statesmen who favored the

French alliance were not more patriotic than those who preferred the English; the policy of the latter was, in fact, the wiser and farther-reaching of the two, but at that time was intensely unpopular. On the other side, calamities enough arose out of the brief union of the two crowns, Scottish and French; and had it lasted the ordinary life of man, nothing but continued calamity could have been expected, possibly the entire subjugation of the weaker country. And yet that the policy of the French party prevailed was nothing more than the natural effect of causes too controlling for the wisest policy to counteract. The clergy were all in favor of France, for France was Catholic and persecuted Protestants; England was Protestant and held Catholics under repression; and the greater number of Scottish people, whatever they might think of their priests, were still Catholic. On the part of the suitors there was a difference of manner, in itself enough to decide the question. England wooed with threats of compulsion and desolating war; France with professions of friendship and military aid.

The shortsighted policy turned out, in the developments of Providence, to the overthrow of the party that chose it and the humiliation and ruin of the unhappy woman personally concerned, but to the best for the nation. Had

Mary been taken to England and educated a Protestant as the betrothed bride of Edward VI., the result, in any conceivable probability, in the death of the young king before marriageable age, and the succeeding reign of the Catholic Mary Tudor, could not have been worse for Mary Stuart personally, and would have put her in harmony with her subjects, when old enough to reign, even if it had not, in the eyes of the Protestants of England, constituted her their most eligible candidate for their throne after the death of Mary Tudor—a candidate whose legitimacy even Catholics could not have questioned. Thus she might herself have done what was actually reserved for her son to do—worn the two crowns. But that would not have led to the measures by which the Catholics so prejudiced their cause in Scotland as to create a tide of revulsion which confirmed the independence of the Reformed Church.

For the then existing present, however, the results tended to peace. The war by which Scotland had been so long harassed was subsequently prosecuted by the English with little zeal, while the Scots and their French allies won rapid victories. It was brought to an end in April, 1550, by a treaty in which Scotland recovered the boundaries which she had before it began.

In September of the same year the queen-mother, Mary of Lorraine, made a visit to France. During her residence there, plans were initiated for the ultimate annexation of Scotland. The first step was to have Mary herself put into the place of regent. With a view to that end high honors were conferred upon the earl of Arran. He was invested with the duchy of Châtelherault, with its town and palace. Nor were the favors from the side of France conferred in such a way that the proud noble should feel them as a price paid for the highest place in his native land, but that the good-natured, weak and compliant man, by receiving unsought and unconditional favors from a friend, in such exalted station, might feel disposed to return an equally exalted and unsought kindness. At the same time, Arran was not ignorant of his own unpopularity among his countrymen. It had been increasing since 1544, and an irregular meeting of some members of the Estates, or Scottish Parliament, had given expression to that feeling in their distinctly stated intention to depose him and put the queen-mother in his place. The annoyance which he suffered, on the one side, from those who wished him to remain in office, and on the other from the action of his opponents, seems at last to have become more than he cared to endure. Things were accordingly so disposed that the duke of Châtelherault gracefully yielded the regency of Scotland, which in April, 1554, was conferred upon Mary of Lorraine.

After France had completed the treaty of marriage with the heir of the Scottish throne, obtained possession of the person of the sovereign and begun to think of the ultimate annexation of that kingdom, and thereby of retaliating humiliation upon England, it became a matter of very little moment to court the favor of a dozen Scottish bishops by holding in custody a hundred Scottish prisoners. Accordingly, the exiles of St. Andrews were soon afterward set free, some in 1549, and the rest after the taking of Boulogne in 1550. A few had escaped by their own ingenuity and enterprise. They all lived to enjoy their liberation, except James Melville, who died of sickness in prison. Knox was liberated in 1549, and immediately passed over into England, where he was employed in the reformation then going on under Edward VI. Appointed to preach in Berwick and about Newcastle, and afterward in London and the south of England, he continued in that service until the death of the king. His salary was then withheld, but he did not cease preaching until the Marian persecution began.

In the five terrible years which succeeded, many English Protestants found refuge in Scotland, seeking safety in obscurity, as did their co-religionist Scots themselves; but for Knox to go there would have been to rush into the clutches of his deadly enemies. The chair of David Beaton was now occupied by John Hamilton, a man of entirely kindred spirit. Hamilton, in his degree, was following the example of Beaton, repressing the utterance of Reformed religion wherever he could obtain information of it. In 1550 he seized Adam Wallace, a plain man of good though not great learning, but of zealous piety, and consigned him to the flames. To have got Knox into his hands would have furnished a sacrifice the pride and boast of his primacy. The Reformer found a shelter, until the storm blew over, with Calvin in Geneva.

Adherents of Reformed doctrines in Scotland had the less difficulty in concealing their convictions that very few of them were clergymen, and that they continued to attend regularly at their parish churches. The number also of those dissatisfied with the Romish religion was now such that they mutually respected each other's reticence. It had not yet occurred to them that their change of opinion was to demand separation from their old places of worship. What they contemplated was reform, not disruption—a revival of pure religion, working in and for the whole, not for a few, to take them away by themselves. Nor had they conceived of more than one Church. To keep silence, when speaking might do harm, was fidelity to the cause. The few clergy of their persuasion could not conscientiously do so. To speak was their calling, and when they spoke they must speak their belief. For them the best course was to withdraw, for a time, to some country where they could labor for truth without injuring its interests. Some of them, like Sub-prior Winram, whose progress was not so far advanced, could say all that they felt called to say and retain their places in safety.

From the reduction of the castle of St. Andrews until 1554, such was the course of the adherents of Reform in Scotland. During all that time Archbishop Hamilton believed that, with the help of his brother the regent, he had succeeded in repressing, if not extinguishing, the troublesome heresy. A few executions, as he and his bishops thought, had intimidated its leaders and sent the more restless into exile.

When Mary of Lorraine began to aim at the regency, it was her policy to secure the favor of the nation as widely as possible, and especially of that party whom the earl of Arran had disobliged in changing his politics, and who had ever since been his opponents. She knew well that the believers of the so-called new doctrines belonged to that party through whom his elevation to the regency had been secured. They, it is true, had also advocated the English alliance and opposed the French. But now that the latter had succeeded, and her daughter was safely in the care of her kinsmen of Lorraine, there was nothing to be feared on that question. They had been completely alienated from Arran. By a little judicious management were not they the men to turn the balance in her favor? Actually, they did so. She was made regent in opposition to the policy of Archbishop Hamilton, and for some time kept on such good terms with those who had so effectually helped her, that many deemed her secretly disposed to their doctrine. In those circumstances men began to express themselves with greater freedom, and refugees from persecution in England sought safety in Scotland, and there promoted the cause for which they suffered.

Among others, two Scotsmen who had long been exiles for religion's sake returned to their native land. William Harlaw, employed as a preacher in England under Edward VI., now ventured to come back and preach the gospel to his countrymen. In Ayrshire he labored from place to place in private houses until after 1560, when he settled in St. Cuthbert's, near Edinburgh.

John Willock, a native of Ayrshire, had in

early youth joined the Franciscan order. Soon afterward converted to the Reformed faith, he abjured his monkish profession and fled into England, where, however, he did not altogether escape persecution under Henry VIII. Latterly, he enjoyed protection as chaplain of the duke of Suffolk. On the accession of Queen Mary he left England and took up his residence at Embden. In the summer of 1555 he was sent by Anne, duchess of Friesland, to the queen-regent of Scotland on some commercial business. While residing in Edinburgh he took occasion to converse fully on the subject of religion with those who for that purpose came to him in his own apartments. Late in the autumn of that year he returned to Embden, but not before a greater workman had taken his place in Edinburgh.

John Knox, when he left England in January, 1554, delayed at Dieppe until the end of February, hesitating whether to go farther or return and encounter the multiplying dangers. He concluded to visit the churches in Switzerland. It was a hasty visit. By the beginning of May he was back in Dieppe, where news could be readily got from Britain. Though strongly desirous of going to Berwick, where his wife and mother-in-law were residing, he perceived that such a step would still be premature, and instead of it went to Geneva.

There he was affectionately received by Calvin, but anxiety about the state of his native country made him restless. He returned again to Dieppe in July. The intelligence was discouraging. Scotland was still biding her time in silence — England was sinking deeper and deeper under Romish intolerance. He returned to Geneva, and devoted himself to study, especially of the Hebrew language, with which he had not been previously acquainted.

But his tranquil pursuits were not long uninterrupted. Invited by the English Protestant congregation at Frankfort-on-the-Main to be their pastor, and strongly advised by Calvin to accept the place, he removed thither in November of the same year. The congregation, though harmonious at first, upon the arrival of other exiles from England divided among themselves. The new-comers found great fault with the worship because it was not conducted after the manner prescribed under Edward VI. The other section resisted the attempt to force a liturgy upon them. No man could please both. Knox left them in March, 1555, and went back to Geneva, where he settled down once more to his biblical studies. They were not again interrupted through the rest of the spring and summer. In August, having learned of the change for the better enjoyed by his countrymen under the new regent, he returned to Scotland.

The place where he landed was near Berwick. After visiting his family he proceeded to Edinburgh, where he arrived while Willock was still there.

At the house of a trusty friend and fellow-Protestant, James Syme, a respectable burgess of the capital city, he continued for several weeks to preach daily. As many more than the apartments could accommodate came to hear him, he divided them into companies, whom he addressed successively at different hours through the day and evening. The attendance went on increasing, and many came in a state of great spiritual anxiety, inquiring what they should do to be saved. In short, he found a profound revival of religion quickening about him.

At that juncture a new step of progress was ventured on. Attendance upon mass now appeared to be inconsistent with the knowledge of the scriptural way of salvation possessed by the people. At a conference of a few of the chief men—among whom, besides Knox, were John Erskine of Dun, an earnest and experienced Christian, and William Maitland of Lethington, a young statesman destined to future celebrity—it was resolved to discontinue attendance upon the Romish service.

Soon afterward Knox was persuaded to go with Erskine of Dun to his residence in Angus, where he remained about a month. During all that time he preached every day to audiences consisting of the principal people of the neighborhood. He then went south to Calder House, where he was kindly entertained by Sir James Sandilands, and preached there with similar results. Among his hearers were Archibald Campbell, Lord Lorn, afterward earl of Argyll; John, Lord Erskine, afterward earl of Mar; and James Stewart, prior of St. Andrews, afterward earl of Murray and regent of the kingdom.

Early next year Knox visited Kyle, that district of the west where believers of Reformed faith first constituted a society in Scotland, and where they were now quite numerous. There he preached in many places, and especially in the town of Ayr, with greater publicity than before. On several occasions, both in the east and west, he also administered the Lord's Supper after the scriptural example. It was thus that his work became known to the clergy. Until now they had not been aware that he was in the country. Attempts were forthwith made to have him arrested, but without success. He was then summoned to appear before a convention in Edinburgh, May 15, 1556. He came to the city, but accompanied by a number of gentlemen resolved to protect him from injustice. In those circumstances the bishops, especially as they were not sure what side the regent might take, must have perceived that to dispose of him without a full discussion of the doctrines in question between them was impossible. With such an adversary public debate of doctrine was not desirable. Accordingly, they met before the time appointed, and on the plea of some informality in the summons set the convention aside. During the ten days following Knox remained in Edinburgh, and preached to larger assemblies than before, no man venturing to hinder him.

The queen-regent being still thought to be secretly inclined to the Reformation, Knox wrote her a letter in the hope of eliciting a declaration to that effect. It turned out otherwise. She took occasion to declare herself on the other side by handing the letter to the archbishop of Glasgow, with a contemptuous remark. It was plain that she had now leagued her interests with those of the bishops. New severities were in prospect for the Protestants. New obstacles were to be thrown in their way. The evangelization of the Scottish Church could not be effected yet. Things were not ripe. Patience a little longer would be better than provocation.

Knox was called to be one of the pastors of the English congregation at Geneva, and returned thither in July, 1556, having first revisited his various preaching-places in Scotland and made a tour into Argyll, reviving in many hearts the spirit of the early days of Iona.

As soon as he was gone the clergy summoned him to appear before them, passed sentence against him in his absence and burned him in effigy.

CHAPTER III.

THE LORDS OF THE CONGREGATION.

THE demand for ecclesiastical reform in Scotland began in the west country, especially in Ayrshire, and on the eastern coast at different places from Berwick to Montrose, with the central Lowlands along the Forth and the Clyde. Farther to the south, and in the northern counties, it grew up more slowly. In Ayrshire the Lollards of Kyle had formed their society before the close of the fifteenth century. When Wishart went into that district he found several of the nobility and gentry prepared to defend him. Subsequently, Harlaw and Knox successively enjoyed the protection of the earls of Cassilis and of Glencairn. In 1556, Knox was taken by one of his Ayrshire friends to the earl of Argyll at his residence of Castle Campbell, where the Reformer remained several days and preached. To the doctrine which he then heard the aged nobleman gave his cordial assent, and remained attached to the end of his life. His son, Lord Lorn, was already one of its adherents. On the east, the earls of Angus and of Morton, whatever may have been their spiritual interest in its truth, chose their profit or their loss with its fortune. Others, as Sir James Sandilands (Lord St. John), and a number of the principal gentry, as John Erskine, laird of Dun, were early its friends from the purest motives. They were all well-educated, well-informed men, and better versed in Scripture than were the Catholic clergy of their day.

On the occasion of Knox's visit to Dun, in 1556, most of the gentlemen of Mearns professed their attachment to the Reformed religion by partaking of the Lord's Supper together. They also entered into a solemn bond by which they renounced the Romish worship and engaged to promote the pure preaching of the gospel as Providence might enable them.

A similar covenant was drawn up next year and signed at Edinburgh, on the 3d of December, by the Protestant lords generally and by many others.

After the second removal of Knox to Geneva, the Protestants of Scotland remained faithful to their profession, but carefully avoided all action which might give ground of offence to the government. In their relations to one another they followed the instructions which Knox had left them, in withdrawing from the Romish service, and constituting themselves into congregations in different parts of the country, with some degree of privacy. For a time, destitute of ministers, they could not enjoy the sacraments, but certain persons of their number were chosen to read the Scriptures, to exhort and to pray in their meetings. They also elected elders for the maintenance of order and supervision in general, and deacons to collect and distribute alms to the poor.

During the war with England, which began in 1556 and continued through next year, the Protestants enjoyed considerable freedom, the authorities of government being otherwise occupied than in harassing their own people. Reformed doctrine made great progress both as to the number of converts and the freedom of their profession. Encouraged by these circumstances, some of them, at whose head were the earl of Glencairn and the Lords Lorn, Erskine and James Stewart, wrote to Knox, informing him of their condition, representing it as hopeful, and expressing their wish that he would return and resume his ministrations among them. He accordingly left Geneva in October, 1557, but upon reaching Dieppe met with other news. Things had assumed a more discouraging aspect, and his friends no longer felt justified in advising him to come home. After waiting and corresponding with them about three months, he became convinced that the way was not yet prepared for him to do any good by visiting Scotland. He returned to Geneva.

The cause of that change lay in the concern with which the Catholic clergy in Scotland had seen the growth of dissent in the parishes. Protected by some of the nobility, Reformed priests had ventured to preach in different places among the dissenting congregations. The vigilance of persecution was quickened throughout the country, while the bishops prevailed with the regent to summon for trial at Edinburgh the ministers who had presumed to preach without their permission. That process, however, was stopped by the appearance of certain gentlemen from the west with a remonstrance, which induced the regent to forbid the molestation of Protestants.

The meeting of the nobles and barons attached to the Reformation, held at Edinburgh in December, 1557, recommended certain regulations to all their people in common.

It was thought by them expedient, for the then existing exigency, "that in all parishes of this realm the Common Prayer be read weekly on Sunday and other festival days publicly in the parish churches, with the lessons of the Old and New Testament, conformed to the order of the Book of Common Prayer.[1] And if the curates

---

[1] Their first substitute for the mass was the "Book set forth by the

of the parishes be qualified, to cause them to read the same; and if they be not, or if they refuse, that the most qualified in the parish use and read the same.

"Secondly: It is thought necessary that doctrine, preaching and interpretation of Scriptures be had and used privately in quiet houses, without great conventions of the people thereto, until afterward that God move the prince to grant public preaching by faithful and true ministers."

The former of these resolutions could take effect, of course, only where the residing barons were Protestant and the people either of the same belief or disposed to comply. But of the disposition of the common people we learn something from the record that the images were stolen away from the churches in all parts of the country, and that the dissenting conventions and councils were held with "great gravity and closeness," uninterrupted by any popular disturbance.

In accordance with the second, the Reformed preachers were taken into the houses of the nobility and protected as chaplains. This was still more alarming to the hierarchy than the former practice of itinerancy. Preachers entertained in the families of the principal nobility of the kingdom were beyond the reach of perse-

---

godly King Edward."—*Letter of William Kircaldy*, quoted by Froude, vol. vii. p. 111.

cution. Attempts were made to withdraw that protection from them.

The earl of Argyll had invited to his house and retained as his chaplain John Douglas, a converted Carmelite friar, and employed him in preaching among his people. Relying upon the friendship existing between the Campbells and Hamiltons, the primate addressed an appeal to the earl, urging, in a very courteous manner, the danger of harboring such men as Douglas in their heresy.

Argyll's reply closed all avenue of hope in that quarter. It was temperate but firm, defended the doctrine preached by the chaplain as that of Scripture, and refused to dismiss him. It mentioned the topics of his moral instruction with high commendation, in language which the primate could not fail to apply to his own scandalous life. The earl added that if his lordship of St. Andrews could furnish him with more such preachers as Douglas, he would gladly, and with thanks to his lordship, provide them with a corporal living. "For truly," said he, "I and many more have great need of such men. And because I am able to sustain more than one of them, I will request your lordship earnestly to provide me such a man. For the harvest is great, and there are few laborers."

Foiled in that attempt, the archbishop turned his rage against preachers still within his power.

Walter Milne, an aged parish priest, condemned as a heretic in the time of Cardinal Beaton, but who had escaped and continued to preach in private from place to place, was now discovered and brought to trial at St. Andrews. He was condemned, and burned to death on the 28th of August, 1558. As the flames began to rise about him he addressed a few words to the spectators, and closed thus: "As for me, I am fourscore and two years old, and cannot live long by course of nature; but a hundred better shall rise out of the ashes of my bones. I trust in God I shall be the last that shall suffer death in Scotland for this cause."

The public indignation created by that execution exceeded anything of the kind that had gone before. People who had hitherto remained quiet and submitted to prudential limitations now bade defiance to ecclesiastical terrors and openly joined the Protestants.

Great national changes do not, in Scotland, proceed upon sudden impulses. Even those which have been precipitated by some unexpected event will be found, on inquiry, to have been long preparing in the peaceful agitation of social intercourse. Apparently, the Reformation was the work of a few months. In reality, it was the growth of more than half a century. History cannot trace all the course whereby it gradually reached maturity. But from the burning of Patrick Hamilton to that of George Wishart, and from that to the burning of Walter Milne, are its two most momentous stages. Boys and youth, startled into inquiry by the first of those events, and thereby enlisted in the controversy which never ceased through all the intervening time, were men of middle age, fully prepared to take public action promptly, on occasion of the last.

A progress is obvious in the sentiment and demonstrations made as the change went on. The surprise, leading to earnest inquiry, in the case of Patrick Hamilton, and which rose to a feeling of revenge and insurrection, which had to be reduced by arms, in that of George Wishart, was changed on the burning of Walter Milne into a national purpose of revolution, waiting only a proper time to break forth into fact. So plainly did that temper make itself understood as national that another execution of the kind was never ventured on.

Reformed ministers now felt safe in breaking over the limitations to which they had deemed it prudent to submit, and began to preach in public and to administer the sacraments. Harlaw, Douglas, Paul Methven and others thus boldly dared forthwith, and in a few weeks they were joined by John Willock, once more returned from Hanover. A new invitation had been already sent to John Knox. But it was slow in reaching him, and because of other obstacles he did not arrive in Edinburgh until the 2d of May next.

Meanwhile the Protestant nobles had laid their complaint before the regent, requesting that, "by her authority and in concurrence with Parliament," she would "restrain the violence of the clergy, correct the flagrant abuses which prevailed in the Church, and grant to them and their brethren the liberty of religious instruction and worship, at least according to a restricted plan, which they laid before her." After repeated experience of her duplicity and unreliableness, they had been brought to the point of open war. At that juncture John Knox arrived. A few days later, the Protestant leaders, once more betrayed by the regent, felt constrained to withdraw from her government.

Means were accordingly taken to ascertain the number of their friends, and to establish correspondence and the strictest bonds of obligation among them. Their covenant was committed to persons who procured subscriptions to it in their respective districts. Thus all the Reformed in the country learned of their common strength and secured organization. In the language of their covenant, they were the Congregation, and the noblemen, who so far had moved at their head, were the Lords of the Congregation.

That body of noblemen included the earls of Argyll, Glencairn, Monteith and Rothes, Lords Ochiltree, Boyd, Ruthven, and the prior of St. Andrews, Lord James Stewart. Some who were friendly to Reformed religion still abode by the regent or remained neutral. "A large proportion of the lesser barons belonged to the Congregation," especially in that belt of country which lies diagonally across the kingdom from Mearns and Fife on the east to Carrick and Galloway on the west.

Leadership on the conservative side was in the hands of no feeble champion. Men enervated by sloth and vicious indulgence occupied places of great emolument in the Church, and ignorance and incapacity prevailed among the clergy high and low; but neither ignorance nor incapacity were charged upon the primate. He was very far from being a man of pure morals, but his learning was respectable, even in that noonday of accomplished scholarship, and his natural ability more than common. Had the Romish system stood in fair esteem before the people, the primacy of John Hamilton would have evinced no signs of weakness. It was his lot to contend against the progress of his time, to stand in resistance to the increasing breadth and light of the national convictions. Consequently, his most energetic measures were defeated and stamped with the brand of inefficiency by the adverse and irresistible current of events.

John Hamilton was the natural son of James, first earl of Arran. He early evinced a taste and capacity for letters, and well improved the facilities afforded him for their culture. He studied at Glasgow, and afterward at Paris, with marked success. Made abbot of Paisley in 1525, he continued his residence in France until his half-brother was elevated to the regency. Next year, 1543, he was appointed keeper of the privy seal, and in 1545 made bishop of Dunkeld, and after the death of Cardinal Beaton, in 1546, promoted to the primacy.

As archbishop he entered upon office with the purpose of suppressing the Reformed faith in Scotland. The cautious silence, so generally observed by persons of that persuasion after the capture of St. Andrews and the exile of their ablest leaders, rendered it difficult to ascertain the opinions of any one of them with sufficient clearness to bring him to trial. And yet many suffered great hardships, from suspicions more or less sustained, under his rule, and demonstrated heresy was subjected without mercy to the death penalty. His first public act, after his consecration, was the trial of Adam Wallace, arrested by his orders on the charge of heresy.

Wallace was accused of having preached

without proper license, of having baptized one of his own children, of denying the existence of purgatory, the intercessory power of saints and transubstantiation of the elements in the Eucharist. He declared that he had never presumed on preaching, and the contrary was not proved; his act of baptizing was only an irregularity; the valid charges were the other three. On all of them he defended himself from the Bible. He was reproved for meddling with the Bible. That was a book which it belonged to the clergy alone to read and understand. Condemnation was passed upon him, and he was burned to death on the Castle Hill of Edinburgh, as if the example were to read a lesson of conformity to the whole nation.

But there was one cause of complaint in the Church, and much in the mouths of Reformers, which could not be encountered in that way, and touching which no man felt the necessity of silence. It was the often-mentioned licentiousness and arrogance of the clergy, in which some of the highest dignitaries were the most notoriously guilty. It had long been a ground of complaint. It was undeniable. No censure had checked it. What was to be done about it? Archbishop Hamilton perceived that his order had lost ground in general esteem, and the few who were guiltless of the common vice were the most humiliated by the degradation.

The people also needed instruction of a nature to counterbalance the Protestant books, which could not be kept out of the country. Some steps must be taken to set forth Catholic doctrine in a way to propitiate public favor.

A national council was called in 1549 to take these matters seriously into consideration. Action was there taken in regard to the clergy, exhorting them to amend their lives, and specifically prohibiting, under severe penalties, the vices of which it was well known that many of them were guilty, and some had no intention of reforming.

"Provision was also made for preaching to the people; for teaching grammar, divinity and canon law in cathedrals and abbeys; for visiting and reforming monasteries, nunneries and hospitals; for recalling fugitives and apostates, whether monks or nuns, to their cloisters;" for silencing itinerant sellers of indulgences and relics; and, in general, for correcting the alarming multitude of abuses which had crept into the Church silently, and retained their place by force of the number of persons interested in them.

But there were other evils, regarded as the most serious of all by readers of the Bible, and which the bishops could not remove. Those were some of the so-deemed orthodox tenets and practices of the Roman Catholic Church.

On such points conciliation was not to be thought of. Heresy was to be sought out and persecuted with increased watchfulness and severity, and heretical books, especially "poems and ballads against the Church or clergy, were to be diligently sought after and burned."

Measures were also taken to bring out a kind of religious literature which the bishops thought would instruct and interest the people and help to retain them in allegiance to the Catholic Church. In this connection the Aberdeen Breviary, in course of preparation perhaps many years before, made its appearance, with its wonderful tales of saints and their miracles and general treasury of Roman Catholic examples. It was printed in 1550—far too late for any effect but to arouse the ridicule of men who had learned from their Bibles.

Another work, sanctioned by the national council of 1551, was a catechism for popular instruction, prepared by some unknown author, but, from the sanction conferred upon it by the primate, called "Archbishop Hamilton's Catechism." It was written in a spirit of charity and great moderation, presenting Catholic dogma in the least offensive way to persons of Protestant persuasion; and for that reason attributed, with strong probability, to Sub-prior Winram of St. Andrews. It appeared in a volume of four hundred and forty pages, small quarto, handsomely printed in Old English black-letter at the expense of the archbishop, and bearing date St. Andrews, August 29, 1552, containing instructions on the Commandments, Seven Sacraments, Creed, Lord's Prayer, Magnificat and Ave Maria; it was in the Scottish dialect, and designed to be read to the people in church by portions. "As much as would occupy half an hour" was to be read from the pulpit every Sunday and holiday with a loud voice, clearly, distinctly, impressively, solemnly, by the rector, vicar or curate in his surplice or stole.

For a similar purpose, but as much inferior in merit as it was smaller in size, was the pamphlet issued by the national council of 1559. Especially designed to be read as a preparation for receiving the sacrament of the Eucharist, it set forth the doctrine of transubstantiation in what was thought to be a popular way. It consisted of only four pages in black-letter, and was sold for twopence Scots. The Reformers greeted it with derision, and dubbed it the "Two-penny Faith."

All such efforts for the inner reform and fortifying of the Romish cause came too late for success. The dissenting Reformation which they were designed to supersede had got too much headway, covered too much ground, to be effectually encountered within such narrow bounds. On the subject of clerical morality not much could be done with any reformatory effect. Who was to inflict the penalty? who to throw the first stone? The bishops were themselves guilty, and the primate most of all. Inner reform of the Church had failed. Recall of Protestants was now hopeless. On their part, rational conviction had been set on fire by the cruelties of persecution; return to their rejected superstitions was out of the question.

The principal business of the council of 1559 was to consider some suggestions offered by certain laymen attached to the Church. The changes which they urged were in discipline and conduct. Down to that date no improvement had taken place. Nor had the action of that council any other effect than once more, by rebuking, to acknowledge the existence of long-censured iniquity, and to drive many churchmen into the ranks of the Reformers. It was the last council of the Roman Catholic establishment of Scotland.

All the primate's efforts to reconcile heretics had proved fruitless, and his burning of some of them, instead of intimidating the rest, had only provoked alienation and wrath. The weapons he wielded crumbled in his grasp. Still, though worsted, he never surrendered, but fought for his ground, inch by inch, to the end. One of his next public acts was in Parliament, in 1560, to vote in a similarly ineffective way against the Reformation. He survived the crisis of that great revolution of faith, and saw himself subjected to some little experience of that restraint he had so often laid upon others. In 1563 he was brought to trial before the Judiciary Court of Edinburgh for hearing auricular confession and celebrating mass, and punished by imprisonment. But again he came up on the winning side by the favor of Queen Mary. For a time he was one of her privy council, and held a commission under the great seal restoring jurisdiction in the probate of testaments and other things pertaining to the spiritual court. He opposed the act of Mary in leaving her kingdom, and, it is said, urgently remonstrated with her to the last.

Under the succeeding regency Hamilton was denounced as a traitor. After hiding for some time among his friends, he took refuge in the castle of Dumbarton, which was then held for France. It was taken by the national forces on the 2d of April, 1571. The ex-archbishop was carried a prisoner to Stirling, and on the ground of complicity in the murder of Lord Darnley, but in virtue of a previous attainder by act of Parliament, was there, in his episcopal robes, hanged over the battlements of the castle on the 6th of the month.

Thus died the last primate of the Roman Catholic establishment in Scotland.

CHAPTER IV.

MARY OF LORRAINE AND THE PEOPLE.

THE second wife of James V. survived him seventeen years and six months. A daughter of Claude of Lorraine, first duke of Guise, and sister of Francis, the second duke, and of the cardinal Charles of Lorraine, she partook of the uncommon ability of her family, in that its best day. With a degree of liberality toward Protestants which her brothers never possessed, she was equally with them attached to the Catholic Church. Her humane disposition and well-balanced good sense, while allowed to act freely, secured her popularity in a land which never loved the rule of a foreigner. The misleading bias of her character was the amiable one of strong attachment to her brothers, whereby she was disposed to put their judgment above her own, and that part of her education which led her to undervalue the truth.

From the death of her husband, in 1542, until her appointment to the regency, in 1554, Mary of Lorraine held no official place in the government of Scotland; but her own personal place and character gradually vindicated for her an influence in its affairs which increased after the death of Cardinal Beaton. And when her daughter had been betrothed to the heir of the throne of France the ambition of her kindred was sustained by that of the French court in seeking for her a constitutional authority.

That was a proud day for Claude of Lorraine. While his oldest son was rising to the position of the first subject of France, and his younger son just created cardinal at the age of twenty-two, his granddaughter, born queen of Scotland, was betrothed to the future king of France, with the prospect of uniting both kingdoms, if not also England, under their rule and in her right. Claude did not live to see the end of those splendid and not unreasonable expectations, nor to know the depths of calamity in which some of them set. The next fifteen years were the summit of prosperity to the house of Guise—a prosperity which in its best estate had more of hope than fruition.

The queen-dowager of Scotland understood well the party differences between the Catholics and Reformed. It was the same controversy in which her brothers were so earnestly engaged in her native land. And it was not difficult to see how the regent Arran had lost the confidence of one of those parties without securing that of the other. Her policy, as well as natural disposition, guarded her against his errors. The head of the house of Hamilton was nearest heir to the Scottish throne in the case of her daughter's death without children. But the leading mind in that house was not the ex-regent, but the archbishop of St. Andrews. To counteract him, operating through and sustained by the clergy, it became her policy to strengthen her adherents among the Catholic laity by a moderate toleration of the Protestants. Nor was it indispensable to alienate the clergy as a whole. There were some among them who could take little interest in the ambition of the Hamiltons. The position of Mary of Lorraine, during the first five years of her administration, was strong in the good-will of the people, and, unintentionally on her part, of of the greatest benefit to the Reformation.

Mistaking her motives, the Protestant leaders expected too much in hoping to bring her over to their cause. Knox's letter, written to her with that view in a respectful but authoritative manner, provoked an indignant remark and the assuming of an attitude to repel all hope of her conversion. They became alarmed, and, from apprehension that premature haste might seriously prejudice their cause, adopted those measures of caution already mentioned. But for two years longer whatever hardships they suffered were not inflicted by the regent.

Of one mistake, however, she never saw the

danger until too late. She persisted in the practice of employing Frenchmen in places of power and emolument in the state. And the attempt, by a new system of taxation, to keep in pay a standing army, instead of relying upon the patriotism of the nobility, although defeated, was followed by accepting from France a body-guard of foreigners.

It had already become a settled purpose of the Guises and the court of France to secure the subjection of Scotland to their interests, if not directly to French dominion. The marriage of Mary Stuart with the dauphin took place on the 24th of April, 1558. Among the preliminaries it was subsequently discovered that the young queen had been persuaded, by her kinsmen, to sign certain papers conveying her kingdom to the royal family of France. Her husband was to be king of Scotland. The commissioners sent by the Estates of Scotland to represent their country in the nuptial solemnities were required to send for the Scottish *regalia*, that the coronation might be complete. They declined. In other respects they were also offended with the evidences of a spirit of usurpation. Upon their way home three of their number, Lords Cassilis and Rothes and Bishop Reid of Orkney, were taken suddenly ill and died at Dieppe. The remaining three, Lord James Stewart, Erskine of Dun and the archbishop of Glasgow, when making the report before the Estates, presented also a request, in the name of the queen, that the "crown matrimonial" should be conferred on her husband. It was granted, but with the limitation that it was to be merely a compliment, and to continue during the marriage alone.

An accidental wound in a tournament carried off Henry II., July 10, 1559, and Francis II. and Mary became king and queen of France and Scotland. They had already assumed the title to England; for Mary Tudor had died the preceding year, and Mary Stuart, in the eyes of Catholics, was the only heir to the English throne. In the mental and bodily feebleness of Francis II., as well as his immature age, being only sixteen, the duke Francis of Lorraine took the management of public affairs, leagued with his brother the cardinal and the queen-dowager, Catherine de Medici.

To the success of their plans the Guises held that the destruction of Protestantism was of first importance. A frightful persecution was commenced in France. Protestantism alone stood between them and the throne of England for their niece, for none save Protestants admitted the legitimacy of Elizabeth. A united Catholic France, with a united Catholic Scotland, upon invasion of England would be joined by the Catholics of that country, still a very large minority of the population; and all three kingdoms were to be subjects of the one crown. It was certainly a glorious plan, and not impracticable, as it appeared to the daring Francis of Lorraine and his ambitious cardinal brother.

Intimation was forthwith communicated to the queen-regent of Scotland of the new scheme. Her judgment rejected it, her feelings revolted from it. She remonstrated. By what method of persuasion we know not, her reluctance was overcome and her whole government changed. Friendship was now sought with the Scottish primate, and the best relations with the Catholic clergy. Protestants were ordered to worship according to the rites of the Roman Church. That order was to take effect immediately upon the ensuing Easter of 1560. Protestant delegates waited upon her, and ventured to remonstrate on the ground that their ministers preached the truth and peacefully. She replied that "they should be banished out of Scotland, albeit they preached as truly as ever did St. Paul." When her former promises were adduced, her answer was that "it became not subjects to burden their princes with promises further than they please to keep them."

About the same time, the Reformed worship was set up and very numerously attended in the town of Perth. The regent sent orders to the provost to suppress it, and also commissioned persons to persuade the people of Montrose and Dundee to observe Easter in the prescribed Romish manner. For disobedience the preachers were summoned to appear before the privy council at Stirling on the 10th of May, 1560. A number of gentlemen resolved to accompany them without arms, as peaceful men, intending only to give their confession together with their preachers. Erskine of Dun went on before them to inform the regent of their intention. He soon reported to them her assurance that, if they would disperse, the citations should be withdrawn. The assembly complied, and many of them returned to their homes. But the promise was not kept. When the appointed day arrived the citations were read out, and the persons cited, not appearing, were outlawed and proclaimed rebels. Erskine, indignant that he should have been made the agent of the regent's perfidy, withdrew from her service.

This was on the 10th of May. Eight days before, John Knox had landed at Leith, and on the day after the preachers were outlawed he preached in Perth. He now found the nation ripe for revolution in religion, and boldly opened the attack upon the idolatry of the Romish Church. By accident, during the interval of worship, while the congregation was absent, a mob was excited which broke down the images in church and destroyed the monasteries.

The regent was enraged, and threatened to lay the city in ruins. The Protestants once more assembled to protect their ministers. An army of seven thousand marched against them. They were not half that number. But a few days before, some of their circular letters had been carried away south-west into Kyle and Cunningham, and came into the hands of the earl of Glencairn, who, together with a large number of his neighbors, convened at the church of Craigie. After some diversity of opinion had been expressed, the earl rose and said, "Let every man serve his conscience. I will, by God's grace, see my brethren in St. Johnston [Perth]. Yea, albeit never a man should accompany me, I will go, and if it were only with a pick upon my shoulder, for I had rather die with that company than live after them." The whole assembly resolved to go with him, and their number soon increased. The earl reached Perth at the head of two thousand five hundred men, of whom twelve hundred were cavalry, and with them the preacher John Willock. The numbers on each side of the conflict were now more fairly matched. The regent consented to a treaty, of which the conditions were that if the people of the town were not troubled for the late change of religion and attack on the monasteries, and if the Reformation were allowed to go forward, and if the French garrisons were removed, she should be obeyed by them in all things.

The terms were agreed to, and next day the Congregation departed from Perth. No sooner were they gone than the regent entered with her troops and priests, in utter disregard of the agreement. The earl of Argyll and Lord James Stewart, disgusted with her untruth, withdrew from her counsels, and with them followed the Lord Ruthven, the earl of Monteith and others.

The Congregation reassembled, and, with Argyll and Lord James at their head, occupied St. Andrews. A force was sent from Linlithgow to expel them. But they were too strong to submit to that process. The result was another treaty, under which the regent withdrew her troops to the south of the Forth, promising to send a commissioner to treat with the Lords of the Congregation more fully. The commissioner never came. Her aim was to gain time until an army should arrive from France.

The Reformers marched to Edinburgh, which they entered without resistance. The regent had retreated to Dunbar. Subsequently, when many of them had scattered to their homes, she came back, and with her French troops enforced a compromise whereby the two parties occupied the city together in peace.

In a short time the expected French reinforcements arrived and fortified themselves in Leith. They were joined by the regent, who by that time had alienated the confidence of her wisest adherents. She was now deserted by the duke of Châtelherault, the earl of Arran and Maitland of Lethington.

Meanwhile, the Lords had formed a treaty with Queen Elizabeth. When the French were commencing their work of conquest by ravaging the coast of Fife, an English squadron entered the Forth. The French had hastily to betake themselves to their camp, which was soon besieged by the united English and Scottish forces.

Mary of Lorraine, suffering under sickness, was removed to the castle of Edinburgh, where she received the utmost respect and attention. Aware that her disease was incurable, she had a conference with some of the Reformed leaders—Argyll, Glencairn, the Lords James Stewart and Marichal—to whom she expressed deep regret for the course she had latterly pursued and the condition to which things had been reduced, but plead that the blame had not orignated with herself. Her remaining hours were given to concerns of religion, in which she willingly held a conversation of some length with the Reformed preacher, John Willock. She died on the 19th of June, 1560, while the siege of Leith was still going on. The faults of her last few months obscured to all future time the wisdom of more than as many years.

A populace, no matter how intelligent individually, as a whole cannot understand themselves without an interpreter, nor move to any wise and permanent result without a leader. To be a true leader a man must fully understand and be imbued with the purpose of the people, and possessed of ability to expound it to themselves and to others, and to regulate their impulses prudently. He may be one of superior rank, but better for his calling is it to be one of themselves. He may be elected by them or moved from within himself, but, in either case, what he is sustained by them in effecting for them must be taken as the exponent of their purpose.

When we find the poems of Sir David Lindsay enjoying a popularity unprecedented in that country, we must infer that they gave expression to sentiments entertained by a numerous portion of the Scottish people. Although those of Dunbar had less extensive circulation, yet, in as far as they treated the same topics in a similar spirit, they met the same favor. The public sentiment, thus signified, may not yet have created a political party, but it is evident that there was something in it which a daring and skillful leader might make use of to that end. Such a leader was slow in coming to the front.

In the Scottish Reformation the first conspicuous men were scholars, preachers of the gospel, humble, modest, retiring and averse to political agitation. Even the statesmen who first belonged to it, such as Balnavis, were, in as far as they were Reformers, more devotional than polemic. In its early days the Scottish Reformation was purely religious and moral, and avoided all complication with politics. The few noblemen who availed themselves of its support for attainment of their own ends took that step at a later time, when its power was more pronounced. Yet, though not forming a political party, the men whose religious views determined the election of a regent after the death of James V., and that in opposition to the plans of Cardinal Beaton, must be recognized as a power in the state. Mary of Lorraine recognized them as such, and for years courted their favor to elevate and sustain herself in office.

And yet there is a way of expression, inarticulate but unmistakable, sometimes adopted by the people themselves. The attacks upon monastic houses, made in 1543 at Dundee and various other places, were not the work of robbers, but of Christian people in detestation of monkish immorality, as American "vigilance committees" sometimes clear out gamblers, debauchees and other corrupters of public morals. They were acts of reformation after the crude, impulsive way of popular justice. When instructed by their wiser men in the necessity of law-abiding quiet and diffusion of knowledge in order to success, all outbreak of violence was avoided for years; for in the death of Cardinal Beaton the public had no hand. Religious knowledge spread rapidly between the death of James V. and the burning of Walter Milne. The act of Parliament passed in the beginning of that interval, allowing people of all classes to read the Bible, was itself an act of reformation, and fertile of all other things rightly pertaining to the cause. When Parliament afterward repealed that act, it could not withdraw the Bibles; it only constrained the people to hold them in closer keeping and to value them more highly.

The first leaders to give the Reformation a political place in the land were the noblemen who latterly became known as the Lords of the Congregation. But such was the progress of Protestant persuasion in that interval that when the Lords sent out the Covenant for subscription, they received the most definite evidence that the greater part of the people of Scotland were in favor of it.

The burning of Walter Milne in April, 1558,

and subsequently the queen-regent's change of policy, and reckless deceit in her dealings with the lords, causing them successively to withdraw from her court, as well as the knowledge of their own numerical strength, rapidly removed the weight of those restraints to which the Protestant people had long submitted. The next few months saw many cases of popular outbreak, though *not a single one of bloodshed* or personal injury. *Idols, not men*, were the objects of violence. Biblical instruction, enforced and applied by their preachers, had well enlightened the congregations on the nature of image-worship. They wanted no more of it. Yet they could not go to church without having their convictions insulted and their devotions disturbed with everywhere-recurring objects of idolatry. Those objects of idolatrous worship were removed by the Christian people. Who was to be injured by it? Congregations who preferred them of course did not remove them. It was the most harmless kind of iconoclasm—people themselves destroying their own idols which they had formerly worshiped, and that without hurt to their priestly custodians.

The images soon disappeared from the churches in most parts of the country quietly. In some of the large cities the change created more sensation. At Edinburgh the great idol of the cathedral church of St. Giles was taken out and drowned in the North Loch, and afterward burned. The priests were in dismay, and urged the bishops to bring the sacrilegious perpetrators to punishment. The bishops applied to the regent. She was not yet prepared to disoblige either party, but consented to summon the Protestant preachers to trial for it. The preachers complied, and with them came many of their friends. The bishops were alarmed, and procured a proclamation that all who had come to the city without orders should forthwith repair to the English border, and remain there fifteen days. It happened that a large number of those present were west-country men, who that very day had returned from service on the border, and who recognized no right in any quarter to send them back. Indignant at the unreasonable proclamation, they made their way to the apartment where the regent and the bishops sat in council. In very plain terms they made complaint of the injustice done to them who had been obedient in all things lawful. One of their number, James Chalmers, stood forward as spokesman, and boldly charged their grievances upon the bishops and the primate there present, and added, "We vow to God we shall make a day of it. They oppress us and our tenants for feeding of their idle bellies. They trouble our preachers, and would murder them and us. Shall we suffer this any longer? Nay, madam, it shall not be." And every man put on his steel bonnet.

"My joys, my hearts, what ails you?" said the queen soothingly. "Me means no evil to you, nor to your preachers. The bishops shall do you no wrong. Ye are all my loving subjects. Me knows nothing of this proclamation. The day of your preachers shall be discharged, and me will hear the controversy that is betwixt the bishops and you. They shall do you no wrong." Then turning to the bishops, "My lords," said she, "I forbid you to trouble them or their preachers." Again to the other party, who were moved by her kind words, she added, "O my hearts, should ye not love the Lord your God with all your heart and with all your mind, and should ye not love your neighbors as yourselves?"

So the summons was set aside, and no account taken of the tragic end of old St. Giles.

But his anniversary, September 1st, was at hand, when he was to be carried in procession; and what was to be done without him, the principal character in the solemnity? The town council was required by the clergy to replace the image destroyed. They replied that to them the requisition seemed unjust. "For they understood that God, in some places, had commanded idols and images to be destroyed;

but where he had commanded idols and images to be set up they had not read." A warm dispute on the subject issued in an appeal to the pope, which was never carried out. A smaller image of somebody was borrowed from the Gray Friars as a substitute for the occasion. It was nailed on a *fertor*, or bier, and borne in the usual procession through the streets, accompanied by a long array of ecclesiastics with the noisiest kind of music. The queen-regent followed it part of the way, and, out of respect to her, the populace suffered the thing to go on. But when she withdrew, their contempt took its own way. In changing the bearers of the *fertor* certain persons took places among them who carried it very disrespectfully. Others, perceiving the image to be fastened in its place, took hold of it and pulled it off, and broke it to pieces on the pavement, many voices exclaiming, "Fy upon you, young St. Giles! your father would have stood four times as much." The priests, thinking that violence was intended them also, took to their heels, each according to his ability, and the solemn procession ended in a ridiculous rout amid the laughter of the multitude. And so ended the tragedy of St. Giles.

Such transactions could not be confined to the godly. Some of their features were too attractive to the mischief-loving element of the populace. On the 11th of May, 1558, John Knox preached in Perth, and dwelt much on the unscriptural nature of idolatry. After the sermon, when the people were gone away, a priest very imprudently, perhaps in bravado, uncovered a rich altarpiece in which were finely carved images, and prepared to say mass. A few people were still lingering about, and among them a boy, who called out with a loud voice, "This is intolerable, that when God, by his word, hath plainly damned idolatry, we shall stand and see it used in despite." The priest struck him. Whereupon the boy threw a stone, which, missing the priest, knocked down and broke one of the images. Immediately other persons rushed in from the street and completed the damage. In a few minutes all the apparatus of idolatry was swept away from the church.

That done, the multitude proceeded to the monasteries of the Black and Grey Friars, and to that of the Carthusians, a very wealthy institution, and demolished them. Their gold and silver plate and other portable wealth the monks were allowed to carry with them; their provisions and furniture were given to the poor, but the buildings were razed to the ground.

None of the leading Reformers were engaged in that affair. Purely an unpremeditated outburst of the lower popular feeling, it was regretted by the ministers, but encountered little or no censure from the general public. It was soon imitated elsewhere, as at Cupar in Fife, St. Andrews, Stirling and Linlithgow; and the leaders were constrained to content themselves with regulating and limiting what they could not prevent. As a general thing, monasteries were destroyed, while churches were spared, but stripped of all objects of idolatrous veneration. The ruined condition of many large and once beautiful churches in Scotland is due chiefly to war and natural decay. Melrose, Dryburgh, Kelso, Jedburgh and others suffered from the violence of English armies in previous invasions, not from the Reformers.[1] Others, in the course of ages, gradually fell into ruin from neglect, because they were no longer needed. After the revenues which once belonged to them were suspended or turned to other accounts, there were no funds to keep them in repair. When the hosts of unnecessary ecclesiastics were disbanded, and where the parish church was large enough to accommodate the parish population, there was no longer any use for such gigantic and expensive piles. Where that was not the case, the great church was retained and adapted,

---

[1] See Veitch, *Border History*, p. 172, etc., which may be called "Henry VIII.'s wooing for his son."

as at Stirling and at Glasgow, to the simpler Protestant worship. At St. Andrews the cathedral, which really was not needed for church accommodation, and served only the purposes of ecclesiastics whom the people wished to expel, was deliberately torn down. It was thought best to "destroy the rookery," so as to leave no inducement for the rooks to return. There were reasons at St. Andrews for exceptional completeness.

CHAPTER V.

JOHN KNOX.

SUCH had been the progress of opinion in Scotland by the year 1559 that a prudent leader had become a national necessity. Had the Reformation not been effected by soberminded men in a regular way, a revolution must have occurred from the impulse of popular indignation, no longer to be restrained. In addition to the corruption of the Romish Church in Scotland, and the incorrigible immorality of its priesthood, their foreign policy had now clearly shown itself as a scheme for subjecting the country to the rule of France. To long suffering under religious oppression and falsehood, and thirty years of more or less gospel instruction and knowledge of the Reformation in other countries, was now added the clear demonstration that their priests were traitors to the independence of their country for the price of support in the enjoyment of their emoluments and iniquity. No leader could have carried that people with him who did not partake of their spirit; and that was the spirit of patriotism as well as of gospel religion.

John Knox arrived in Scotland on the 2d of May, 1559, at the very juncture in which he was needed. The breaking up, next day, of the council in Edinburgh, whose action would in any case have proved the one thing more than endurable, the newly-assumed attitude of the regent toward the nation, her reliance upon French arms and Scottish ecclesiastics, and the outbreak which occurred a few days after at Perth, all evinced the premonitory feeling of a national crisis and the inflammable state of the public mind. Knox, as well as other members of the Congregation, was grieved by the public violence at Perth. Desirous to see the people remove their own idols in an orderly way, he regarded it as a serious injury to the cause of truth that it should be done for them by a mob. But all that remained for him or any other at that juncture was to regulate the commotion by order and limitations.

It was the design to abolish monasticism, and the destruction of the monasteries was therefore perfectly rational. Those structures answered no purpose but to accommodate monks. It was because they were built that monks were brought into the country. In the days of St. Margaret and her sons monasteries were erected, and then monks were brought from abroad, from England and France, to live in them, and estates were appropriated to their support. The whole thing was, from the first, foreign to Scotland. Monks never had anything to do in that country but to live in the houses built for them and draw the revenues provided for them. When the people of Scotland wished to have done with the idle crew, who had also become profligate and an injury to public morals, the most rational, or at least the most natural, course, in their eyes, was to tear down the houses whose existence had brought them there, and to turn the revenues to better account. A perfectly reasonable distinction was accordingly made between the monasteries and the churches, excepting that in some places abbey churches had been constructed where they were not needed for any other purpose than that of monastic or prelatic effect. Those were, in one or two cases, put in the same class with the monasteries, but upon the whole they were spared, though stripped of their idolatrous objects of worship.

The presence of John Knox, who sympathized with the people far enough to have a strong control over them, did much to retain them within those bounds. He reached his native land, on this occasion, very fully furnished with practical knowledge of all the different systems of government existing in the Western churches. He had labored about five years in the Anglican Church under Edward VI. and Mary, and not less than four years had he been a resident of Geneva, and a great part of that time a pastor there. His residence in Germany had also brought him into some relations to the Lutherans. He had labored in co-operation or conflict with all of them. When, together with these facts, we take his long and severe study, under the Romish system, until he was thirty-seven years old, continued on a broader ground five years longer before he began to preach, and his habit of persistent study in all circumstances, we shall admit that none of the great Reformers of his time came to the work with a more complete equipment for it than John Knox.

It had now been resolved by the Lords of the Congregation that the full time was come to make an effort to relieve the nation from its long-endured grievances by abolishing the Romish religion and setting up the Reformed in all places where the people were prepared for the change. It was apparent that if not done in an orderly way and simultaneously, it would be attempted in a disorderly and scattered way. The regent had declared her purpose to drive the Reformed preachers out of the land, and was actually then employing French forces, and forces in French pay, to defeat their cause, and had ceased to observe any regard to truth in her dealings with them. Nor were the Lords ignorant of the design to reduce Scotland to the condition of a dependency of France. Lord James Stewart and Erskine of Dun had been members of the delegation to Paris on the occasion of the queen's marriage. They were fully impressed with the conviction that stronger force would soon be brought against them from abroad, and that no time was likely to be more favorable for their purpose than the present. It was also resolved that the seat of the primacy was the right place to begin.

The earl of Argyll and Lord James Stewart (who was the prior of St. Andrews), after their final separation from the regent on the 1st of June, 1559, repaired at once to St. Andrews, giving notice by writing to Erskine of Dun, and other Protestant leaders of the neighborhood, to meet them at that city on the 4th. They observed the appointment, and with them brought John Knox, who went on farther south to preach at Crail and Anstruther, and returned to St. Andrews on the 9th.

The Lords had assembled only a small body of followers, and still knew nothing about the disposition of the citizens. Archbishop Hamilton, hearing that the Reformer was expected to preach in his cathedral city next day, arrived in great haste with a body of soldiers, and after consultation held with some of his clergy, sent a messenger to say to the Lords that if John Knox should present himself in the pulpit of the cathedral, he would order the military to fire on him.

The Lords were alarmed. The life of such a man must not be rashly exposed. Among themselves they deemed it best to postpone the preaching until their own force should be more numerous or circumstances more favorable. Knox, when the proposal was made to him, thought otherwise. He had come there to preach the gospel; he had no intention to preach "in contempt of any man nor with the design of hurting any earthly creature; but to delay to preach on the morrow (unless forcibly hindered) he could not in conscience agree." "My life," said he, "is in the custody of Him whose glory I seek, and therefore I cannot so fear their boast nor tyranny that I will cease from doing my duty, when God of his mercy offereth the occasion. I desire the hand nor weapon of no man to defend me. I only crave audience; which if it be denied here unto me at this time, I must seek farther where I may have it." In short, his resolution was that, though actual force might prevent him, threats should not.

Accordingly, next day, Sunday, the 10th of June, 1559, John Knox preached in the great church of St. Andrews before a large assembly of all classes of people, lay and ecclesiastical. The military did not fire, nor was any other disturbance offered. His text was the Lord's expulsion of profane traffic from the temple at Jerusalem. Twelve years before, in that same city, he had publicly proved that the Jewish religion in the time of Christ was not more corrupt than the Romish Church was in the sixteenth century. He now took up the theme at that point, and showed that, after the example of the Lord, it was the duty of those to whom God had given the power, especially the magistrates, to cleanse the Church by removing "all monuments of idolatry."

A deep impression was produced upon the the audience, which continued to increase under the preaching of the three following days; and on the 14th of June the magistrates, with entire consent of the inhabitants, peacefully removed from their churches all objects of idolatrous veneration. They also destroyed the monasteries and set up the Reformed religion.

Intelligence of these events, sent by the archbishop to the regent, who was with her French troops at Falkland, about twelve miles off, led to the meeting at Cupar Moor already mentioned. Under the truce, there formed, the regent retired to Stirling. In a few days, the Lords were apprised of her intention to fortify the passage of the Forth at Stirling, and cut them off from connection with the Reformers of the south. To prevent that, they hastened to Perth, drove out the garrison which she had put there in violation of her solemn promise, then turned on that rapid march whereby they took Stirling and every other place on their way, until they entered Edinburgh. Knox was with them all the way, and preached in the church of St. Giles on the day of their arrival. When at Perth he had used his utmost effort to save the abbey of Scone, where the bishop of Murray was then residing. But it was burned to the ground by the multitude, in spite of all. The reason of that public persistence, perhaps not known to every one, expressed quietly by a woman in the hearing of some of those who were laboring to allay it, was perfectly sufficient.

On the 7th of July, 1559, the citizens of Edinburgh, in a public meeting in the Tolbooth, chose John Knox as their minister. That action being approved by his brethren, he accepted the charge, and continued in its duties until the Lords returned to Stirling with the Reformed forces. John Willock then took his place, while he spent the next two months on a preaching-tour. In that time he visited the country south of Edinburgh as far as Kelso and Jedburgh, proceeded westward to Dumfries, then into Ayrshire, and through the west country round to Stirling, thence northward as far as Brechin and Montrose, and back to Dundee and St. Andrews. That journey was a band of fraternal sympathy thrown around the Lowlands, not to the creation of excitement, but of a sober confidence, promoting the orderly and quiet progress of the revolution in hand. That progress, although in most places so peaceful as to attract no outward notice, was very rapid. In little more than three months from Knox's first sermon at Perth, already eight principal towns were provided with Reformed pastors, while others were vacant only because of the fewness of preachers.

CHAPTER VI.

THE FRENCH INVASION.

THE queen-regent had latterly put forth all the powers conferred upon her by Parliament to subvert the national independence. Foreign arms, under her command, were employed to enforce upon Scotland a foreign policy. From early in her term of office her influence and dignity had been sustained by the presence of a small body of French troops. As the scheme of making Scotland subservient to French designs upon England took shape, the number was increased by such small additions as seem to have attracted little attention. Some Scots were also enlisted on French pay. About the time when the conflict with the Reformers began, in May, 1559, the regular foreign force must have amounted to three thousand men. They were under command of M. d'Oysell, a partisan of the duke of Guise. At first, the regent could also, upon emergency, call together four or five thousand from the native population. The progress of events, however, soon alienated that element, and latterly her dependence rested entirely upon the French. Increased by successive reinforcements, they took possession of Leith and fortified it, as their gate to and from the sea. One thousand more were added to their number at that time, the first detachment of an army which was expected soon to follow.

Courage and capacity for military training were not lacking to the Scottish people, any more than in earlier days, but their resources had been drained by long-continued and heavy exactions. They were reduced to poverty. A few weeks in the field exhausted their means, and they could not endure taxation for support of a standing army. A small, well-trained regular force, in possession of a fortified port in communication with abundant supplies by sea, had great advantage over them.

On returning from Dunbar, the queen-regent made her head-quarters at Leith. Advancing thence to Edinburgh, she was encountered by the Reformers. A truce was agreed upon between them, to last until the 10th of January next. Among its conditions the queen was to occupy Edinburgh, while the Protestants in the city were to enjoy the freedom of their worship, as then observed. The Lords accordingly left Edinburgh on the 26th of July, 1559, and retired in the direction of Stirling. John Willock remained as minister of St. Giles, and Knox went on his tour of visitation.

The Lords could not fail to consider the increase of French troops and the continued work on the fortifications of Leith violations of the truce. French soldiers were also employed to interrupt or to disturb the Protestant worship in Edinburgh, so that often the preacher could not be heard by the congregation. Remonstrance was made with the queen in reference to these things. She replied by sending two messengers, who had nothing to propose except that "if things were submitted to the queen's will she would be gracious enough." By proclamation she also attempted to justify the increase of French troops, and by private means to create division among the Lords. Within the same time a group of French ecclesiastics arrived, consisting of Pellevè, bishop of Amiens, with three doctors of the Sorbonne. Le Broche, a French knight, accompanied them with two thousand infantry. They professed to have come to dispute with the Protestant preachers. But as they never really sought an occasion of debate, it is more probable that their mission had a view to reviving and strengthening the Romish interest in Scotland by some other persuasions, which they never had a chance to exercise.

In reply to the queen's proclamation the Lords

issued a statement, in which they again protested against the continued increase of foreign troops, and the occupation of the best harbor in the neighborhood of Edinburgh for the purpose of a foreign power, which could serve no other end to Scotland than the ruin of her independence. Having issued that declaration, they returned to Edinburgh, and took possession of it on the 18th of October. They had meanwhile been strengthened by the accession of the earl of Arran, who, having escaped from the court of France with more knowledge of its designs than was consistent with his safety there, found his way home through England. As soon as he arrived he persuaded his father, the duke of Châtelherault, to join the Reformers.

On the same day on which the Lords re-entered Edinburgh the regent took refuge in Leith, followed by the archbishops of St. Andrews and of Glasgow and other Romish ecclesiastics. The conflict had now clearly decided itself to be between the Scottish people and the Reformation on one side, and the ambition of the Guises, sustained by French arms and Romish ecclesiastics, with the regent at their head, on the other.

The demand of the people was freedom in the observance of their religion and the dismissal of the French. On the other side, subordination to the policy dictated from France, and compliance with the religion of Rome were the objects in view.

On the day after they re-entered Edinburgh the Lords sent a message informing the regent that they were convened to redress the disorders in the nation, and especially to relieve the port of Leith, that it should be free for its proper use in the national traffic, and desiring her to dismiss all foreigners and mercenary soldiers then obstructing it, and to demolish the forts erected by them; otherwise they should take it to be her intention to bring the kingdom into servitude, against which evil they must provide in the best way they could. The answer came by the Lion herald king-at-arms, and, as was to be expected, conceded nothing. It closed with ordering them all to depart from Edinburgh, under the penalties of treason if they disobeyed.

The herald was detained a few days while the Lords took counsel with a number of the barons and burgesses as to what course they should next pursue. The king and queen were still minors in a foreign land, and in the hands of the very persons creating these national troubles. A regular Parliament could not meet in the circumstances, but the imminent danger of the country called for some action on the part of its natural representatives. To human eye that danger never was greater, not even under the aggressions of Edward I. If less violent, it seemed to be more complete in the strong links of its chain of causes.

A numerous assembly of nobles, barons and representatives of boroughs met in Edinburgh to consider the state of the country, and the proposition laid before them was the expediency of deposing the regent. Already had the regency been transferred by the authorities of the nation; might it not be transferred again? Could any case more urgently demand it? There was a difference of opinion. After discussion had proceeded to some length, the two ministers, Willock and Knox, were called on for their advice. When they closed, the assembly resolved unanimously, in the name of the absent king and queen, to suspend the commission granted to the queen-regent until the next Parliament that should be called by the royal advice and consent. Proclamation to that effect was made by sound of trumpet, and information sent to the queen-dowager by her returning herald on the 23d of October.

Next day the Lords summoned Leith to surrender. But their operations before it were unsuccessful. On the 5th of November they were repulsed, and their troops so disheartened that on the following night they left Edinburgh and retreated to Stirling, which they reached on the evening of the next day. But they carried with them two men who proved the safety of their enterprise. William Maitland of Lethington, offended and endangered by the policy which ruled in the regent's court, escaped from Leith and joined the Lords in the midst of their disasters. And on the morning after their arrival at Stirling, Wednesday, the 7th of November, John Knox preached before the defeated and despondent forces. His text was from the eightieth Psalm, the fourth to the eighth verses inclusive, and the sermon had a wonderful effect to lift up the hearts of his hearers, to confirm their faith and encourage them to further effort and hope of success. In the afternoon of the same day the Lords held a meeting, at which they invited Knox to be present, and agreed to send Maitland to London to lay their case before Elizabeth, believing that so eminent a ruler could not fail to perceive the danger to herself in a French occupation of Scotland. As the strength of aggression was the Romish religion, the most obvious method of resistance was to combine the Reformers. Such an alliance had occurred long before to both Scots and English, and might have been effected sooner but for the obstinate animosity of Elizabeth toward Knox, who with Balnavis had hitherto managed negotiations on the side of Scotland. Until the results of the new embassy should appear, and during the depth of winter, the Congregation dispersed; while one-half of the council were to reside in Glasgow and the other in St. Andrews. With the former Balnavis, and with the latter Knox, were to remain and act as secretaries, to maintain constant communication between them. With Knox it proved a period of great intellectual labor, in constant preaching, correspondence and otherwise.

As soon as the retreat of the Lords was known at Leith, the French took possession of Edinburgh, except the castle, which was still held by Lord Erskine. More troops were sent for, to make their victory complete. A French expedition sailed from Dieppe, but was encountered by a storm at sea. Part of it was driven back to France, and the rest cast away on the shores of Holland. Subsequently, the marquis D'Elbeuf succeeded in reaching Leith with a thousand infantry and some cavalry.

Toward the end of December news came from England favorable to the Reformed cause. It was soon known also to the French, who forthwith hastened to make an end of the war before the English could interfere. Marching upon Linlithgow and Stirling, and then to Fife, where the Protestants were strong, they must have been disappointed to find no army there. All they could do was to burn and destroy. Only on the coast of Fife were they harassed in their camp and on the march by the companies organized under Lord James Stewart and some of the local gentlemen. On the 23d of January, 1560, when on their march to St. Andrews, from the high ground looking south-eastward they espied a fleet sailing into sight up the Forth. They rejoiced, for the first thought was that it must be the expected reinforcement from France. But in a short time, from a boat which landed near them, they learned that it was an English squadron in aid of the Reformers. It now became necessary for them to hasten back to Leith with all expedition. A detachment which went out to Glasgow was also recalled. The English ships took up their position before Leith, blockaded the harbor and cut off all communication by sea.

A treaty between the queen of England and the duke of Châtelherault, as head of those representing the native government of Scotland, was signed at Berwick, February 27, 1560. The English army, consisting of six thousand infantry and two thousand cavalry, under Lord Grey of Wilton, set forth immediately and joined the reassembled forces of the Lords at Preston, about eight miles from Edinburgh, on the 4th of April. The French shut themselves up within their fortifications, which were now invested by land and sea. At the same time the regent, in impaired health, was received into the castle of Edinburgh by Lord Erskine, who, although a Protestant, still maintained his singular neutrality. The siege of Leith continued from April 5 three months. On the 10th of June the queen-regent died.

Meanwhile, the princes of Lorraine were losing their absolute control of public affairs in France. Among the nobility a party was formed against them, to defeat their dangerous ambition and protect French Protestants. Under that pressure, the cabinet sent delegates to Edinburgh to make peace with England. The treaty agreed upon by the representatives of the three nations was signed on the 7th of July, and on the 16th the French embarked at Leith, and the English commenced their march to the south, and on the 19th the Lords of the Congregation, with their followers, assembled in the church of St. Giles to render thanks to God for the restoration of peace.

CHAPTER VII.

THE VICTORY.

SCOTLAND was now relieved from foreign interference. The question of religion remained to be settled, but the order of events had prejudged it. The Protestants had transacted the business for the national protection. Their cause had identified itself with the national independence. For their cause had the victory been won, and, now that the foreigners were gone, in their hands had the national authority been left. The Roman Catholics had reposed their hope upon the French, and were now helpless and without position. The Protestants were also the most powerful in rank and number. Most of the nobility, barons and gentlemen and the great mass of the commons were on their side. In numbers the Catholics were not so feeble as they seemed, but the unnational policy of their leaders, long persisted in, and finally so completely exposed and defeated, had for the time utterly prostrated their influence. Upon the whole, except where it had been enforced by the regent, the services of their religion were almost deserted. Priests of their own accord ceased to celebrate the rites which few or none attended. The people, now free to follow their choice, peacefully set up the Reformed worship, wherever there were ministers to conduct it.

In the treaty of Edinburgh it was stipulated that a Scottish Parliament should be held in the month of August following. Notice was accordingly given to all persons entitled to a seat in the national council. Many of the members came together before the appointed day. During the interval a meeting of the commissioners of boroughs, with some of the nobility and barons, undertook to assign the Reformed ministers to places of regular preaching and pastoral labor, Knox being appointed to Edinburgh, Goodman to St. Andrews, Heriot to Aberdeen, Row to Perth, Methven to Jedburgh, Christison to Dundee, Ferguson to Dunfermline, and Lindsay to Leith. As for many places no ministers could be provided, certain persons were selected to read the Scriptures before assemblies of the people, and such as were deemed competent were encouraged to offer practical remarks on what they read. Over such districts, where no better provision could then be made, some well-known and fully competent men were set as superintendents to preside, and travel from parish to parish and see to their order and spiritual interests. Not over all the kingdom were superintendents set, but only where they were needed—only over the five districts of Lothian, Fife, Glasgow, Angus and Mearns, and Argyll and the islands. The device was only temporary, and continued no longer than until the number of ministers increased sufficiently to complete the permanent design.

On the 1st of August, 1560, an unusually large attendance on Parliament assembled in Edinburgh. What had formerly been shunned by many as a burdensome and expensive task was on this occasion eagerly claimed as a privilege. Most of the higher clergy, the nobility, the barons and representatives of boroughs were present. Knox was not a member, but was at hand, with some other Reformed ministers, to aid in such manner as Parliament might require. During the time of the meeting he continued to preach on the prophecies of Haggai, with application to the times.

First among the articles of business brought before Parliament was the petition of the barons, gentlemen, burgesses and other subjects of the realm concerning religion—first, that "the doctrine of the Roman Church, professed and tyrannously maintained by the clergy, should be condemned, and by act of Parliament abolished." Some of its doctrines and practices they represented as "pestilent errors, which could not but bring damnation upon souls therewith affected." They desired, therefore, a punishment to be appointed for the teachers of such doctrines. Secondly, that "a remedy should be found against the profaning of the holy sacraments by men of that profession, and the true discipline of the ancient Church revived and restored;" and thirdly, that "the usurped authority of the pope of Rome be discharged, and the patrimony of the Church employed to the sustentation of the ministry, the provision of schools and entertainment of the poor, of a long time neglected."

Before taking up the discussion of these topics Parliament requested the ministers to prepare a statement of the doctrines which they proposed to substitute. That was promptly done, and the first Confession of the Scottish Reformed Church was laid before Parliament. It consisted of twenty-five sections, covering the main heads of theology, church government, relations of the Church to the State, and the duty of the latter to maintain the former and to be conformable to its doctrine. It was read before the Lords of the Articles, and with their approval read before Parliament. It was then laid over several days, that the members might have time to give it deliberate consideration. On the 17th of August it was again taken up, and read for discussion and vote, article by article. Only three persons of the temporal estate voted in the negative—the earl of Athole and the Lords Somerville and Borthwick, whose only reason given for so doing was, "We will believe as our fathers believed."

Some of the ecclesiastics voted with the Reformers. When the revolution had secured victory on its side, men like Winram of St. Andrews were emboldened to speak their minds openly. The bishops of Galloway and Argyll had already joined the evangelical connection. The primate and most of the bishops opposed the Confession, but made no defence of their ground. They knew that if they ventured on debate they would be overwhelmed with argument from the other side, and that, however the merits of their cause might be presented, they were sure to be outvoted. Already they had ceased to hope for victory by that means. Moreover, they still cherished the probability that France would recover her hold of the country. Francis and Mary had not yet ratified the treaty, nor was it likely they ever would, especially as it contained an article whereby they were to be bound not to assume the title or emblazonry of England. That the claim of Mary Stuart upon such a throne would be so tamely surrendered was exceedingly improbable. But the grand design upon England required the possession of Scotland as an important preliminary. France would certainly send another army, and a stronger, and England might not be ready to come north again with an adequate force. The present triumph of the Reformers could only be temporary. In a short time it must certainly fall before the vengeance of outraged royalty and the superior prowess of France. It was perfectly rational so to think at that time, but History, in her subsequent complications, reasoned in another way.

Parliament recognized the Confession as truly stating scriptural doctrine, and so accepted it as the faith of the Church of Scotland. Acts were also passed abolishing the dominion of the pope within the kingdom, annulling all statutes of earlier time "for maintenance of idolatry," prohibiting the saying of mass, and enacting punishment for those who should persist in it.

These acts of Parliament were sent to France for ratification by the king and queen. But the commmissioner, Sir James Sandilands, Lord St. John, was coldly received, treated with indignity, and ratification was not granted. The acts, however, went into force as laws by popular choice, for they expressed a previously determinate purpose of the people, which had become actual before they were passed.

After the dissolution of Parliament a committee of ministers was formed to prepare a Book of Discipline. The work was soon completed and presented to the nobility. But it was found too severe for most of them, and never received more than a partial approval.

Meanwhile, the Catholic leaders in Scotland were plotting another invasion from France. The archbishop of Glasgow, the abbot of Dunfermline and Lord Seaton were already in Paris for that purpose. The plan to overthrow the Guise domination in France had been discovered, and the conspirators were suffering in multitudes beneath the merciless vengeance of their enemies. When that impediment should be out of the way it was counted on that the energies of France could be concentrated upon the great enterprise in Britain. But just at this crisis, and while many of the victims were still awaiting execution, King Francis died.

The link was broken which connected the administration of government with the family of Guise. Another son of Catherine de Medici ascended the throne, to whom that family had no relations. Catherine, who never loved the princes of Lorraine, or their niece, was relieved from the necessity of being secondary to their ambition. Her power was still a compromise with theirs, but their niece's claim to the thrones of Scotland and England was now nothing to her and her sons, save a probability to be deprecated. Nor had the princes of Lorraine any longer a family interest in aggrandizing the throne of France as held by the house of Valois. The designs upon Scotland from that quarter came to end. Their motive was extinct. Such stupendous interests, so deeply affecting three kingdoms, rested on the life or death of a feeble boy. Francis II. died on the 15th of December, 1560, and the burden of anxiety was lifted from the heart of Scotland.

About the same time a number of the Reformed ministers and leading laymen agreed to meet together, and "consult upon those things which were to forward God's glory and the weil of his Kirk in this realm." They met on the 20th of December, 1560. Simple and rudimentary in its structure as it was, that meeting represented the existence and purpose of an already practically established Church, which recognized it, and has ever since, when unhindered by violence, maintained its succession, as the first Assembly of the Reformed Church of Scotland.

Whatever importance may attach to it in the order of cause and effect, it is at least worthy of remark that the strength of the Scottish Reform movement appeared in those parts of the country which in earlier ages had been the special scenes of the evangelical work of Ninian, of Kentigern, of Columba, and of their respective followers, and where Palladius found believers in Christ. Though much of the intervening time is dark—worse than dark, covered with deceitful clouds of fable—with such a history before its beginning, and unveiling itself at the end, one cannot resist the obtruding conjecture that fond hankerings after the earlier faith had survived through all the obscurity, as one slumbers in the night, and awakened again to activity in the warmth and light of the liberated gospel. Nations have memories—hereditary memories—amazingly long, holding on, dreamily it may be, for centuries, but sure to come to consciousness when a proper occasion arrives.

THE END.

www.ingramcontent.com/pod-product-compliance
Lightning Source LLC
Chambersburg PA
CBHW032009300426
44117CB00008B/958